MUST SUCCESS COST SO MUCH?

MUST SUCCESS COST SO MUCH?

Paul Evans

&

Fernando Bartolomé

Basic Books, Inc., Publishers

NEW YORK

First Published in the United States
by Basic Books, Inc., New York, 1981
Copyright © 1980 by Paul Evans and Fernando Bartolomé
Library of Congress Catalog Card Number: 80–68964
ISBN: 465–04746–7
Printed in the United States of America
10 9 8 7 6 5 4 3 2 1

Contents

Acknowledgements

We wish to thank the many executives who talked to us about their professional and private lives, about their success and failures in the past and their hopes and fears for the future. We owe a particular debt to the men whom we asked to fill out our questionnaire in the knowledge that this might lead to some painful self-questioning. Above all, we express our gratitude to the 44 couples who allowed us to interview them at length on deeply personal issues. We have felt obliged to protect their confidence by combining quotations from different people and by disguising their true identities, while maintaining the integrity of what they told us.

This is also an occasion to thank people who have played key roles in our professional development. For Paul, two people stand out, Henri-Claude de Bettignies and Ed Schein, who in different ways have been sources of stimulation, support and guidance. Fernando would like to express his deep gratitude to the late Fritz Roethlisberger and to Tony Athos for all the gifts, intellectual and emotional, that he received from them.

This book was completed thanks to the assistance, expertise and support of many people who were involved in different stages of our research. Tony McNulty, our research assistant, cooperated creatively in research design and data analysis; Olivia Grayson and Catherine Leblanc skillfully conducted the interviews; their intuitions, which often proved to be correct, guided part of our analysis. Our colleagues at INSEAD acted as sounding boards, in particular our next-door neighbour André Laurent; Annick Alzieu and Sharon Hastings spent weeks typing at the office and at home to meet our impossible deadlines, while Henriette Robilliard in addition to that coordinated the project administration for most of its duration. For Paul, however, the person who has played the greatest role in the project has been Bente Evans, his wife. A woman with her own professional life, she has lived with the project in one way or another for several years, assisting it often, commenting on its unfortunate effects on *real* family life, but never standing in the way of its completion. For her, the over-involvement of Paul in a study of the balance between professional and private life has been a paradox. The final test that this book has had to pass is its credibility in her eyes.

We gratefully acknowledge the financial support of CEDEP (the European Centre for Permanent Education at INSEAD), INSEAD, the Exxon Foundation, and Berndtson International.

Some parts of the book are adapted from articles we have previously published: 'Professional Lives Versus Private Lives—Shifting Patterns of Managerial Commitment', *Organizational Dynamics*, Spring 1979; 'Must Success Cost So Much?', *Harvard Business Review*, March–April 1980; and 'The Relationship between Professional and Private Life', published in a book entitled *Work, Career and Family* edited by C. Brooklyn Derr (Praeger 1980). May we thank the editors of these for their past assistance. Finally, our thanks go to Andrew Best, our agent, who guided us to the right publisher; and to our publisher himself, Grant McIntyre, for cooperation beyond the call of duty.

Fontainebleau, France
May, 1980

Prologue

Clichés about managerial lifestyles abound: the workaholic and his supportive but neglected wife; the stressed, coronary-prone executive; the organization man ready to uproot his family at the order of the company; the young executive caught in the rat-race. Novelists and essayists have shown us the executive as 'the man in the grey flannel suit', 'the pyramid climber', 'the gamesman'. The stereotype is of an individual ready to endanger, even sacrifice, his marriage, his children, and his health, in order to achieve success. The underlying assumption is that professional success does necessarily exact such a price.

The evidence for this assumption seems contradictory. Maccoby's 'gamesman' achieves professional success but risks losing his capacity for intimate relationships (Maccoby, 1976). George Vaillant, on the contrary, finds that the men who become company presidents and leaders in their fields are those who have developed stable marriages and rich friendships (Vaillant, 1977). Some authors use statistics to describe widespread stress-related illness among executives; others use them to demonstrate that executives suffer less from stress than blue collar workers do.

It was this contradictory evidence that originally intrigued and drew us into our research. Must success cost so much? The title of this book raises the question and implies our answer. It is a nuanced answer, since our findings and conclusions are the result of a wide inquiry, and survey in depth.

How the study came about

We have not invented the ideas in this book. We developed them from managers' responses to a questionnaire which dealt with matters that appeared of vital concern to most of them. We came to our conclusions after listening to hour upon hour of interviews with executives and their wives, men and women who allowed us to look into their lives in order to understand an issue *they* felt was central. We have worked them out in

1

discussions at nearly 150 management seminars, and at several dozen seminars with the wives of managers, where we tried to find out what made sense to people and what did not.

The venture, with its origins in our prior research, formally began four years ago with a yellow questionnaire entitled, 'A study of the professional and private lives of managers'. It was filled out by 532 managers, and you'll find it in abbreviated form at the end of the book, in Appendix 1. You may wish to fill it out yourself now. In that way, you'll be able to judge our conclusions from a personal perspective, seeing what makes sense to you and what doesn't. The questionnaire was designed to provoke and interest people, and it will take about half-an-hour to complete.

But answers to a questionnaire can be misleading, so we contacted 45 of the managers and asked if we could interview them and their wives about their careers and family lives. Only one said no; thus we carried out interviews with 88 people. Half lived in the London area, and were British by nationality. The other half were French living in and around Paris.*

Who were these managers? They are profiled in the box on the opposite page. They have some particular characteristics, which indicate that our ideas and conclusions may only apply to certain types of people.

First, they were *successful* people. The majority were middle managers running some department or project, though many were general managers or senior executives. Most worked for large corporations or medium-sized enterprises. They were all people regarded by their companies as sufficiently important, or as having enough personal potential, to be worth sending on an executive development programme. It was on such general management seminars that we met them and asked for their cooperation in our survey.

And secondly, they were all *men*. We have not yet studied women managers – rare participants on our programmes – though our exchanges with the few women on these courses and our reading of the literature on women executives make us believe that our ideas do also apply to them. In fact, the dilemmas and conflicts they face in trying simultaneously to manage their professional and private lives may be even more difficult than those faced by men. Even though more and more married women are choosing to pursue careers in dual-career families, it is our impression that it is generally still the woman who is expected to take special responsibility for the quality of a couple's private life. She is thus under strong pressure to manage skillfully the boundary between work and home.

Some may find it strange that at a time when the dual-career family and the career woman have emerged as so important, most of the couples

* For a more complete description of the research methodology, see Appendix 2.

THE SURVEY

The participants in our survey were 532 men, middle managers who attended various executive development programmes at the European Institute of Business Administration (INSEAD), at Fontainebleau. All were married, 93 per cent of them had children, and their ages ranged from 27 to 58, with an average of 39. The majority worked for international companies, and their jobs spanned all functions. The largest group worked in marketing or sales (29 per cent).

In terms of cultural background, they were a very diverse group, representing more than 20 different nationalities – 95 per cent were Europeans; the remainder came primarily from the United States or Latin America. Of the Europeans, the British represented the largest group (23 per cent of the sample), followed by the French (22 per cent), the Scandinavians (15 per cent), and the Germans (8 per cent). However, except where we comment specifically on cultural differences, none of the ideas presented in the book varies much with national background. We believe that the ideas apply equally to the American and the European manager.

Two sources of data were used. A questionnaire that took one to two hours to fill in was completed by the 532 managers. In most cases this was followed by a half-day discussion on the theme. Separate interviews were also conducted with 22 British executives and their wives in London, and with a similar sample of 22 French managers and their wives in Paris. Each of these 88 interviews lasted $1\frac{1}{2}$ to $2\frac{1}{2}$ hours.

in our study were traditional families with one salary-earner. The lives of the women we interviewed, whether young or old, whether they had jobs outside the household or not, usually seemed to focus on their husbands. This reflects the nature of our sample rather than any prior intention of ours to study such couples in particular. Although social trends may change, we find that this type of marriage is in fact still the commonest among the middle class of most cultures.

These ideas and conclusions have been influenced by discussions with nearly 4,000 other managers and 600 wives of managers at seminars where we have presented the ideas, in Britain and the United States, in Northern and Southern Europe, in Central and Latin America. At these seminars and presentations, we have collected further data on key issues, such as on how managers invest their time and energy in professional and private life, and on how they feel about their lifestyles. With some differences, the results have been consistent across cultures. The reactions of people to our presentations have also been similar, endorsing our belief that the problem of achieving balance in professional and private life is of concern to managers and their families throughout the Western world.

An overview of the book

There's no such person as the 'typical executive' or his 'typical wife'. For this reason, among others, we felt doubtful about the truth behind those clichés about executives and their families. We set out to survey how managers really invested themselves in their careers, their marriages, and their children, and how they balanced these different aspects of their lives.

Part One on 'Life Investments' presents the facts we found and introduces the rest of the book. Here we raise and answer questions of the following types. How do executives invest their time and energy? Is 'workaholism' indeed as widespread as some suggest? Why do some managers grumble about not having enough time and yet feel that they waste each weekend? Why do others feel dissatisfied with the way they balance professional and private life, and yet have no intention of changing their behaviour? How does work affect family, and *vice versa*? Indeed, what is the relationship between professional and private life, and is it different in the early and later career years?

Part Two, 'Finding Professional Identity', describes how men up to their mid-thirties launch their careers, and how their families react at this time. What are different managers searching for in their careers and why do many fail to find it? Why is work so stressful for some, while others who work the same hours and achieve the same results feel highly satisfied? What are the wives' complaints, and how do the men respond? Is the executive wife in a family with children free to determine her own life? And what does research say about the consequences of paternal absence for the development of the children? Probably the most important issue that this part of the book raises is how some managers appear successfully to launch their careers without paying an excessive price, while others both fail in this task and do pay such a price.

Part Three, 'Private Life', then examines how couples in their mid-thirties and early forties try to balance their lives. The question of what constitutes a 'happy marriage' is a theme that runs through some of these chapters, and the answer from our study and from the research of others is clear but nuanced. Why do many couples go through a stormy period at this time, and what happens if this does *not* occur? What happens to private life when work becomes pleasure and family obligation? What is the meaning of the common complaint by some wives that their husbands never express their personal feelings? Is there any relationship between the type of work a manager has and the type of leisure pursuits he prefers? What is the research evidence on whether the wife of an executive is likely to be happier working or not? Why do some executives find it easy to make emotionally tough decisions at work, for example those leading to layoffs, whereas others find less tough decisons more stressful?

Part Four on 'Lifestyles' focuses on the behaviour of the men at work and with their families, after their early forties. The period of life around the age of 40 has come to be identified with the 'mid-life crisis', and we ask the question whether this crisis is myth or reality. Ours is one of the few surveys undertaken of this period, and we believe the results lead in very interesting directions. They also lead to other questions. Why do some people feel so positively about themselves, while others appear to lack self-esteem? What happens to managers when their careers reach a peak? How do very successful men cope with private life at this time? What is the link between the years of early adulthood – and behaviour in these years – and the shape of life after retirement? Questions such as these lead on to the 'Conclusions' in Part Five, where we comment on implications for managers and their wives, for organizations (should the corporation care about the private lives of its employees?), and for society at large. Must success cost so much? – By this time we hope the reader will have answered the question for himself, and understood why some people *do* pay a high price while others do not.

Part One

Life Investments

'Life investments' may sound like an odd concept. Blue chip and speculative investments, short- and long-term returns, profitability ratios are all familiar enough. But life investments, what are they?

Certainly the scarcest of one's resources is one's own time. The business cliché 'time is money' recognizes that and every executive complains about not having enough time to do all he would like. But one chooses to do one thing rather than another – one is making time investment decisions every day. In this way, one is also making life investments. In doing so, most male executives try to maximize returns on at least three different areas of their lives: their professional lives, their lives as husbands, and their lives as parents. They hope not only to enjoy making those investments but also to enjoy a good return.

Some people do succeed relatively well: they make the right choices at the right times, and make not one but three fortunes. Others, on the contrary, make every possible mistake, and end bankrupt in all three ventures. Our research shows that in the business of life investments there are a few who end up as millionaires. Many do more or less well. A considerable number at one time or another in their lives have to recognize that they have exhausted one or several of their three capital funds.

This observation is in itself interesting since it counters the cliché that success in all aspects of life is impossible – the cliché that the successful executive pays a price for his success in the currency of stress: an ulcer or a divorce. What our survey shows is that only for some executives does investment in one area of life undermine investment in another. Our inquiry provides some insights into what it is that distinguishes these from those who manage two, or even three, areas successfully.

We begin with a more specific cliché, that of the workaholic. It is true that executives invest too much of themselves in their work? How much of their available time and energy do they invest in their careers relative to their family and leisure lives? Is it true that executives value above all professional success? Or do some of them work simply to pay the bills and have a good time in life outside work? We attempt to answer these questions in Chapter 1.

This chapter shows that many managers in our survey are disatisfied with how they are investing their time and energy in life. But this dissatisfaction doesn't necessarily mean that they intend to change their behaviour in the immediate future. One of the reasons for this paradox is a phenomenon we call 'emotional spillover', which we explore in Chapter 2.

Other than emotional spillover, there are several ways in which managers experience the relationship between professional life and private life. What is indeed the relationship between the two? In Chapter 3 we show that there is no single way of viewing that relationship: it is experienced differently at different times in life – sometimes as one of spillover, sometimes as one of conflict, sometimes as one of complementariness, and sometimes as one where one side of life maintains the other.

We find that the lives of executives fall into definite phases, and these form the theme of Chapter 4. At each phase, managers' preoccupations are different. Their investments are made in one area of life at a time, and in sequence. Further, having made good investments in one phase facilitates good investment decisions in the next. Poor investment decisions in the past handicap new investment choices in the present.

Part One as a whole introduces the next three parts of the book.

Chapter 1

Time and energy

Your wife tells you that you work too hard, that you travel too much, that you don't concern yourself enough with your private life. You too feel dissatisfied with your current lifestyle. Are you the typical manager? Or are you the exception?

The first purpose of our survey was to provide an answer to this question. We wished to describe the lifestyles of managers by surveying their values, their behaviour and their feelings. The results indeed emphasize that tension and ambiguity are widespread. They exist in the lifestyles of nearly half of the people in our survey.

What managers value

We were interested in finding the relative importance managers ascribe to work and family. According to the stereotype, the executive's life revolves around his career. Work is his central interest; home is a haven, a place where batteries can be recharged for the next day's work.

To survey their values, we asked managers to consider various areas of their lives: work, family relationships, running a home, leisure activities, social activities, and civic participation. We asked them to indicate which of these activities they rated highest, and second highest, in terms of satisfaction. We did not find at all the career-centred managers we expected. Figure 1.1 classifies the responses: it shows small percentages of managers whose lives revolve dominantly either around their professional world or their private world. On the other hand, it reveals 80 per cent of managers attaching a high value to *both* work-career and family-leisure, half of them giving the preference to their professional, and half to their private lives.

There is apparently no dominant value orientation. We believe there is a simple reason for this – that both career and family are important to the manager. We found in discussions that many people resisted saying which was more satisfying, particularly those from the middle 80 per cent

Figure 1.1
Managerial values

Orientation		Percentage*
Dominantly career centred		7
Dual orientation		79
career oriented	38	
family oriented	41	
Dominantly private life centred		14
*N (number of respondents) = 453		

in Figure 1.1. 'Both career and family are equally important and satisfying', they said, 'but in quite different ways.'

This is consistent with what other researchers find. A British couple, J. M. and R. E. Pahl (1971), studied the relationship between career and home life of 86 managers and their wives. They observed that the manager viewed his family as the most important aspect of his life, but obtained his greatest sense of achievement and mastery from his work.

Are managers peculiar in seeming equally attached to both professional and private life? Professors Schein and Bailyn of M. I. T. have for some years been studying the career paths and life concerns of people in different business-related occupations. They find that scientists and academics are in general highly involved in their work, with low family involvement. Engineers tend to be the reverse. Managers, however, show high involvement in both (Bailyn and Schein, 1976).

The 24 hour day

However, if we look at the manager's behaviour, we find a very different picture, one that fits much more closely with the career-centred stereotype. The typical manager sees himself as investing twice as much time and energy in his professional as in his private life.

Since people must divide their waking hours between these two areas, we asked the managers in our survey what proportion of their time and energy was invested in work and career relative to family and leisure during a typical seven-day period. This, of course, was a purely subjective assessment, asking people to describe how they experience their time and energy expenditure. (See Appendix 3, Note 1).

Energy investment is different from time investment, and yet perhaps the more significant of the two. Most people know intuitively what we mean by the difference. A manager comes home in the evening and spends time with his family, but his thoughts remain with the work problems of the day; in that case his energy is still being invested in professional life.

Our managers saw themselves spending an average of 62 per cent of their time and 71 per cent of their energy on their professional lives. Nearly twice as much time and three times as much energy was seen to be going into work as compared to family. Although there was a substantial range in perceptions – from 40 per cent to 90 per cent for energy investment in work – we found these averages to be very consistent across groups of managers. One in eight of the managers reported spending 90 per cent of his energy on his professional activities – these were all married men, almost all of them with children. Moreover, we frequently had the opportunity to ask their wives about their perceptions of their husband's behaviour, and their views consistently endorsed these averages to within a couple of percentage points.*

Most of the managers upheld as an ideal lifestyle one in which professional and private life were both separate and independent (reflecting their dual values). The actual boundary between the two aspects of life was naturally flexible, but only in one direction. While private life concerns rarely interfered with work, job concerns did pervade family and leisure lives. Two thirds of the men saw themselves as either gradually unwinding from work after they left the office or as spending considerable amounts of spare time thinking of professional matters. Most conceded that their minds were sometimes or often on other things when their wives or children talked to them in the evening. Imagine the consequences of a wandering mind at the office!

For many of them, even the weekends were coloured by their professional lives. One third of them viewed weekends as a time to relax and build up energy for the next week. Only one in four saw the weekend as a time to leave work behind and follow his own private interests.

Values say one thing, behaviour another. The result of this difference was a considerable degree of dissatisfaction that these managers felt with respect to their lifestyles.

---

* To put these subjective figures into perspective, one might calculate the following norm. These managers have a five-day working week, and they indicated in the questionnaire that they work for an average of $9\frac{1}{2}$ hours per day. Thus they have a 48-hour week. One can add to this five hours per week for commuting, giving 53 hours. On the other hand, out of a 24-hour day they sleep an average of $7\frac{1}{2}$ hours. If one allows an extra hour per day for activities such as going to bed and waking up, they have about 108 active hours available per week.

The norm would thus be that professional life represents about 50 per cent of one's time and energy investment. More than 70 per cent of our group see themselves as exceeding this norm in terms of time investment in professional life. And when considering energy, more than 90 per cent see themselves as exceeding the norm.

Feelings about lifestyles

The Pahls' study of career and home life – one of the few survey investigations into managerial lifestyles – centres on the themes of ambiguity, paradox, and tension. While managers often declare that their families matter most in their lives, they frequently report experiencing most satisfaction at work. And while they describe themselves as deeply attached to their wives and children, they also admit worrying that they do not devote enough time and attention to them.

How they feel about these apparent contradictions is expressed in Figure 1.2. In fact only half of the managers in our survey declared

Figure 1.2
Feelings about lifestyle

	Percentage*
Very satisfied with my present distribution of time and energy	5
Satisfied	44
No feelings one way or the other	6
Unsatisfied	42
Very unsatisfied with my present distribution of time and energy	3
*N = 522	

themselves satisfied with their current distribution of time and energy. All but one of those dissatisfied felt they were investing a disproportionate amount of themselves in work.

One should not jump to the conclusion that the dissatisfied manager necessarily intends to change his lifestyle, to turn more toward his private life. Frequently he feels that he cannot, and often, after deeper reflection, he realizes that he does not really want to. If you ask him why he maintains a lifestyle with which he declares himself discontented, he will probably list for you the demands of his job and the pressures from his boss. If you you point out that it sounds as if he is a puppet dangling on the end of strings manipulated by others, he will concede that indeed he maintains his lifestyle because it provides him with satisfying experiences in his professional life. For example, consider pressure. At one point in an interview, a manager will talk with exasperation about the havoc his job pressures create for his family life. Ten minutes later, he will talk about how he likes those pressures, for indeed, we found that the vast majority of managers want constant though reasonable pressure in their jobs:

Well, I like the pressure – the pace, the action, being in the centre of things. A job without pressure wouldn't be a challenge. It keeps you on your toes.

The dissatisfied manager acknowledges his disgruntlement, but produces in the next breath a host of arguments and reasons for why he must for the moment live with his dissatisfaction. In trying to understand his dilemma we will meet these arguments frequently in subsequent chapters. For he does indeed live with a dilemma. He feels that if he were to reinvest in his private life, he would compromise his career. And this would be as bad or worse. than his present situation. Searching for balance, he is unwilling to make choices.

Our discussions show this dissatisfaction as an expression of one of two wishes. There is the simple wish to have more time available to invest in one's private life and to profit from it. And then there is the wish to improve the quality of how one uses private time – the feeling that work drains so much energy that there is little left to invest actively in family pursuits. In the early days of our inquiry, we explored the first of these wishes. Time is perhaps the villain, we speculated.

The law of diminishing life returns

We started from a hypothesis that professional life and private life stand in inevitable conflict one with the other. Since time is finite and must be shared between the two, the investment of time in one must be made at the expense of the other. There is no way of disguising the conflict, though people may deny it. The problem is, we said, that managers invest too much in their careers. An investment of only 30 per cent of one's time, let alone a mere 10 per cent, is simply not sufficient to maintain a satisfying private life.

In our seminars we often proposed what we called the marginal return on investment argument represented in the Figure 1.3.

The numbers in this table were not intended to represent any exact measure of return on investment. The purpose was to illustrate the idea that increased investment in professional life probably leads to an increase in work satisfaction and productivity, but above a certain point with decreasing marginal returns. Increases in work investment lead to smaller and smaller increases in work satisfaction. In general, executives seemed to agree with this idea. Some went as far as to say that beyond a certain limit increased investment in work might even result in decreased satisfaction.

But the side of the argument that touched them most was the

Figure 1.3
Diminishing life returns

Professional life			Private life		
Investment (percentage of time and energy)	Satisfaction* (return on investment)	Marginal increase	Investment (percentage of time and energy)	Satisfaction (return on investment)	Marginal decrease
40	40	+10	60	60	−10
50	50	+ 8	50	50	−12
60	58	+ 6	40	38	−14
70	64	+ 4	30	24	−16
80	68	+ 2	20	8	−18
90	70		10	−10	

* The 'satisfaction units' indicate, in schematic terms, what personal return one might expect from a particular investment behaviour. Total life satisfaction has arbitrarily been set at 100 units if one invests 50 per cent in professional and 50 per cent in private life, giving 50 units of satisfaction to each.

parallel effect of progressively decreasing their investment in private life. Increased investment in work means less time to spend with the family. Our argument was that each additional reduction leads to bigger and bigger decreases in the satisfaction obtained from private life. Beyond a certain point, one ends with negative results of one's investment. Thus, for example, if insufficient time and energy is devoted to wife and children, the relationship with them will necessarily suffer: the little time and energy devoted to them may be full of conflict and misunderstanding.

Some executives argue, however, that time and energy are not the crucial variables, that what is important is the *quality* of the time spent together. We agree, but would add that quality in fact depends in part on time and energy. In order to create a satisfactory private life, in order to have a good relationship with another person, one must have invested in it. If an individual's private life is in very good shape, because he has put enough into it in the past, he may maintain a satisfying private life for short periods with little investment. If, on the other hand, private life is not in the best of condition, then we do not believe that positive results can be obtained that way. Suppose you went to your boss and told him that you could obtain the same quality of work by investing only 20 per cent of your time and energy instead of the 60 per cent that you are investing today. What do you think would be his answer?

There must be an ideal level of investment that will produce maximum total satisfaction. Where, we asked, is this point where the sum of professional and private life satisfaction is the greatest? It will probably vary from person to person, and be different at different stages in their lives.

When we tried out on managers our 'law' of diminishing returns, most of them agreed with it. So we expected to find it confirmed through the statistical analysis of our data. But that did not happen. People with 50–50 investment lifestyles were no more happy with their lives than others. Some people investing 80 or 90 per cent of their time and energy in their careers were happy with their lifestyles, their work and their family lives, contrary to our expectation.

These results puzzled us, and at first we had only two hypotheses to explain them. *First*, having enough time and energy to invest in private life is a necessary, but not sufficient condition, for a good private life. Some people have enough time and energy, but they don't know how to use it creatively in their private lives. People indeed show much more creativity in their professional lives than in their private lives.

Secondly, our picture of time and energy investment was a snapshot taken at one particular moment. Those people who were investing a high percentage of time and energy in professional life and still had a high quality private life may have created the foundations for this in the past.

But then the analysis of our data led us to what we think is the best explanation. What makes the fundamental difference to the quality of an individual's private life is not just the amount of time and energy that he devotes to it, but the presence or absence of a phenomenon we call emotional spillover. We explore this phenomenon in the next chapter.

Chapter 2

Emotional spillover

Work can spill over into family and leisure life through the negative feelings that it produces – worry, tension, fear, doubt, stress. If the executive brings these feelings home with him, they will have a negative effect on his private life. If on the other hand things go well at work, then he is at least psychologically available at home.

After countless exchanges with managers and their wives, and after careful analysis of our research data, we conclude that the most powerful influence on private life is the influence of negative feelings aroused at work. The manager who is unhappy in his work has little chance of fulfilment elsewhere – no matter how little he travels, how much time he spends at home, how frequently he takes a vacation.

We can in fact distinguish four different types of spillover. The first is *emotional*. Worries and concerns, satisfactions and joys, linger on in the evenings well after the working day is over. After a bad day at the office, the manager returns home moody and depressed and tries to unwind. After a good day, he comes home excited and happy. Emotional spillover influences the energy he has available to invest in private life.

Perhaps more obvious is the *physical*, the consequence of sheer fatigue. After a hectic and stimulating day at work, the executive returns home exhausted. All he wishes to do is eat and sleep, and he has not time or energy for an active private life.

Thirdly, there is *attitudinal and behavioural spillover*. Much of adult socialization takes place at work, and the skills and attitudes that have been learnt there may influence behaviour in private life. Bartolomé (1972) shows that executives whose jobs demand that they play tough roles have difficulty in expressing feelings of dependence and tenderness toward their wives and children. If one gets used to masking feelings when at work, it may become difficult to express feelings when at home.

Fourthly, one may also talk of a more insidious spillover – the *existential*. As alienation theorists suggest, estrangement from work may have general consequences for the psychological health of the individual. Studying people living in Midtown Manhattan, Langner and Michael

(1963) found that those who were dissatisfied with their jobs were more likely to show signs of mental illness. Career failure may provoke a depression which colours all aspects of life.

Are you at home when you are at home?

Our study reveals that of all types, emotional spillover is most widespread. Ask a manager how his work life affects his private life, and he is likely to tell you something like this:

> When I started working for my boss, four years ago, that affected my family life. He was very different from my previous boss. He was a bit of a tyrant. From working with someone who was terribly easy-going, to someone who's an absolute dynamo, that certainly had an influence on my family life. It made me slightly – how can I put it? Well, I'd come home to my wife talking about him, about decisions he had reversed on a certain proposal I'd made. I'd talk it over with my wife, and I couldn't get it out of my mind because it was so different as a way of operating from my previous boss.

The experience of this 36-year-old manager typifies the emotional spillover phenomenon. Sometimes the feelings may be quite specific – tomorrow's difficult assignment, an unsolved problem, today's disastrous meeting. Often they are more general: the difficulty of adapting to a new boss's unpredictable behaviour; worry about an impending reorganization; overall dissatisfaction and uncertainty about future prospects.

Under normal circumstances, we find that emotions spill almost entirely in one direction – from work life to private life. In discussions, interviews and questionnaires, we searched for evidence of spillover the other way, but in fact few managers think about their families or leisure while on the job; if they do, it is about mundane details such as errands on the way home. Many managers have highly developed skills in listening to their wives while thinking about something else; they have an even more developed skills in switching off private life when they enter the world of work.

What created this spillover is clear: *stress*! Nearly 40 per cent of the wives we interviewed felt that their husbands' tension about work had the most damaging effect on private life – far more damaging than other behaviour – working at home, long evenings spent at the office, or travelling away from home for much of the year.

In the early days of our study, we believed that the problem for these

17

managers was that their work consumed too much of their time and energy. But later we had to qualify this view. Time investment in family is important, but it is not the most problematic aspect. Most of the wives, even though they complain, adjust to the fact that their husbands spend long days at the office or are often away travelling – as long as they keep the weekends and holidays free. (If the wives feel very strongly about these absences, it is often because they have young children. The wives see the younger children above all as needing that active time investment from their fathers for their development.)

What damages family life most is the spillover of worry and tension. It is the inability to 'switch off' that hurts – through the passive family orientation and the psychological absence that this creates. When work generates stress, home becomes a simple refuge – the word which managers often use is 'haven'. Under those conditions, most time spent outside work is spent in sleep or activities akin to sleep, such as snoozing on the couch under the pretence of listening to music, or mooching out in the garden without any real purpose.

The following remark of a wife in her early thirties, married for 11 years, describes this situation and its effects:

> What annoys me is when he comes home tense and exhausted. He flops into a chair and turns on the TV. Or else he worries and it drives me up the wall. If he's happy, that's OK. But three years ago he had a very tough job. He was always at the office, even weekends. We had no holidays at all and he was always tense at home – when he was at home, that is. But it's slightly better now. . . . I really wish his life were completely different. He shouldn't always say 'Yes' to everything his company wants him to do. I think he should get out of the commercial USA-type rat race. I don't see the necessity for all that pressure, speed, tempo.

A more typical comment was the following:

> I don't really mind the amount of work he has to do. That is, if he's happy in his work. What I resent is the unhappiness which he brings home.

If you ask the wife of a manager 'What is the *most* pleasurable aspect of being married to a business executive?' what sort of reply would you expect? Six of the 44 wives we interviewed replied that it was the fact that their husband's work did not at present spill over into private life in a negative way:

Well, the best thing is that he is happy. I'm glad he's happy – he really enjoys his work. A lot of my friends' husbands are miserable and it's sad for them. It's so much easier to live with someone who is happy!

'It's easier to live with someone who is happy.' Most (not quite all) of the wives said this. It is not that they are dependent women, whose lives centre on their husbands. It reflects the fact that the careers of many men generate persistent stress which pervades their non-work lives. Only when this stops happening do many wives feel that family life begins.

The sensitivity valve

Perhaps the best way to describe how spillover works is to view tension as turning off a sensitivity valve to all other parts of life except that which generates the stress. During periods of work stress, either short or protracted, the manager becomes less sensitive to what is going on in his private life. Tension dulls his awareness of his wife, children and friends. It clouds his capacity to enjoy his private life, which becomes essentially passive. The weekend is sacred only because then he can recuperate – not because he can get actively involved in other pursuits. Joy, sorrow, anger, pleasure, and fun are suppressed; they simply cannot be experienced.

Typically, the wife's reproaches are not overt and specific. Her husband is rarely aggressive, deliberately inconsiderate, or abusive. Her reproaches are more general – that she is left alone to bear the responsibility for the home and family. Almost all the French wives used the phrase, '*Il n'est pas disponible,*' which can best be translated as 'He isn't available psychologically.'

One woman, in her fifties, was married to a man who had been dissatisfied with his work for many years and who, in her view, brought his dissatisfaction back home with him:

This is the most sensitive issue of all because *I* think his work has an enormous effect on our family life, but he doesn't. We've often had violent arguments about it. He thinks of himself as one of those men who doesn't rant and rave and destroy his family, even when he *is* having problems at work. And I agree. He isn't one of those men who vents all his frustrations on his family. I can't reproach him for being aggressive or for beating his wife – and there are some people like that.

Instead, he closes up like a shell. Total closure. And then there's not even the 40 per cent of energy. He just doesn't exist. He's completely absent. It's quite clear that you can't reproach him for being disagreeable or aggressive, but it's just as bad in its way. And that's the biggest effect of work on our family life. [pause] It's a big burden for the wife to bear.

One cause of marital separation may be the psychological absence of the husband. His career generates such preoccupation and tension that he is largely unaware that anything is amiss in the relationship with his wife. He is insensitive to her feelings, her problems, her developmental needs as a separate human being, her affairs on the side. It is only the penultimate clash that breaks through this lack of sensitivity. By this time it may be too late – the relationship has deteriorated to the point where anything said will be misinterpreted.

This was true for four of the five people in our interview sample who had divorced and remarried. One of them ascribed the failure of his first marriage to his preoccupation with work:

It happened during a two year period when I was in a situation which was very fast changing, very fast developing. We were doubling our turnover and I agreed on that objective. Normally I work a twelve-hour day from Monday to Friday. But it was taking even more time during that two year period. I just sort of got completely absorbed in what was required in the job. To the exclusion of everything else. I didn't realize what she was feeling until the day she walked out.

Another manager was currently at this stage, and we do not know whether his marriage has broken up or has been patched together. His wife told us that she had recently considered leaving him, since he brought little but misery into her life. She had been put off this decision only by the messy divorce proceedings of the couple next door. Her present lot, she felt, was better than that ordeal. Her husband was dissatisfied and frustrated with his work, and yet felt trapped by it. The stress he experienced dulled his sensitivity – he had difficulty in getting concerned about his family life even though he knew something was amiss. Describing a recent period when his wife had been very unhappy, he said:

Her unhappiness didn't really bother me, I suppose. I tend to cut off. But I knew it from our relationship. It was obvious that things were going downhill. . . . Something has produced a distance in our relationship with each other. I don't know what it is. It only happened after the first child was born four years ago. Maybe she diverted her feelings towards him?

I suppose it's me that needs to put effort into the relationship. But I'm not sure I will. I don't know why. I suppose I'm simply not inclined to do so.

Lack of sensitivity is particularly damaging when the wife is experiencing stressful events at the same time. While the manager is preoccupied with his own worries, his wife's pass him by, which aggravates her pain, and the result may be a protracted crisis. More than a third of the managers we interviewed had experienced a situation like this. In retrospect they usually saw it as the lowest moment in their marriages – if not their entire lives.

Here is one 40-year old manager:

'It was just after the birth of the third child, eight years ago. The birth coincided with a move to another part of the country and with a complete change in job. And there I have to admit that I was completely unaware of the consequences which all that had for my wife. She was absolutely overloaded with work and worries. It went on for some time and I just wasn't aware of what was happening. Finally she fell ill and had to be hospitalized, and it was only then that it began to dawn on me. I was quite unconscious of everything I was doing.'

'You were overloaded in your work?'

'Yes. Well, not really overloaded. I was worried about my work. I didn't feel very sure of myself. It was that. I wasn't sure of myself and so I was very worried. It was the time of a merger between two companies and so a period of great uncertainty. That had led to my new job and the move. And I just couldn't get my work out of my mind. I think back even today, and the uncertainties of the time were real. It was normal, but anyway I couldn't get the work out of my mind. Today I'm much more sure of myself. I find it easier to switch off.'

Yet, as the wife looked back on it, this experience, however painful, had been a turning point in their lives together. The crisis had obliged her husband to react.

The stress that creates spillover

What creates stress in professional life? The focus of research in organizational behaviour, since the days of Roethlisberger and Mayo in the twenties, has been work satisfaction. Even today, the 'quality of working life' debate singles out satisfaction as its indicator of quality. Yet life is made up of satisfactions and sorrows. Bradburn (1969), Andrews and Withey (1976), and others have shown that satisfaction and tension are two separate dimensions of human feeling. It is possible for a person to feel very satisfied with one of his life roles, such as work, and free of tension. But it is equally possible for him to feel very satisfied *and* very tense – or any one of the four combinations.*

It is the presence of tension rather than the absence of satisfaction that generates spillover, and not all tension at that. Just as one can distinguish between positive and negative feelings, so one can distinguish between positive and negative tension. Most managers and professional people appear to thrive on a certain degree of positive tension. It is part and parcel of their achievement orientation. A striking example of this is their attitude toward *job pressure*.

In the interviews, the managers were asked to describe their ideal and their actual jobs in terms of a number of dimensions. One of these was job pressure – the extent to which the manager wanted a 'job where I work under constant though reasonable pressure' versus 'a job where there are no pressures and I can take things as they come'. Sixty four per cent of the executives described their ideal job as one with constant or fairly constant pressure – all but two desired at least a moderate amount. One manager, dissatisfied with his present job and intending to leave to start his own enterprise, told us:

> This job provides me at least with a reasonable income. So I am using it as a springboard to start something else. I suppose I live a stress-free life at the moment, *but really that can be a plus or a minus.*

Not all stress should be considered as destructive. Hans Selye, the Canadian endocrinologist who has devoted his life to the study of stress, emphasizes the point that complete freedom from stress is death (Selye, 1956; 1975). All forms of activity invoke the biochemical process in the body which scientists see as the stress syndrome – do not avoid stress unless you wish to lead the life of a vegetable! The distinction that is the crux of Selye's later work on stress is between *eustress* (good stress) and *distress* (bad stress). Pleasant experiences and unpleasant experiences are virtually indistinguishable from a physiological point of view. One day at

---

* Hofstede (1976) has some interesting findings here. In a study of 88,000 employees in 38 occupations within a multinational corporation, he found that managers alone of all occupational groups experienced high satisfaction and high stress at work.

the office, you pull off a major contract. Another day you make a catastrophic blunder. In both cases, your body will be hyped up by adrenalin. Your blood pressure will soar. You will feel tired at the end of the day.

What scientists know (though they do not fully understand why) is that eustress stimulates body and mind while distress is likelier to produce disease. 'Stress is the spice of life', says Selye, while the distress of frustration, anxiety, guilt and doubt leads to ulcers, migraine, and high blood pressure. Eustress invigorates and vitalizes. It opens up private life unless it reaches the point where it becomes an ego drug, where professional stimulation and excitement overpower private life. (We discuss this in the next chapter.) Distress, on the other hand, spills over into private life.

Distress

Work generates more than its fair proportion of distress in the lives of our managers. One of the questions in our interview schedule asked the men to tell us about sources of worry during recent years. They were asked about anxieties in six different areas of life – work, wife, children, friends, relatives, and other areas such as illness or questioning of one's life-style. The distress of these worries was evaluated on a five-point scale, running from a minor irritation to a major crisis.

Two-thirds of the major distresses came from the world of work and career. If one also included life style preoccupations, usually provoked in part by career concerns, then more than three-quarters of all major distresses stemmed directly or indirectly from professional life.

While some of these distresses were quite specific, others had a more pervasive quality. For example, a successful young marketing manager spoke of his dissatisfactions and worries:

I suppose I have to say that there aren't any sources of dissatisfaction sticking their necks out. You are *perpetually* dissatisfied because of little things rather than because of the *big* event. That's why I have problems in finding particular examples. The daily frustrations never stop . . .

. . . My biggest worry in the area of work? It's the fact that assignments and deadlines which I have given are not respected. There's a certain planning process which is part of my work, leading to assignments and deadlines and the realization of certain targets. If these assignments aren't achieved, it matters. The worry that this will happen is a continual source of anxiety for me. That's the major area of worry for me. And yes, it often stops me sleeping at night.

Insidiously, tranquillizers present themselves as a support against the day-to-day pressures of life. Likewise, alcohol has also been viewed as a socially acceptable way of coping with the stresses of life (McClelland *et al.*, 1972), and the young manager quoted above is conscious of the dangers here:

I have some worries about my health. That's to say that I'm extremely tense and nervous at the moment – having worries and anxieties all the time. It's obvious that a rhythm of work like this has repercussions on your health. I try not to resort to artificial expedients. I don't smoke. I don't drink too much. I have to admit that alcohol lifts you above the worries of the day – it has a euphoric effect which you can easily get attached to. Well, I don't want to, but obviously [laughs] when you have a lot of worries you look for an outlet!

The 'euphoric effect' of alcohol. Tranquilizers and alcohol speed up the closing of the sensitivity valve. Awareness of the world outside oneself is dulled and numbed. In one case the person withdraws into suspended animation, in the other case into the world of his own fantasies.

The causes of distress

Both alcoholism and a poorly functioning private life may be manifestations of distress in professional life. But what creates that distress?

The stressors that were mentioned in the interviews varied widely from manager to manager. Some expressed general feelings of insecurity or failure, others were linked to specific events or situations. They ranged over the following sorts of concerns:

Feelings of general insecurity, of fear for one's future; worries about the possibility of unemployment created either by the layoff of other managers or by the uncertain future of a particular industry

Feelings of career failure or disappointment with career progress; frustration at being passed over for promotion in a recent organizational restructuring, leading a manager to question his own image of himself

Ambiguous or inconsistent policies affecting one's job; headquarter policies that show a lack of concern for or knowledge about the difficulties of one's particular department

Pressures created by a recent change in job or a new assignment; the fear of not doing well enough

Failure or lack of achievement in some assignment or some aspect of one's work

Problems in one's relationship with one's boss – the fact that he is unusually demanding or hostile

Problems with subordinates, that they cannot be trusted or are not adequately motivated

The quality of work itself – that it is boring, not meaningful, or very unstructured, or that the value of the work one does is not sufficiently recognized

Feelings of isolation or loneliness at work; the absence of friendships, or the fact that all relationships are tinged with competitiveness

At first sight, these appear to be very different sources of distress. But we believe that they can be seen as manifestations of two underlying causes. The first cause is environmental uncertainty. The second is difficulty experienced in matching personality to environment.

Overall, the uncertainty of our environment is increasing rapidly. Conducting our research in the troubled mid-seventies, we noted widespread spillover tension stemming from what Alvin Toffler calls 'future shock'. Economic recession has brought lay-offs, subtly disguised, even among managerial personnel. Reorganizations have been more frequent as companies have tightened up to face hard times. Alternative jobs are harder to find. For many managers, this creates semi-permanent spillover tension. The more changing and uncertain the environment of the manager, the more likely it is that he will experience a sense of insecurity that carries over into private life.

The second fundamental cause of distress is more personal, the lack of fit between one's personality and job. This can be illustrated by pointing out that distress is subjective. The same experience, for example being driven very fast in a car, can be eustress for one person and distress for another. What is experienced as conflict, overload and anxiety by one person may be a source of challenge and satisfaction for the next. Schein (1978) shows how the interpersonal processes in organizational life (bargaining, negotiation, the process of group decision-making, facing conflict, bringing about change) may be experienced negatively by a technically-oriented manager as 'damn politics getting in the way', and

25

generate distress. Yet someone managerially oriented may be stimulated by these same situations.*

The process of exploring one's personality and matching it to a job is a major life task that we call 'launching the career'. Considerable spillover is created by this process, and private life inevitably suffers from time to time. Part Two of this book is devoted to a discussion of this process and the consequences of spillover for private life. Among the issues we raise there is that of how far spillover affects the life of the wife (Chapter 8). Some adjust to it with difficulty, like those we quoted in this chapter. But others do not feel that spillover has a particularly negative effect on family life.

Of course, managers do not live in a perpetual state of distress! Spillover is not the only way of experiencing the relationship between professional and private life. It alternates with other relationships. In the next chapter, we turn to consider the extent to which spillover colours the lives of managers, and to explore other relationships between these two sides of life.

---

* One might expect certain objective job characteristics to create distress (Bailyn and Schein, 1976; Kahn *et al.*, 1964). We investigated this in our interviews. The jobs of the managers were evaluated on 13 different dimensions. Examples are: the extent to which the boss was unfairly demanding; the qualifications of the subordinates; the uncertainty of the work; the extent to which work results could be ambiguously interpreted; and the fairness of company policies affecting work. While some of these job characteristics were statistically associated with increased work tension, it was apparent that individual reactions to these job characteristics varied widely. On this and other grounds explained in Part Two, we were led to conclude that distress is created by lack of job-personality fit rather than by job characteristics alone.

Chapter 3

Professional life and private life

In this chapter we wish, firstly, to describe how managers experience and perceive the relationships between professional and private life. Secondly, we intend to present a map of the different patterns of that relationship.

Spillover is one way of experiencing the relationship, but it is not the only way. To guide our interviews with the 44 managers, we widened the list of alternative ways. Drawing upon a scheme suggested by Payton-Mayazaki and Brayfield (1976), we tentatively formulated five such ways:

Spillover
Independence
Conflict
Instrumentality
Compensation

How does each of these describe the boundary between professional and private life, as experienced by successful business managers?

Figures 3.1 and 3.2 show how the alternative relationships were presented to the managers interviewed; their wives were also asked to describe their husband's lifestyles. Many found this task to be the most provocative part of the lengthy interview and discussion. Most had no difficulty in singling out one of the five descriptions, though some felt that a combination of two descriptions best captured their own experience. In each of these cases, it was a combination of spillover and one other description that they chose.

1. The spillover relationship

Among those we surveyed, the relationship between professional life and private life was most commonly seen as one of spillover, both by the

Figure 3.1
Five relationships between professional and private life

Managers and their wives were asked in the interview to describe the relationship between professional and private life by choosing one of five descriptive statements:

Spillover: *One affects the other – in a positive or negative way.*
If I am satisfied in my work, this will contribute to my family life, while if I am unsatisfied in my career, this will have a negative effect on my family life. In a similar way, satisfaction with my family life may affect feelings about my career and work.

Independence: *They exist side by side and for all practical purposes are independent of each other.*
It is quite possible to be successful and satisfied in my career and my home life, in one or the other, or in neither.

Conflict: *They are in conflict with each other and cannot be easily reconciled.*
Success and satisfaction in my career will necessarily entail sacrifices to my home life; and to have a satisfying home life entails making compromises with respect to my career.

Instrumentality: *One is primarily a means to obtain something desired in the other.*
Work and career are primarily ways of obtaining the means to build and maintain a satisfying and successful family and leisure life; or vice-versa.

Compensation: *One is a way of making up for what is missing in the other.*
The less satisfying are my work and career, the more I look to my family for fulfilment and development; or, if my family life is less satisfying, then I turn more to my work and career.

husbands and also by their wives describing them. Nearly 60 per cent of the men saw spillover as wholly or partly characterizing the boundary between the two sides of their lives. The form that this spillover took has been described in the previous chapter. What Figure 3.2 emphasizes is the *extent* to which it pervades and colours lives. If one is to investigate the tension and ambiguity that exist in the lifestyles of managers and professional people, one must focus first and foremost on the causes of emotional spillover.

Figure 3.2
Perceptions of managers and their wives

Perceptions of 42 managers and their wives as to the relationship between the professional and private lives of these managers.

Relationship	Percentage of husbands	Percentage of wives (describing the lifestyles of their husbands)
Spillover	45	31
Independence	17	26
Conflict	10	5
Instrumentality	7	14
Compensation	7	0
Spillover & Instrumentality	12	5
Spillover & Conflict	2	2
Spillover & Independence	0	17
	$\overline{100}$	$\overline{100}$
	(Total Spillover = 59 per cent)	(Total Spillover = 55 per cent)

But Figure 3.2 also emphasizes that spillover is not the only experience. There are no black-and-white ways of describing this relationship. Sociologists have argued for many years over what *the* relationship between work and leisure might be (Wilensky, 1960; Kando and Summers, 1971; Banner, 1974). This seems a futile debate. Different people experience the relationship in different ways. The important question is what leads one person to experience the relationship in one way and another to experience it differently? Let us explore the other relationships. One in six of the men (and a higher proportion of wives) experience the worlds of work and non-work as independent.

2. The independent relationship: parallel worlds

Those who choose independence as a description of their current experience are generally managers who feel competent and at ease in their work. On the infrequent occasions when they are concerned and worried, they succeed in switching off when they leave the office.

These executives are involved in their jobs – but their involvement is not excessive. It is neither the anxious involvement of the spillover manager, nor the excited involvement that characterizes the conflicted manager, as we will see. They are also involved in their private lives, sensitive to their wives and children. Both sensitivity valves are open. Clearly, most managers strive towards this type of relationship between their professional and private worlds.

Several of the wives commented that independence described the relationship for their husbands *at the present time*, now that their husbands were content and at ease in their jobs – now that they were 'happy'. They spoke of periods in the past where their husbands had been tense and frustrated in a new job or a former company. At those times work and non-work were certainly not independent. As one 42-year-old wife put it:

> The very best moment in our marriage is without doubt right now. We have never before had such a complete life together. The children are interesting to my husband and he is very happy with his work. On the other hand, the most difficult moments have been when he wasn't happy with what he was doing.

The husband fully agreed with this view. He spoke of feeling secure in his job and confident in himself for almost the first time in his career. The present period was the high point of his life, and his only doubt was as to how long this state of balance could last into the future.

Several of our interviewees (the wives in particular) could not characterize the relationship between professional and private life either in terms of spillover or of independence. It was *both*, as another 40-year-old woman said:

> When his work goes well, it is much better. He is more human. But if he is frustrated with his work, then we feel it strongly at home. That happens less often than it did ten years ago, but I still can't say that his work and family are separate. Sometimes they are, sometimes they are not. It varies from month to month.

Indeed spillover and independence are not separate relationships; we view them as opposites on a continuum. The greater the degree of spillover of tension, the less independence exists. The less spillover there is, the higher the degree of independence.

Some wives talked of how they have to adjust to the swing between spillover and independence. 'I have to adjust to my husband's moods', they say. 'When he feels like making love, I'm expected to be instantly loving, sexy and available. But during the long periods when he doesn't feel like making love, I'm expected to fade into the background. I have to be dependent on him when he wants me to be dependent, when he is aware of my presence. At other times I have to lead my own independent existence.'

One should not infer that independence is the guarantee of a happy and fulfilling private life. In fact a marriage is not necessarily happier at times when the two life domains are separated. In the same way as we viewed the spillover effect as dulling psychological sensitivity to private life, so we see independence as the opening up of psychological sensitivity. One becomes *aware* of one's family and leisure existence. This may be a painful process. One may become aware of feelings, behaviour and events that previously had only been partially acknowledged. That there is growing distance between oneself and one's wife. That one has few interests in common with her. That the relationship with the children is less close than one would like. The data for these conclusions existed before, but the awareness of them was clouded by the spillover of career stress. The heightened sensitivity that accompanies independence may be a cue for a period of repair of private life. For others, it may indeed signal a period of fulfilment outside work as well as in the career.

3. The conflict relationship: when work becomes a drug

Another way of experiencing the relationship between professional and private life is that of conflict between life domains. This is the basis for the leading stereotype about managers – that career achievement requires sacrifice and compromise of family and leisure life. The two worlds are experienced as mutually incompatible. Realization of dreams for both of these requires more time and energy than is available.

The man who experiences conflict is likely to be exceedingly involved in his career – his work gives him immense satisfaction and self esteem. He is tense, but this tension is that of excitement, stimulation, activity. It is positive tension – eustress. Absorbed in a work life for which he is most suited, his professional world does not simply invade his private world – it *excludes* the private world.

One of the managers expressed his dilemma thus: 34 years old and very successful, he felt secure, confident and satisfied in his work, though his family life was in a mess. Talking about cancelling family holidays and the upset that this generated, he went on to say:

> The conflicts that these sort of situations create, anyway for me, I find them the most painful things in my life. And some of the most difficult decisions. I find my business decisions very simple compared to those . . . My wife feels that I should work less hard, travel less, and be content with a smaller salary. Sure, we don't need the money that much, but that isn't the point. What she doesn't realize is that I work for the satisfaction that it gives me. If I didn't work as hard, I'd be much less satisfied. I'd be miserable when I'm at home and things would be even worse than now.

Less than 10 per cent of the total group of husbands and wives saw the relationship between professional and private life in these pessimistic terms. All these men felt very enthusiastic about their jobs, working long hours because 'the work is so interesting'. They had problems in finding anything negative to say of their work, except to say that it was so demanding. They came home – *when* they came home – not with worries and preoccupations but in a state of exhaustion. The spillover that pervaded their private lives was not emotional but physical. There were just not enough hours in a day to do everything they wished to do.

When they were at home, their most urgent need was to relax, to unwind and recharge batteries. Their wives did not complain about their husbands' worries but about their working long hours – about their being late, being passive family men during weekends, and travelling too much. There was conflict at home about this – open discussion, confrontation and argument. Both husbands and wives found this distressing, for they did not feel that the conflict was moving towards a resolution. On the one hand, the wives felt they had no impact on their husbands' behaviour. On the other hand, the husbands said that their wives did not realize that they would be even more unhappy if they were to scale down their work involvement. They worked for the satisfaction that the work brought them.

This small number of men experience a profound dilemma. They are intensely conscious of the satisfaction and fulfilment that their work brings. They are equally aware of the havoc that their lifestyles are wreaking in their private lives. They have no immediate solutions and often feel trapped – the pain of confrontation at home makes them want to withdraw (to sleep or rest or watch TV), or escape back into the world of work. Yet they know that either course just postpones the solution and aggravates the dilemma.

4. The instrumental relationship: money for the family

'Work is something I have to do in order to afford the kind of life I want to have.' For people adopting this life position, work concerns have ceased to spill over into private life. The two worlds are independent. But while the managers who experienced the relationship as one of independence *care* for both worlds and are still involved in both, the manager with the instrumental view has given up any psychological involvement in his career.

This relationship is the converse of the conflictual one. In that, private life is instrumental to the career. In the instrumental relationship, work serves a maintenance function to private life. Work does not generate much stress, but on the other hand it is not a source of great fulfilment and satisfaction.

One would expect to find the instrumental pattern among men who recognize their own career failure and have given up striving. Since our sample of managers were people who were sufficiently successful to be sent on a management development programme, we had not expected to find many describing their lives in this way. It is certainly a biased sample in this respect, yet in reality 14 per cent of the men described the relationship as either instrumental or compensatory. An additional 12 per cent saw it as instrumental at times and as one of spillover at other times. Most of these men were older, in their late forties and fifties. The common denominator among them, young or old, was indeed that they were turned off by their careers. Most were beyond the point of frustration. Most commented they had probably chosen the wrong sort of career, or regretted not creating their own businesses. But it was too late to change, and they felt bitter. Read the reply of one of these men, a 54-year-old production manager, when we asked him what sort of things satisfied and dissatisfied him in his professional life, and what sort of things he found stressful:

> 'Professional dissatisfaction? There isn't even that. [pause] For the moment everything is a state of grey. Work doesn't even give anything to be dissatisfied about. It's grey. One just waits, waits for I don't know what. Everyone talks about March 1978 [the forthcoming French elections when the Communists and Socialists were predicted to win], but I don't know what that will change. Hmmm. Not much.'
> 'There's nothing that worries you or makes you preoccupied?'
> 'Worries and preoccupations. Hmmm. Work. [pause] It isn't worries. Or preoccupations. It's – look, I do my own thing. I get on by myself and don't bother about other people. I was just saying this to one of my colleagues the other day. He's a guy who gets upset every

week about this and that and complains about his fate and the injustice of it all. He says that he's done this and he's done that and it's now one and a half years without any reward or gratitude. And I told him, "Look, I'm the same age as you are. You've only got one objective. And that's to exit. Retirement!"

'It isn't motivating at all. Him – well, he's a good friend, and that's why I told him that.

'It isn't a worry, it isn't anything at all. What counts isn't salary or promotion or things like that – it's *self-respect* that counts. They've shunted me into a corner. The last person who had this job was a director. And a director had the job before *him*. And – well, they have even given me the responsibility for another sector since I took over, and *that* was previously held by a director. But they tell me that they aren't giving director titles to anyone these days.

'But that doesn't stop me from seeing memos every other week that Mr So-and-So has been appointed director. But in my case they say no. That's the way it is. Yes, I suppose it's a little bit disturbing. That's my only preoccupation.'

However successful they are from the outside, however well they do their jobs, the work lives of these instrumentally oriented managers are bland: void of satisfaction and even void of stress. To experience stress requires some psychological investment, the feeling that something is at stake.

Significantly enough, although these managers invested more in their private lives, none of them had particularly fulfilling family or leisure worlds. Here too, their lives could best be described as bland. It is this group of people who most clearly embody the description of the '*alienated*' human being – estranged from his own existence.

5. The compensatory relationship: when work offers too little

The only people among the instrumentally oriented individuals who led fulfilling lives outside work were those who explicitly saw themselves as *compensating* in private life for lack of gratification in their careers. One was a young man who had little satisfaction from his job in finance. He had positioned his career here rather than in the sales area (which he liked better) since he felt his career would progress more quickly. The focus of his life was his wife, and they led a very happy family life together. What he should do with his career was a deep source of worry, but never one which kept him awake at night. The more troubled he felt, the more he would put into his family life.

The other two people who spoke of compensation were managers in their late thirties who had undergone particularly marked experiences of career failure, so clear cut that neither could deny having 'failed'. In one case, the man had owned a business eight years ago which had gone bankrupt. To support his family, he had been obliged to join a large corporation, but his work since had given him little satisfaction. In the other case, the manager felt that he had done poorly in job after job and, as he put it, his career was 'quite out of control and swimming'. Both viewed private life as a compensation for lack of fulfilment in work; both invested very heavily in their private lives – particularly in their relationships with their children. Yet, interestingly enough, neither of them was in the least satisfied with his present situation. Both were actively thinking of breaking out – the former man was taking steps to start another business of his own, the latter was thinking about buying a farm and changing career. We had the impression that it was because they had with time come to recognize the relationship as compensatory that they were now taking steps to break out – so that in the future the relationship would *not* be compensatory.

The relationship between professional and private life

We began this chapter with a tentative typology of five different types of relationship. Each of these five descriptions – spillover, independence, conflict, instrumentality and compensation – seems to describe the relationship between professional and private life for one group of people.*

Can one say that these five descriptions of relationship constitute an all-inclusive typology? Probably not. They certainly permitted us to describe the lifestyles of the 44 managers we interviewed. But one can imagine other types of relationship – such as an *integrated pattern*, where professional and private life are so interwoven as to be inseparable. This would describe the couple who work together, jointly running the corner grocery. But our investigation of managerial lifestyles did not lead us to generate new conceptual categories.

The five different patterns of relationship are associated with

---

* Sociologists since the time of Marx, and particularly since the time of Wilensky (1960), have tried to define the once-and-for-all relationship between work and leisure. Review studies proudly conclude that the weight of evidence favours, for example, the spillover description over the compensatory description (Rose, 1974). But no one can deny that for some at least leisure and family are a compensation for what is lacking at work. Sociologists argue over whether work and leisure are 'segmented' (independent) or 'holistic' (interdependent) (Parker, 1971). But clearly they are independent for some and interdependent for others. And at one stage in the life of an individual they may be independent, and at another stage in conflict.

different work and career states. This is shown in Figure 3.3. We have summarized our observations by linking three aspects of the way in which work is experienced to the likely relationship between professional and private life. These three aspects of work are the subjective feelings about work and career (the degree of satisfaction and subjective success that a person feels); the emotional state characterizing professional life (the exent to which he feels tense); and psychological involvement in work and career.

The spillover relationship predominates where the manager is struggling to be successful. The independent relationship is one of equilibrium, where he is satisfied with his career progress. He feels confident in his abilities and has a sense of inner success. As evaluated by traditional work satisfaction measures, he is not likely to be more satisfied than his colleague who experiences spillover – the difference is that his professional life is free of the distress that is created by struggling. The conflict relationship develops where the manager feels highly satisfied and successful in his career, which feeds his sense of self-esteem. He too leads a professional life of high tension, but one characterized by stimulation and excitement rather than by the stress of insecurity and anxiety. Locked into a professional ego trip, his psychological involvement is directed almost exclusively to his career. This contrasts with the instrumental manager whose sense of career failure has led to his gradual disengagement from his work.

We can speculate as to another type of relationship, or in this case of non-relationship. This will be found where work and career generate a very high degree of stress but a very low degree of satisfaction. What we expect to happen is *breakdown* or *crisis*. This will most likely occur for a manager who has lived for many years with intense spillover. Making little progress in his career and finding himself in a job ill-suited to his nature, he becomes progressively less and less satisfied with what he is doing. At the same time this preoccupation takes a heavy toll on his private life. Gradually the sense of crisis and breakdown grows. He *may* break out into a new career and life structure, or he may gradually come to combat his tension by resigning himself to a failed career, joining the managers who are instrumentally oriented.*

---

* This conceptual model was indeed supported by data from our questionnaire (see Evans and Bartolomé (1980) for the results). The managers were asked to indicate the extent to which they felt satisfied and tense with respect to their work. Obviously, simple measures of satisfaction and tension do not capture the difference between the excited satisfaction of the conflicted person and the calm satisfaction of the person experiencing independence; nor do they measure the difference between the distress of spillover and the eustress of conflict. Nevertheless, the results for managers viewing the relationship between professional and private life in different ways exactly match the predicted pattern. Our model is confirmed statistically.

Figure 3.3 Work states and the relationship between professional and private life

Subjective feelings about work and career	moderately satisfied (struggling to be successful)	moderately satisfied (content with his success)	very satisfied (very successful)	somewhat dissatisfied (resigned to his failure)
Emotional state characterizing professional life	stressed (anxious, tense, insecure)	free of stress (calm, relaxed, feels secure)	stressed (very excited, tense, feels secure)	free of stress (resigned, fatalistic, accepting)
Psychological involvement in work and career	very involved	reasonably involved	over-involved	disengaged
Likely relationship between professional and private life	EMOTIONAL SPILLOVER	INDEPENDENCE	CONFLICT	INSTRUMENTALITY or COMPENSATION

The model opens the way to understanding the evolution of the adult lifecycle – the way in which professional life and private life are related at different stages. A particular manager might experience a spillover relationship at one time in his life, experience a sense of independence between work and leisure at a later time, and ultimately turn to an instrumental orientation. The periods of spillover would be periods of high stress and tension, where professional and private life coexisted in uneasy equilibrium. This would prevail during the early work years where the manager was trying out successive jobs and companies and struggling to launch his career. Later, the periods of independence would be more frequent – periods of stability where for a time professional and private life proceeded along separate but parallel paths. If the struggle to launch one's career were too bitter and protracted, the person might for a time invest in a compensatory manner in his private life, or turn with resignation toward an instrumental lifestyle.

Is there such a rhythm to the course of life? This is a question that we will address in the next chapter.

Conclusions

In conclusion, we wish to emphasize two propositions about the relationship between professional and private life. Both of them stress the overriding influence of professional life over private life. First, we argue that for managers at least a healthy professional life is a precondition for a well-functioning private life. Secondly, we ask whether private life indeed has any significant effect on work and career.

The conditions for a well-functioning private life

Most managers are deeply concerned at one time or other about the quality of their private lives – about the proportion of time and energy they are investing in their careers at the expense of their private lives. But it is useless to advise them to invest more in their private lives as long as they experience a situation of spillover or conflict. The equilibrium has first to be found in the career. *For an ambitious male a well-functioning professional life is a necessary, though not sufficient, condition for a well-functioning private life.*

This is an important conclusion, and one which many wives will not be pleased to read. But in our society today and among male managers in particular, private life is to a great extent at the mercy of professional life.

Equally, one could say that a high degree of independence is necessary for the development of a family and leisure life that functions well, though it is not enough. It is necessary, because only under these conditions can one have the necessary sensitivity to what is going on in private life. But it is *not sufficient*, because one may not like what one becomes aware of. Sensitized to a situation at home that is far from ideal, one may indeed decide to invest actively in developing one's private life. Or one may instead decide to escape back into one's career by finding new professional challenges there. One postpones indefinitely the day of active investment in private life.

Independence is a state of balance – but of balance that lasts for limited periods of time. We do not feel that there is any once-and-for-all resolution to the dilemma of professional and private life. After some period of experiencing independence, a feeling of boredom and monotony sets in at work. One accepts or creates a major job change. Or corporate events bring about that change with a major reorganization. The spillover relationship comes to the fore once again. This leads us to our second conclusion.

The dominant influence of professional life

In day-to-day life, professional and private life are not interrelated reciprocally. The influence is one-way. It is the feelings generated by work that determine the quality of the relationship, and not the reverse. The influence of private life on the relationship is felt in only three ways: first, it has a strong influence on major life decisions as opposed to the day-to-day reality of work and leisure (we discuss this below); second, the strong attachment to private life influences people's values in the sense that the independence of the two worlds is upheld as an ideal; and third, private life dramas may affect professional life if they are sufficiently traumatic – for instance, separation, divorce or death.

This conclusion is consistent with the orientation of research during this century. Countless studies have shown that work satisfaction and the emotional feelings aroused by work are associated with mental health and psychological well-being. This indeed was the assumption behind the 1971 Task Force of the US Department of Health, Education and Welfare on 'Work in America' (1973; see also O'Toole, 1974).

Our observation can be put in another way. The fact that the manager has a career is apparent day in and day out to his wife and his children. It is apparent not simply in the number of hours spent away from home each day, but in his moods and attitudes at home, in where that home is located, and in the quality of his investment in private life. The fact that the manager has a wife and children is rarely if ever apparent to the corporation. Certainly he spends a certain number of hours away from the office, but it is possible to work effectively with a colleague and not even know that he is married.

When we discuss this with personnel managers, some of them strongly disagree. 'I have a problem on my hands at the moment which proves the contrary,' they say. 'It is a sales manager who is having problems in his marriage. He's so upset that he can't keep his mind on his job – things are falling apart in his professional life.'

But on further investigation, this often turns out *not* to be a contrary case in point. Why is it that even the extreme of divorce appears to have a powerful effect upon the professional behaviour of some people, but not on others? If we explore further with the personnel manager, we invariably find out that the sales manager was not doing too well in his work in the first place. He was already insecure and anxious in his job; his marital problems aggravated that tension and insecurity. This creates a general feeling that life is falling apart – both professional and private life. This is the situation of quasi-paralysis, of depression and despair, of the traumatic life crisis where nothing has any significance. It is what we have described as breakdown crisis (page 36). In contrast, we believe that the person who is confident and involved in his work may more easily ride through the storms of divorce and private life tension. Separation and divorce lead him to invest even more earnestly in his work and career, at least temporarily.

Does our investigation thus imply that private life is entirely subordinate to the twists and turns of professional existence? Most readers will intuitively reject this conclusion. Work-leisure research has been critized for making this assumption, but we nevertheless find it largely justified – provided we are talking about the *daily experience of professional and private life.*

When queried about the ways in which private life affects work, many managers – particularly those above their mid-thirties – will give an example of the following kind. Being unwilling to relocate abroad because one's wife did not wish to move. Wishing to move one's job from Paris to the French provinces, or from the north of England to the London area. Turning down a promotion and a new job because of the demands it would place on family life. Leaving a company owing to, among other factors, the demands that were placed upon family life. Looking for an assignment overseas because the family wanted the excitement of living there.

Virtually all the examples which were mentioned were instances of *major career and life decisions.* While we have little evidence that private life affects work in daily life, there is ample evidence that private life considerations have a major influence at those critical decision and choice points. It is these moments where the general structure of one's lifestyle in the immediate future is implicitly chosen. That lifestyle may be one which creates a high degree of spillover – the professional challenges opted for may be at the limits of one's capacities. Or it may be a lifestyle that fosters a relationship of independence – one of parallel development in both worlds.

This leads us to our second proposition: *Professional life affects the quality of private life on a day-by-day basis. But the reverse is not true; private life only affects the quality of professional life in extreme situations. The effect of private life on professional life is through its influence on major career and life decisions.*

In his recent book on *The Seasons of a Man's Life*, Daniel Levinson of Yale University describes the development of adult life in terms of phases in life where an *individual life structure* is chosen (Levinson *et al.*, 1978). This structure is the basic pattern or design of a person's life at a given period of time – a set of choices that give life meaning and direction in the years ahead. For example, in the early twenties a first life structure is tentatively chosen. A major decision point here is the choice of occupation and career. What Levinson calls 'the age thirty transition' is a period where this life structure may be questioned; getting married and having children may have undermined earlier choices. Similarly, the 'mid-life transition' is viewed as a period of questioning of lifestyle choices, often leading to the emergence of a new life structure and a reorientation of professional and private life.

It is at these major choice points, where a life structure is opted for, as well as in other life decisions, that private life influences professional life.

This moves us on to our next theme of inquiry. Does age matter in the relationship between professional and private life? Daniel Levinson and others argue that clear stages exist in adult life. Do these stages express themselves in a life rhythm of spillover and independence, conflict and instrumentality?

Chapter 4

Three life phases

In the ten years between 20 and 30, most men launch simultaneously not one, but three careers. Their working lives begin in earnest. At the same time most get married, and launch their careers as husbands or partners. The first child is born sometime after, and so starts the career as parent as well.

Tentative choices on how to live one's adult life are made at this time. Most men choose to invest and realize themselves in all three sectors of life. Each contains challenges, opportunities, crucial choices, moments of success and failure. Each therefore can be considered as a 'career', in the sense of its original meaning as movement along a specific path.

What interests us is how these three careers relate to each other. Sometimes they clash and conflict, most frequently at predictable points in life, for example when one is trying to *launch* those three careers simultaneously – struggling in a new job, dealing with the misunderstandings and tensions accompanying the first years of marriage, being woken up in the middle of the night by a crying baby. Fortunately, periods like this alternate with others where all three careers coexist harmoniously.

The events in the lives of individuals vary infinitely, as do their lifestyles, but the question that has increasingly intrigued people during this last decade is whether there are general patterns to the adult life-cycle. Is spillover marked at certain stages in life as a manager struggles with his career? Are there periods where an individual is likely to be most preoccupied with the quality of his private life? Research does indeed suggest the existence of stages or phases in the adult lifecycle.

Life stages

Developmental psychology is devoted to the study of these stages in the lives of people.* While this discipline was focused originally on the study

* The pioneers in this area are well known – Freud, Jung (1934), Erikson (1968), Neugarten (1968), Lidz (1976). A specialized field called 'life-span developmental

of children and adolescents, it has recently expanded to explore the developmental phases of adults also. The last ten years have seen the publication of important work expanding and enriching our ideas about the adult life cycle. Two leading contributors in the area are Daniel Levinson with *The Seasons of a Man's Life* and Roger Gould with *Transformations*. Their ideas have been popularized above all in *Passages*, a readable and dramatic presentation by Gail Sheehy. The 'terrible twos' and 'noisy nines' of childhood are paralleled by similar labels to describe phases in adulthood: the trying twenties, the catch-thirty trap, the deadline decade from the mid-thirties to mid-forties, the age forty crucible, and so on.

There is much similarity and convergence of ideas in these studies. There is agreement that an individual's life consists of alternating phases of stability and conflict, turmoil and reassessment; that this process never ends, that it continues well into old age. Gone is the idea that with adulthood one finds once and for all who one is, settles down into a profession for life, marries a person with whom one will stay to the end of one's days, raises children, and settles down to the business of living the serious and stable life of an adult. Our own research on the relationship between professional and private life provides one more illustration of the paradigm of developmental stages in adult life.

Sequencing life investments

Our research supports strongly the notion that there are phases in adult life.

The concepts of spillover and the sensitivity valve rest on the proposition that people focus their psychological attention above all on their work careers until such time as they find a sense of fulfilment there. The family is important, but major preoccupations are elsewhere. Sensitivity to the family and to private life awakens later – when spillover tensions become less severe, when the career is felt to be underway. Or when some rhythm in the cycle of life calls a man to turn to his family life. Or when some crisis forces him to.

We believe that the manager copes with the conflicts that are inherent in his lifestyle – that is, the conflicts of trying to run simultaneously his three careers as manager, parent, and husband – by concentrating his attention predominantly on one of them at each phase. Our evidence shows that his professional career is placed centre-stage early in

psychology' emerged in the late sixties to bring together the ideas of researchers interested in adult development (Baltes and Schaie, 1973).

his adult life, while family is back-stage. It would be too much to say that he is impervious to conflict, tension and unhappiness in his relationship with his wife, though he is certainly less sensitive to these issues than to the satisfaction and tension of his career. His self-image and self-esteem are more wrapped up in his professional life than in his private life.

Yet, at a later stage, it is the family that becomes the centre of his attraction. After years of heavy career investment, he becomes more sensitive to the quality of the relationship with his wife than to the gratifications, trials and tribulations of career progress. If the career is still on an uneasy path when attention turns to private life, these will be difficult years. The spillover of career tension will persist and may block constructive investment in private life.

What we call life phases are, in fact, defined by different central preoccupations at different stages in life. These life phases mark different balances of concern, investment and sensitivity to professional life and private life at different times in life.*

The three life phases with their different preoccupations were apparent in the different reactions of managers to our discussions with them about their lifestyles. We discussed the theme of professional and private life with management students on an MBA (Master of Business Administration) programme, average age 28, typically with three to five years of work experience. We found them to be concerned, but in general they were not ready to translate this concern into action that would protect their private lives. They agreed to the principle that they should invest in their private lives, pay more attention to their wives' needs, and so forth. But when the time came at the end of the year to find a job, all these 'concerns' were put aside. Securing the best job to launch a career was the main preoccupation. As for private life, they planned to take care of it *mañana*.

Older managers in their late forties and fifties, on the other hand, reacted in a different way. Many were deeply provoked by the discussions, and by some of our tentative speculations about the relationship between home and career. But one typical attitude was that of defensive and dogmatic rejection, as if we had touched a sore nerve. This was particularly true when we talked of the relationship between a manager and his family. The other attitude was one of enthusiasm, though usually with a resigned comment at the end of the discussion, 'But why didn't

* For a psychological theory of human functioning that supports this idea of sequenced preoccupations in life, see Erik Klinger's book *Meaning and Void*. The core of Klinger's theory is that 'people are sensitized to those cues in their environment that relate to their current concerns. . . . One travels through one's world of stimulation ignoring most of it, processing primarily those features of it that fit into one or more current concerns.' (Klinger, 1977, pp. 53, 54).

someone raise these issues at an earlier time in my life, when thinking about them could still have made a difference?'

It was among the managers in their mid- to late thirties and early forties that we found the most preoccupation when we began to discuss the question of the manager's relationship to his private life. The men seemed deeply concerned. Often the atmosphere in a seminar room would become highly charged, a sign to an instructor of having touched on an issue fundamental to listeners' lives. Often we found it difficult on the following day to address any other theme in the more traditional repertoire of an executive development programme.

We believe that there are three different phases in a manager's adult life, three different modes of resolving the tension inherent in his life-style. Each phase is named for a manager's major preoccupation at a particular point in time. The first phase, from the mid-twenties to the mid-thirties, is a time of overriding concern for *launching a work career*. The second stage, from the mid-thirties to the early forties, is marked by *turning towards private life*. The third phase, from the early forties on into the fifties, is characterized by an integration of professional and private life and a renewed sense of life purpose (*generativity*) or by resignation to a more fragmented style of life (*maintenance*).

These life phases were evident in our statistical data, where the pattern of changing preoccupations and sensitivity showed up in how people felt about their lifestyles – in whether or not they were satisfied with how they were investing their time and energy. The issues which were linked to a questioning of lifestyle changed from one life phase to another. Let us explain how this was apparent.

Each area of life gives rise to certain feelings – feelings about one's career, feelings about one's relationship with one's wife, feelings about one's relationship with one's children. These feelings can be categorized into two broad types. There are feelings of *satisfaction* – of joy, pleasure, enjoyment, stimulation, reward and excitement; and there are feelings of *tension* – of conflict, stress, guilt, anxiety, difficulty, and doubt. The general attitude of a person towards a particular aspect of his life (his career, for example) is the result of a combination of positive and negative feelings about that area of life. This is clearly so with respect to our feelings about other people; they tend to be mixed, a combination of positive and negative sentiments which we often experience as ambivalence. It is also true of our feelings about other aspects of our lives.*

One would expect feelings of satisfaction in any area of life to reinforce a person's lifestyle, leading him to invest more in that area of life.

* Life is a cumulation of satisfactions and sorrows, and what matters is that satisfactions outweigh sorrows – such was the conclusion of a major investigation into well-being among citizens of the United States (Andrews and Withey, 1976; see also Bradburn, 1969).

Conversely, one would expect that strong tension in a given area would lead the person to question his lifestyle. But this is not so. We have found that at each phase in life the individual does not pay equal attention to *all* his feelings. As a consequence, his *global* feeling of satisfaction or disatisfaction with life at a given time is not equally influenced by his feelings towards all aspects of his life, but very specially by his sentiments about that aspect which is the centre of attention during that phase. Thus, for example, while the young manager's feelings about life are disproportionately influenced by his feeling towards his career, the feelings of the man in his mid-thirties or early forties towards life are influenced above all by his relationship to his wife.*

We did not find, however, any clear pattern for the manager in his mid forties or older. For him the life investment perspective is no longer relevant. These men face different dilemmas, and we will address them later in this book. Let us now begin by considering the younger manager.

The young manager: launching his career

The young manager in our survey is a man, aged 27 to 34, who has succeeded in crossing the threshold into the ranks of management.

Of his three 'careers' we find him to be obsessed with launching himself at work. His career as father is in distant second place, and his wife plays an indirect background role – she is a minor character in the life script now, and will become central to the plot only in a later act.

Professor Douglas Hall of Northwestern University has, through his research on careers, outlined how the successful young manager launches his career, showing how he becomes more and more involved in his professional occupation. Let us imagine a young business graduate, aged 25, who joins a company with big ambitions. He is given a responsible and challenging first job. He works hard at this and performs well. The result is a sense of personal achievement as well as praise, recognition, and even promotion. His sense of self-esteem is boosted and he begins to feel some sense of competence. Since most people are motivated to try to enhance their self-esteem, it is probable that he will now set himself a higher goal and work even harder at its achievement. And this is indeed likely to lead to a renewal of the same cycle, where effort generates performance, and performance generates the personal satisfaction and external rewards of

---

* This explains why career failure is not found to lead to decreased career commitment among younger people, contrary to what one would expect (Hall, 1971; Schneider and Hall, 1972; Faunce and Dubin, 1975). Career failure leads to renewed career striving at this stage since the individual is wholly preoccupied with launching his career. Only at later phases in life will career failure lead to decreased career motivation.

success, which in turn leads to bigger targets and more effort. Progressively, the young man is becoming more and more interested in seeking success and developing his competence in his work career.

Hall describes this cyclical process as the 'success spiral syndrome': early career success generates both the opportunities to be more successful (promotions and bigger assignments) and the desire to be more successful. The net result is that the manager becomes progressively more involved in his professional career – at least for the first eight years or so. (Hall, 1971, 1976; Bray, Campbell and Grant, 1974).

The increasing involvement of the successful young manager was clearly revealed in our survey results by a pattern of steadily increasing time and energy investment in work up until the age of 35, where balance between professional and private life appeared to stabilize. For example, three-quarters of the younger managers, less than 33 years old, saw themselves as investing more energy in their work relative to their private lives than they were doing two years earlier – compared with only a one-quarter of all managers above this age. And while nearly one-third of those younger men saw themselves as continuing to increase their energy investment in work, this was only true for one in ten of the others.

These are the years where spillover is the rule rather than the exception. Periods where professional and private life are independent are few and far between. For the young manager has few guidelines to assist him in launching his career. He can only discover his strengths and weaknesses, his work likes and dislikes – his career path – through trying himself out in different jobs. He is unsure of his capacities and potential. He is often faced with challenges that he has never faced before. When his work goes badly and he feels his career to be in jeopardy, he is tense and preoccupied. He puts even more energy in his job. Emotional spillover from work pervades his private life. On the other hand, when his work goes well and he is on a success spiral, this is not a cue to attend to his private life – it is an encouragement to set higher targets, to outdo himself further, to notch his career one peg further up the chosen ladder.

His wife experiences this spillover – his spiralling career involvement and the negative consequences that this has had for their marriage:

> I think work has always been absorbing for him. But in the last five years, because he's become so successful, it's become a major bone of contention between us – simply because of the extra demands on his time and energy.

Many of the wives of the younger managers who we interviewed were clearly dissatisfied with their husband's lifestyles. Although the couples were still in the early stages of married life, our survey showed that there were almost as many unhappy marriages among them as among the older groups. One would expect that if a manager perceived his marriage to be unhappy, if he experienced a lot of conflict in his relationship with his wife, and if he found little satisfaction and fulfilment in the relationship, then he would feel disturbed. This would be reflected in growing dissatisfaction with the way in which he was balancing his professional and private life. Yet our survey results show this *not* to be the case. He might be disturbed, but the young manager was relatively insensitive to what happened in his marriage. Marital life was a peripheral preoccupation that became central only on the rare occasions when spillover stopped.

Our results showed that the manager's lifestyle feelings were not affected by experiencing satisfaction, either with respect to his marriage or his children. Ambivalence at this life stage appeared to originate from the tension and struggle that he might experience in the process of launching his career. That tension led him to question his increasingly career-oriented behaviour. Most of the young managers whom we interviewed spoke of career anxieties that they experienced: Will I be a success at my new job? How can I outmanoeuvre other people, find my own role, and get recognition for what I do? Shall I stay on in this company? Have I blown my own horn loud enough? This tension led them to question whether the lifestyle was worth the pain. For the present, his answer was almost always yes.

The *mañana syndrome*

We cannot simply discount the wife and family in the young manager's life. The marriage *is* important to him. He may be dimly aware of the consequences of spillover – his wife may complain, though some wives build their lives for the moment around supporting their husbands in pursuing their careers. But what obsesses him are the *causes* of spillover: the doubts, problems and demands that he faces in his work. If his wife complains, he feels disturbed. His doubts and dissatisfaction about his lifestyle may grow, but are channelled into a hardened concern to launch his career. Tomorrow things will be different . . . the *mañana* syndrome. Investing in the family must wait.

One of the younger managers describes his reaction as follows:

I'm obviously not a totally satisfactory family man, and that creates a series of conflicts. But on the other hand, if I gave up work, I'm not sure I'd be better. It would be worse. I'd do all sorts of things that wouldn't be any better for them. Basically, I feel that when I'm there, it should be good for them, but I don't *have* to be there all the time.

He is not concerned with 'developing' his private life; the very idea makes little intuitive sense to him. His orientation is essentially utilitarian – regarding private life as a support system. If tension appears in his marriage his dilemma is not: 'How can I regain a gratifying private life,' but 'How can I pursue my career . . . without destroying my family life.'

Our statistics showed that the area of private life of most concern to the younger manager was his relationship with his children. He was more likely to question the balance between professional and private life if he experienced tension with them. Some managers we interviewed had tried to limit travel time spent away from home, but less because it upset their wives than because of the need for 'continuity' in bringing up their children. Those managers who tried to keep their weekends free of work typically did so to be able to devote themselves above all to constructive activities with their children. But it was particularly the combination of tension in raising the children *and* in the career that was upsetting – rather than worries about the children alone. The stress of launching the career is *aggravated* by worries about the relationship with small children.

In Part Two of this book, we will explore in detail the process of finding a professional identity, both as the hallmark of this first life phase and as a task which for some lingers on to colour peoples' whole lives. For indeed the essence of launching a career is the process of discovering, crystallizing and maintaining a professional identity. Learning to cope with spillover is an ancillary life task at this time, one which is experienced in a more urgent way as the mid-thirties pass.

From the mid-thirties: turning towards private life

By age 35, the manager's career is launched, for better or worse. If successful, he is now likely to invest 70 to 80 per cent of his energy in his work. He begins for the first time to become genuinely concerned about the consequences that this lifestyle is having for his family.

The wife of the young manager has willingly or reluctantly played a secondary role in his life. Her assertion of her own independence or her realization of a family dream may have been frustrated by the tension that the husband feels in getting his career underway – though without her having any apparent impact on his lifestyle and behaviour. However, from the mid-thirties onward, life outside work begins to acquire a meaning for him that it did not have before. The idea of private life investment and the development of a non-work self begins to acquire as much meaning as the idea of career development, even though there may be no formal arena for such development. The ambivalence that the manager may feel about his lifestyle no longer reflects private life getting in the way of work and career. It reflects ambivalence about the effect that his work and career is having on the quality of his marriage.

The central preoccupation of early midlife is the search for a meaningful and gratifying private life. As the manager becomes more sensitive to what is happening in his private life, the first thing that comes to his attention is the state of his marriage. One of the signs of this change in perspective is his view of the trade-offs, choices, and sacrifices made in balancing professional and private life. Ask a young manager if he has made any sacrifices in his home or leisure life for the sake of his career. In most cases, his answer will be no (the only one we interviewed who said yes had been through a divorce). Push him farther on this – pointing out that his life appears to revolve around his work – and he may concede that he has given something up. He may admit that in an ideal world, he would like to spend more time with his family. But, more likely than not, he will argue fervently that choices have to be made in life and that he has made a conscious and deliberate to give up a certain amount of leisure and family time.

Yet ask a manager in midlife this question, and the typical reaction is very different. Most will spontaneously say yes, and half will also say that in retrospect they do see this as a sacrifice. A 38-year-old executive answered as follows:

> Yes, my family life. Yes! Because of the sheer time pressures. And I feel more and more that they are sacrifices. Earlier, I thought they were the normal price that one has to pay in the early stages of one's career. But in ten years the children will be off my hands altogether, and the amount of time that I've spent with them – although there have been good moments – has certainly been too little.

One could ask whether this is merely an effect of realizing that one is not likely to be as successful as one had hoped. But if this were the case one would find a strong link between perceived career failure at this point and the phenomenon of turning towards private life. Our results do not support this view. While some who turn energetically towards private life have indeed experienced failure, many successful people also turn at this time.

Turning towards private life is a turning in awareness and sensitivity. But whether this heightened awareness is translated into a change in investment behaviour or lifestyle is quite a different matter. In Chapter 9 we will argue that the manager who has most difficulty in translating awareness into action is neither the individual who has clearly succeeded nor the person who has clearly failed in launching his career – it is the manager who feels outwardly successful but inwardly unsuccessful.

For young and older managers, our statistics showed virtually no relationship between marital and lifestyle feelings. There is a clear relationship, indicating heightened sensitivity, only for those aged 35 to 42. At this time, two thirds of those who have a positive assessment of their marriages (seeing their relationship to their wives as satisfying and free from tension) are satisfied with their lifestyles, viewing them as balanced. Only one in seven of those who view their marriages negatively are similarly satisfied. Feelings about the marital relationship and feelings about lifestyle balance go hand in hand at this phase in adult life. This distinct early-midlife preoccupation was confirmed by all points of our survey analysis. For example, it was the manager who felt unhappy with his marriage who was most likely to feel various types of emotional strain at this time.

There is more to life than work

Marriage is not the only part of private life to which the manager turns, however. Although there is no evidence from our survey that he is particularly sensitive to his feelings about his children at this time, it was clear from our interviews that most midlife managers were preoccupied with the active development of their leisure lives – with sports, hobbies intellectual interests, and in particular with physical fitness. This markedly contrasted with the managers in the preceding stage, who either took such pursuits for granted or, more typically, simply neglected them. This concern for leisure symbolizes the proactive rather than reactive orientation of the manager toward his private life at this phase. Nevertheless, it creates a new dilemma for the individual: How should I use my private life time? With my wife? With my family? With friends? On sports or individual activities?

> I'd like to have more time perhaps to play golf and participate in sports. I'd like to do more than I do or have done. But I have a choice. The weekend is either for my family or for sports. And I've decided that the weekend is more for the family so I can't get involved in sports.

This 40-year-old manager chose his family, but others whom we interviewed chose golf or their musical interests, and thereby created tension within the family. This is a central dilemma in midlife for the man who does allow himself to turn toward private life. As the manager saw himself earlier having to make choices between work and nonwork (and then often looks back and sees these choices as sacrifices), so the midlife manager typically sees himself as having to make choices between various private activities – between time spent with his wife, his children, his friends, or himself.

What all this indicates is a clear realignment of what is important in the life of a man at this time. Private life now occupies centre stage. Consequently the source of self-esteem changes. The career calls for special attention only at times of crisis. Senses of well-being and of self-esteem depend fundamentally on the health and development of private life.

We believe that the midlife 'crisis' is avoided if at least one fundamental area of the individual's life is working well. On the other hand, if things go poorly in two or three areas, a real life crisis may build up at this time.

Passages into generativity or maintenance

The two phases of adulthood oriented toward making life investments end in the early forties. After age 42, managers have very different concerns. Carl Jung talks of the events at this 'noon of life' as leading toward what psychologists call *individuation* – become uniquely individual. Certainly our data analysis did not reveal clear patterns, and this distinguishes it from previous stages. While we found confirmation of the different preoccupations of the younger and midlife managers from all points in our survey, while the transition points of 34–35 and 42–43 were suprisingly clear, we found few indications of common lifestyle preoccupations among the older managers.

Their most notable development preoccupation appeared to be their relationship with their children – not with their wives or careers. As young managers, they felt disturbed if they experienced tensions in bringing up their children; now as older managers they tended to question their lifestyles if they did not experience satisfaction in their relationships with their children, now adolescent or grown-up. It is as if they were taking stock belatedly of their careers as parents, which were now coming to fruition or failure. As a 44-year-old manager put it:

I suppose that if I deliberately spend more time with the youngest child on the basis that I seemed to have missed time with the other three. And I probably spend more time with them all now that they are getting older. It was during that in-between period that we lost a lot.

We also observed that a certain disengagement from the career appears necessary at this phase. Sixty per cent of the older managers who felt very 'active' toward their careers and who found this area of life extremely 'interesting' were dissatisfied with their lifestyles – compared to a mere 28 per cent of those managers who felt only moderately active and interested. This relationship with feelings about lifestyle was not found at either of the preceding life phases. Over-involvement in the career seems dysfunctional after the midlife point. And this observation has nothing to do with reaching a career plateau, for the over-involved managers see themselves to be no closer or farther from the position to which they aspire than the less involved managers.

The need for some career disengagement is a sign that this phase of life is quite different from the preceding two. We found the older managers less concerned by lifestyle dilemmas, by the relationship between professional life and private life, or by the question of how to invest their time and energy, than in the years before the early forties. As Jung suggested, the early forties do seem to herald a qualitatively different era in life. In the words of the California psychiatrist, Roger Gould, people come to terms with time and with their own personalities. The early forties are a period of reassessment, of questioning one's values, achievements, and lifestyle. Indeed, when we interviewed the managers, these turned out to be the questions that ran through their minds and kept them from sleeping at night.

The transition, contrary to the widespread view, is not typically experienced as a point of crisis unless the process of reassessment provokes deep depression or a major change in life path. Nor is it a separate life stage. We view it as extended period of soul-searching, brought about not only by a sense of time – of being at a midlife point – but also by the fact that in the late thirties and early forties both professional life and private life development are salient in a person's preoccupations. The transition is the product of the previous two phases in life: the man who has been investing in work and in family now seeks an integration of the two.

The search for integration can best be illustrated in terms of what we see as the two polar outcomes of the midlife transition. These represent two lifestyle paths through the later forties and fifties – the path of *generativity*, or renewal, and the path of *maintenance*, or resignation.

The generativity path

Generativity is the successful outcome of the previous phases. Bringing together the professional and the private self creates a sense of 'wholeness' not experienced before. We use Erikson's word 'generativity' not only because of its connotations of turning towards other people and the next generation, but also because it implies a renewed internal sense of purpose and of confidence, a renewed self and fresh enthusiasm. There is a fusion of the task-oriented, achievement side of life (the struggle to master the world and succeed that has in particular characterized the career) and the affective, emotional, relationship-oriented side of life that in particular has been expresses in private life. The manager comes to view his career in more affective terms; he is more prepared to recognize the organization as a 'family' to which he has a responsibility as a senior member, rather than simply as being a vehicle for his career. Conversely, he is more prepared to recognized his private life as a 'career', as a developmental challenge that requires investment, thought and management.

As an illustration of this integrative path, we might cite the words of the divisional manager of a large company. He was the only person we interviewed who was 'very satisfied' with his investment behaviour; he was also one of two people who spoke with quiet assurance of making it to the topmost executive level. His comments about his work emphasized how much he liked the responsibility for people, not just the challenge of tasks, and yet his comments stressed the need for balance in life. On the other hand, he will probably look back on the recent years of his life as ones of transition, having been through an extremely stormy period in his marriage that led to finding great fulfilment in both his professional and private life. His view of his work:

'I like a job that gives me a chance to stretch myself, a job that has a lot of change and variety. My ideal job is one that keeps me going – but not excessively. That's why I answered that last set of questions about my attitudes toward my job as being in-between. I don't like the terms "extremely" or "totally". I don't want a job to be "extremely absorbing" – only fairly absorbing.... I like responsibility, having people report to me, and shaping a department, influencing people ...'

'Would your ideal job be in a large company or a small company?'

'I'd prefer the large company. I'd rather, in a sense, be a small frog in a large pond than a big frog in a small pond. But ultimately I'd like to be a big frog in a big pond.'

'And do you expect to be this'?

'Well, if you had asked me twenty years ago, I would have said there's no way. I didn't really want to be a big frog in a big pond. But as I get older, I quite enjoy the idea and I guess I probably will be.'

The maintenance path

The change in this manager's aspirations illustrates the concept of integration. But contrast the managers above with another man who is the same age and has a similarly responsible position in another company. Neither he nor his wife are particularly happy about their marriage, although she is not overly concerned. Recently the wife has developed her own outside interests, for as she said: 'He is so involved in his job that I must have my own life.' This manager seems himself as investing the same amount of time and energy in his work as the man above, but he says of his lifestyle:

> My lifestyle? Yes, I have growing feelings of unease at occasional moments. I feel anxious about my idleness outside work. I feel that I'm wasting my time. And there have been long periods of stress in this new job – I'm not yet fully confident of my abilities. And our relationship is rather distant at home.

Notice how his comments flip from talking of private life to talking of professional life, and back again. It is this type of reflection that is essence of the midlife transition. Will he succeed in finding a life which gives him a sense of balance, of confidence, of renewed purpose? Who can say? If it does not happen, what would be the outcome?

We describe that outcome as 'maintenance' or resignation, and it is probably the most typical passage into the forties and fifties. Indeed, 'maintenance' is the word that the sociologists have used to describe this stage in life. It implies accepting the *status quo*, accepting that life has reached a plateau, accepting a lifestyle that is to some extent fragmented and certainly not integrated – accepting these things with the growing sense of resignation that researchers have found to characterize the fifties. Gradually, the attitude of bitterness, which contrasts with the prevailing ambivalence of earlier life stages, is muted – changing to one of fatalistic acceptance, the resignation that is the most characteristic sign of the maintenance path. One preoccupation may grow – a concern for the relationship with now adolescent children; this probably is coloured by a belated hope of helping them to realize themselves in the fulfilling way which has not proved possible.

The distinction between generativity and maintenance is captured in one of the central findings of George Vaillant's *Adaptation to Life* study. Vaillant found that the 'best outcomes'; – the people who at age 50 were the best adapted to life as measured by a score of tests – were people who looked back on the years from 35 to 49 as the happiest in their lives, but nevertheless they saw the seemingly calm period from 21 to 35 as the unhappiest. Not surprisingly, these 'best outcomes' are people who are on the generativity path, individuals who in the turmoil of the late thirties and early forties have discovered a sense of purpose and of selfhood which makes the earlier years of their life seem pale, fragmented, and one-sided in comparison. In contrast, the 'worst outcomes' in the Vaillant study, those people least adapted to life in the forties, longed for the years of younger adulthood, regarding the storms of later life as too painful. These are the people on what we call the maintenance path, the people who are no longer going places but who are caught up in the day-to-day struggle to maintain a precarious lifestyle.

It is probable that few people achieve generativity as we have defined it. The view of phases in the lives of managers to which our survey has led is akin to Erikson's. His description emphasizes the different conflicts at different phases in life, and how the resolution of each conflict is dependent on how conflicts have been resolved at preceding stages. Achieving a generative lifestyle in the fifties presupposes that one has successfully launched one's career in the twenties and early thirties – that at this first stage one found a career that fitted with one's personal skills and orientations, and succeeded in launching oneself on that path. It presupposes that in the late thirties if not before, one became concerned about one's marriage and leisure development, and succeeded not only in improving the relationship with one's wife, and in balancing career, family and leisure interests, but also in taking care of one's wider personal development. And it presupposes that one has not defensively turned a blind eye to the painful questions of 'Who am I?' and 'What do I want to do with my life?' that this latter process raises.

Life phases and life tasks

Preoccupation with launching a career . . . preoccupation with marital and leisure development . . . preoccupation with the need to discover an integrated and purposeful lifestyle. This changing pattern of preoccupation is less a pattern of changing investment behaviour than one of changing sensitivity to different areas of life. The cycle of preoccupations appears as a rhythm that runs through the lives of many of our managers. It is a rhythm that probably in part reflects processes of psychological development. The development and maintenance of a sense of profession-al identity takes priority over investment in the quality of private life. Work comes before family, as the British study of workless people in the years of unemployment after 1972 shows (Marsden and Duff, 1975). Without work men slowly lose their morale and all sense of who they are. When unemployment brings working life to a halt, the holiday lasts for a week. Then gradually people fall apart, not only as providers but also as partners and human beings. Thus we find the same priority of work over family at the level of life-cycle development as we found when defining the relationship between professional and private life.

In part this rhythm reflects the ambitions of our group of successful managers – as well as the structure of careers and families in modern society. Lotte Bailyn, a professor of management at MIT who has long been interested in the adjustment problems of dual-career couples, points out how organizations place a premium on very high work involvement in the early career years. The route to the top is a 'fast burn' path – those who show early evidence of their potential become the focus of attention, while those who do not make it fall by the wayside – burnt out by a race that begins with a sprint (Bailyn, 1978).

But let us stress that this life rhythm is not a deterministic rhythm. It is not a rhythm that says, 'Launching your career will be a tense and painful process in your early thirties', or 'You will have a midlife crisis!' Instead it is a pattern whereby a person's sensitivity to different areas of life changes. It is a rhythm whereby certain events, *if* they happen, have great significance at one phase in life, but are of subsidiary significance at another phase. Let us discuss an example. Various studies, including our own, show statistically that marital happiness is at its lowest in the late thirties. The results are reported as if the truth were simply this. But is this a 'real' phenomenon, or is it rather that people are most sensitive to the problems in a marriage at that age? Our analysis suggests the second. At a later stage in life, those same people may perceive their marriages to be very happy, not because their behaviour or that of their spouses has changed, but because they have learned to accept their marriages for what they are.

We call these periods in adulthood *'phases'* rather than 'stages'. Perhaps this is just a subtle nuance. The word 'phase' is less deterministic. What we wish to reflect is that although the transition points from phase to phase are clearly marked by statistics, these are *average* patterns. So do not envisage suicide if you are 39 years old and still wholly preoccupied with your career! Some people may continue well into the fifties coping with launching their work lives, and hardly turn to private life.

The phases reflect different life tasks – what our analysis shows is a sequencing of life tasks. In the first twenty years of adulthood they are separate – psychologically separated. Few people can focus on such different tasks at one and the same time. One life task is that of *discovering professional identity* – yet it will be affected by private life and will influence the quality of that private life. Another life task is *building the quality of private life* – and it will be affected by the strength of professional identity. A third life task is the reinvocation of the adolescent identity crisis – when

57

the period of life investing is over, there is the need to *rediscover a personal sense of purpose.*

In the next three parts of this book, we turn to explore those three life tasks through the lives of our managers. Our intent is to provoke the reader into thinking of the personal challenges that he faces at different moments in life. And the different dilemmas in relating professional and private life. And if our life phases are indeed life stages, the 30-year-old reader will be instantly drawn to the next chapters on professional identity. The 38-year-old manager will want to skim through to the subsequent chapters on the quality of private life. And the 45-year-old person will be most drawn to the later chapters on lifestyles.

Part Two

Finding Professional Identity

Why is launching the career such a demanding process? Research, ours included, shows that vocation is rare – like love at first sight. Usually professional identity crystallizes slowly as a result of a long and painful process of trial-and-error. For some it never does. For example, the U.S. Department of Health, Education and Welfare reported in 1978 that the average American citizen can be expected to change jobs once every eighteen months, to change *career* three-and-a-half times during a lifetime! (*Psychology Today*, 1978). These changes are most likely to occur in the early adult years (Sommers and Eck, 1977), reflecting the intensity of the search at that time.

There can be few people among the millions of men and women who work as 'managers' who ever felt a calling to management. Management does not exist as a profession; the word covers a myriad ways of life. Some children may feel a calling to become doctors – they usually have some stereotyped notion of what that involves. But all a child sees of business and management is the cereal packet with its free offers on the carton and daddy's new car. Even if his father is a businessman, it is doubtful whether a son understands more of his profession than a briefcase full of papers spread out on the dining room table.

The fact that management consists of multiple careers is the attraction of business to many people. Others enter business after a process of eliminating other careers. Once in business, some particular role must be searched for and discovered. In the next four chapters we wish to map out this search process and its consequences for private life. As was often the case in our inquiry, many insights into husbands' careers derive from remarks made by wives. It was as if the husbands were immersed in the details of their career progress, whereas their wives could see the bigger picture. Their comments led us to conclude that *launching the career is a search for a job that fits with one's personality*, rather than a process of adapting oneself to fit a chosen career path.

In the interviews, each wife was asked how she felt about her husband's job. Most of their answers were couched in terms of whether the job made him satisfied or frustrated – *whether it suited him and his personality or not*. They experienced their husband's frustration as spillover, their satisfaction as independence.

Here is a typical positive reaction:

> His job really suits him and his temperament. It gives him a great deal of satisfaction, and he's very involved in it – sometimes to the exclusion of his family. He's much more happy now than he was a few years ago when he was in research.

At the other extreme, nearly 30 per cent of the wives felt that their husbands' work was so ill-suited to them that they wished they would break out and change work, company or occupation. Thirty per cent is rather a high proportion. But our discussions with the wives of other managers lead us to believe that it is representative.

Many of the husbands were aware of these feelings and sometimes interpreted them as ambition on the part of their spouses. But this was rarely accurate. The feelings usually represented a perception by the wife that her husband was not fulfilled in his current work.

> I'm very proud because he is successful. But it's not what I think he wants to do. He isn't really satisfied with what he's doing now and gets uptight. I strongly feel that he should get out, and I would support him if he ever does decide to do so. You see he wants to do more using his own initiative. Everything there as an accountant is so planned out for him. And he's so talented – it's such a waste. He carries on and doesn't want to talk about it because he hasn't got any clear ideas about what else he wants to do. But it niggles me that he's tied down to this job. I hate to think that he's spending the best years of his life in a job that isn't perfect for his talents.

'His work suits him.' 'His work doesn't suit him.' If a man who is impulsive, decisive and action-oriented finds himself in however important an analytic staff position, what is one to expect? Lack of sense of achievement; problems in his relationships with his subordinates and possibly with his boss; a feeling that his work is unstructured and lacking in meaning; a projection of these feelings onto the company producing a view that company policies and guidelines are inconsistent; uncertainties about his performance and future. What one expects to find is a host of concerns and preoccupations – concerns which will pervade his private life.

But what about the influence of a job on a man's personality? Launching the career could also be seen as adapting and developing one's personality to a chosen job path. As Kohn and Schooler (1973) have argued, the characteristics of the job affect a man more than the man can influence the job. People working in complex jobs develop intellectual flexibility; people with intellectual flexibility find it difficult to make simple jobs more complex. This is certainly true. A job influences one's perceptions, skills and thinking processes because of demands that must be met. The job affects one's psychological functioning – the various types of spillover are an example.

Each job develops or changes the person in some way. But in one job the young man finds that he dislikes certain important tasks. Work generates more distress than satisfaction – distress that will contaminate private life. This may lead to a job or career change. The new job generates a higher proportion of satisfaction relative to distress. The man feels closer to launching his career because what he is now doing is what suits him better. As we will show in this next part of the book, the launching of the career can be viewed as finding a job path that above all suits the *emotional* aspects of one's personality.

After 50 years of the study of stress, Hans Selye arrives at the same conclusion:

> The best way to avoid harmful stress is to select an environment (wife, boss, friends) which is in line with your innate preferences – to find an activity which you like and respect. Only thus can you eliminate the need for frustrating constant re-adaptation that is the major cause of distress. . . . The art is to find, among the jobs you are capable of doing, the one you really like best – and that people appreciate. Man must have recognition; he cannot tolerate constant censure, for that is what – more than any other stressor – makes work frustrating and harmful. (Selye, 1975, pp. 82–3, 99)

Find an activity which you like and respect. This is the essence of the process of finding professional identity. The path is long and difficult. It is the first major task of adulthood.

Chapter 5

The fit between personality and work

Common sense tells us to avoid putting square pegs into round holes. But the 'shapes' of people are difficult to evaluate and we often make costly mistakes. The fit between a person and a job is usually judged in terms of skill, ability and competence. Although it is natural for organizations to stress this aspect of fit, it is actually only one of three.

Let us define what we mean by the fit between man and job. A perfect fit occurs when three things are true simultaneously. One feels competent, one enjoys one's work, and one feels satisfied in living according to one's values. Thus a job should fit not only with one's skills and abilities, but also with one's motives and values (Schein, 1978). When such fit exists, one feels naturally confident and at ease. The feeling of authenticity results in increased self-esteem. Distress disappears and is replaced by calm or by eustress.

Whenever one of the three conditions is absent, there is a misfit. In the case of the total misfit, none of the conditions are fulfilled. He is not particularly competent or skilled at what he does. There are very few aspects of his work that he enjoys. And he feels ashamed of doing things that go against his values.

Tension and deep fear of failure are the natural consequences of going against one's own grain. Not feeling particularly comfortable with what they are doing, men who take jobs for which they are ill-fitted are often afraid that their weaknesses will show, that they will be found out. These inner doubts can be so intense that no amount of external recognition, no external acknowledgement of success, can eliminate them.

The competence misfit

The competence misfit is the man who enjoys his work and who is proud of what he does, but who is unsure of his skills and competence to do the job really well. He feels insecure, and this sense of insecurity may also diminish his enjoyment of the work. Nevertheless, he views the job as a substantial challenge. He is in a line position, for example, but finds it difficult to make decisions. Or he has moved into a personnel job to broaden his skills, but he knows little about recruitment, compensation and training issues. As a consequence of his doubts about his own competence he suffers from spillover.

These are three types of competence misfit. The *first* is the person who clearly and undeniably does not have the skills for the job and who is unlikely to develop them. Here is the very successful sales manager who is promoted to marketing director, in charge of formulating marketing strategy. He loves his new job because it gives him the opportunity to be in contact with an even wider range of clients than he had before. But this is not what the company is looking for: they wish him to formulate a new marketing strategy. But the new director, finding himself bogged down in this task, replies that the only way to do this is through direct client contact. Nevertheless, the signals he is receiving make him feel vaguely uneasy. Sales managers start complaining that he is doing their work. Reluctantly, the company decides that they made a mistake in promoting him. They concede that they judged his potential skills badly – they promoted him above his level of competence. This type of person may not last long in his post. Spillover may have been strong for a time, but then he moves and it ends – if he can digest the disappointment.

The *second* type of competence misfit performs sufficiently well to keep his job, but does not feel confident. Lacking natural skill for the work, he gets by through a massive investment of energy, where his more skilled counterparts would be more relaxed. He works long hours, follows every detail, and takes a briefcase of papers home each night. He may even be proud of how hard he works, and he enjoys the fact that results come out well. He holds onto his job through the investment of energy rather than skill, he trusts nobody else because he is not even confident of himself.

New jobs imply new tasks and activities, which especially for a young manager require skills and competences that one has never proven. The new position is an opportunity to develop those skills, believing but not knowing for sure that one has the capacities. Until those skills have been developed, one feels unsure of oneself; this is natural since that sense of insecurity pushes one to develop and adapt. This is the *third* type of competence misfit, one that is purely transitory. It is the product of learning and development, and the spillover gradually fades away. If it does not, then the pattern of misfit comes to resemble one of the two above.

Most organizations are highly sensitive to the competence of people in their jobs. The performance of the organization is at stake. Consequently vast amounts of time are spent in judging whether a person is competent for a promotion, and on whether a younger person has potential to develop or not. This is time well spent. But there are two other types of lack of fit which are equally important and that most organizations fail to recognize. These reflect the emotional aspects of fit. We call them *enjoyment misfit* and *moral misfit*.

The enjoyment misfit

The enjoyment misfit is competent at his job and proud of it, but he does not like doing it. Unlike the competence misfit who twists the job to what he enjoys doing, this manager competently does what has to be done – he may even be a good performer – but he does not derive intrinsic enjoyment from his work.*

This, for example, is the case of the man who has the necessary qualities to be a manager and who is promoted into a managerial job. He is highly respected for his technical competence and for his ability as a team member to mobilize others to action. But he would rather have remained in a technical position – he prefers individual challenge to the laborious process of working though other people. His colleagues and superiors, however, recognize his human and managerial skills. He is pressured into accepting the promotion, agreeing out of a sense of duty reinforced by an improved salary. But he is unhappy in his role. He buys a new house, but his wife remarks that he is more often moody than in the past.

There are other common causes that may lead a person to become an enjoyment misfit. Staying in a job too long is one example. Time can transform enjoyment into routine. The manager is competent but his job has become nothing more than predictable variations around a humdrum theme. In a study that has implications for job enrichment, Katz (1977) shows that the relationship between work satisfaction and productivity and job commitment increases sharply after the first six months of moving into a new job. This presumably reflects the increased satisfaction that comes with acquiring competence. This relationship levels off and the declines with longevity of tenure. It dips sharply in the fifth year, levels off, and then declines steadily after the tenth year in office. Feeling satisfied no longer depends on being committed and productive in the job.

---

* Many people are attracted to new jobs that they will not enjoy by the lure of extrinsic rewards (money, status, recognition, material well-being). One of the more exciting recent developments in motivational theory focuses on the interplay between these two sets of forces – the force of extrinsic rewards and the force of intrinsic rewards (see Deci, 1975).

At other times enjoyment is destroyed by work overload. Some people find it very difficult to say no to challenges and tasks that indeed they enjoy. As a consequence, they accept too many tasks or are given too many assignments. Separately, these assignments would be enjoyable, but taken as a whole they add up to stress and tension. Problems, deadlines and pressures on one assignment are always interfering with work on other assignments. The struggle to simply finish overrides any intrinsic enjoyment, and creates an enjoyment misfit.

The moral misfit

The moral misfit is the man who enjoys his work and is competent at it, but who does not feel proud of what he does. It forces him to compromise his values. He is a sales manager, for example, but he does not believe in the product he is selling. He would not buy it himself and cannot whole-heartedly recommend it. This discomfort spills over into his private life. After a successful and important sale he comes out feeling, 'thank goodness that is over'.

How comfortable does someone who has been involved in bribery to sell goods to a foreign country feel at home? Uncomfortable. The moral spillover created by unethical business practices has two additional twists: fear of legal consequences, and condemnation to secrecy which prevents all expression of feelings.

From an individual point of view, each of these forms of lack of fit is dangerous. If a manager accepts a task for which he lacks the competence, he risks losing his job. If he accepts a job for which he is skilled but which he does not like doing, he will be unhappy. If he accepts a job in which he does not feel pride, he will not feel at peace with himself. The organization may be only able to spot the incompetence misfit, but all three types of misfit will suffer, and in all three cases their families will be affected.

Professional identity as a sense of positive fit

A state of positive fit, something that gives one a sense of confidence, enjoyment and pride, a sense of congruence and ease, *is* difficult to achieve. That is why launching the career can be a long process. It is so difficult that for some people the process continues well into later years. Others never succeed in discovering this sense of fit, and end by abandoning all career oriented values.

Launching a career is generally a history of successive jobs, successive companies, and even successive occupations. In all of these, a man finds himself to be – in some degree or another – a misfit, but each new job leads to greater awareness of skills, needs and values. Jack

Williams can serve as an example of someone nearing the end of this process. At age 34 his sense of professional identity is beginning to form.

Jack was a business school graduate attracted by the prestige and earnings of a consulting career. For three years he worked as a consultant, solving problems of his client companies. He did well, and his sense of confidence in his problem-solving skills grew. But although people had told him about the long hours of work and the large amount of travel in the consultant's job, he never understood what this meant until he had experienced it. After marrying he came more and more to feel this as a burden. Moreover, he realized slowly that he disliked competitiveness in his relationships with his colleagues. He jumped at an unexpected offer to join one of his client companies as assistant to a divisional general manager. This was an unhappy experience which lasted for more than a year. Granted, the work was less competitive and entailed less travel, which he appreciated, but it was too unstructured. It gave him little sense of accomplishment. He missed having close contact with a team of people and felt himself to be in the backwater of corporate events. It was a low ebb in his career, and from time to time he yearned for the 'exciting' consulting days – now idealized in his memory.

One day, there was an opportunity to work as a senior analyst in the corporate planning team, an opportunity he grabbed with zest. He began this assignment with enthusiasm; the problems on which the team was working were important and taxed his skills. He felt very successful; he felt part of a team. His self-confidence increased.

One day at lunch, his boss commented on how he had seemingly begun to take over the leadership of the team of planners – how his colleagues called on him for advice and assistance, and how he had contributed to the creation of a strong team spirit. This side observation, this compliment made in passing over lunch, was for Jack a flash of insight. To be seen as a 'leader' . . . yes, indeed, perhaps! From that day on, he began to focus more consciously on leading his peers. He asked to attend a corporate seminar on management and felt confirmed and invigorated by the experience. Gradually, the ambition of taking over the formal leadership of the planning group emerged in his mind. Three years after starting in the planning department, he was promoted into that position.

Jack Williams is now eight years into his career, and we will leave him at that point. His professional identity has begun to emerge as a result of success and failures, experiences he liked and experiences he disliked, the positive feedback of some and the negative feedback of others. Although he may not express it in precisely these terms, he sees himself as liking and being good at problem-solving, but disliking competition and a high-pressure style of work. He prefers to work as part of a stable team, and relationships with other people are important to him. He sees himself as having the capacities to motivate and lead other people, and obtains satisfaction from doing so. His self-concept can be summarized by some label – as a 'planner' or more likely a 'planning manager', or even as a 'manager' of a certain type of problem-solving activity. In the future, he may even find that his self-concept matches even more closely the requirements of a position in charge of business development for his firm or another corporation.

Ed Schein has called the professional self-concept that emerges a *career anchor*, for it progressively comes to anchor the person to a particular type of job or a certain career path. This anchor is a collection of self-perceived talents and abilities, motives and needs, attitudes and values. The more professional identity has crystalized, the more these act as an anchor. If Jack Williams were to move back to his former consulting job, he would probably feel frustrated and ill-at-ease: his self-concept anchors him to a very different career path. He has the feeling of fitting more with his present job than he ever did as a consultant. He enjoys it more, he is more skilled, and he feels more proud of it.

In his book *Career Dynamics*, Schein outlines five different career anchors, five professional identities that emerge from the years of launching the career. Each of these anchors represents a different type of fit between man and job. In describing them, he singles out the central skill, motive or value that characterizes these professional identities. The five different central concerns he found are technical competence, managerial competence, creativity, autonomy and security.

Technical and managerial anchors

Schein studied 44 management graduates for 12 years, interviewing them last in their early mid-thirties. The largest group, 43 per cent of them, were anchored to their *technical or functional competence*. What linked their personalities to their jobs was the technical content of the work they were doing. What they valued, liked doing and were good at was exercising their technical expertise in their particular functional area – be it engineering, marketing, research or accounting. Although most had managerial responsibilities, their prime satisfaction did not come from leading other people but from the wider scope that this responsibility gave them to exercise their technical skill. They may well have liked the managerial role as leader, but only when they were leading people with technical values and interests similar to their own – their technical competence placed them in a dominant role, which would not have been the case had they been managing people in a different area of work. The importance they attributed to their expertise meant that they would have felt uncomfortable in another functional area. They would not have welcomed a general management position.

In the early career stage, the second group of managers may have looked outwardly the same. They too were functional managers. But whereas the men above were managing their own functional areas, 18 per cent of Schein's small group of graduates held positions specifically as managers – of whatever functional area. They had no strong attachment to that function; instead they were attached to picking up experience in different functions. These were people who were described as having *managerial competence* itself as a career anchor. Their aspirations were to attain general management jobs, for instance as 'product-line managers', 'divisional general managers', or 'general managers of a subsidiary', and specific technical jobs were only stepping stones. The early careers of these men could thus be particularly stressful.

Schein sees the core of the managerial anchor as being a combination of three types of competence. The first is analytic competence: the ability to identify, analyse and solve problems under conditions of uncertainty, and the liking for such problem solving activities. The second is interpersonal competence – exercising influence, control and leadership over other people in the pursuit of specific targets and goals. The managerially anchored person, thus, is stimulated by the problem of analysing what achievement is possible for a group of people, and by influencing them so as to bring that achievement about. If one defines 'management' in classic terms as the process of bringing about results through other people, this is not surprising. The third element of this anchor is emotional competence. This is the capacity to be stimulated by interpersonal and other events which other people would view as crises; the capacity to bear power and responsibility without being plagued by paralysing feelings of guilt, shame and doubt. As Schein notes, the very things which the men 'anchored in technical/functional competence feared or deplored as "politics in the executive suite" or the "jungle" were seen by the managerially anchored ... as "stimulating" and the "place where the action is". Politics, in-fighting, wheeling and dealing, making things happen, having the ultimate responsibility was seen by them as the very thing they wanted and would be stimulated by.' (Schein, 1978, p. 136). What is a source of shame for one person is source of pride to another.

It is the combination of these three qualities – analytic, interpersonal and emotional – that fits the requirements of a general management job. Analytic competence alone may be enough for a technical or corporate staff position, but not for a leadership role. Interpersonal competence alone may be associated with a fulfilling role in a supervisory job. The combination of analytic and interpersonal competence fits with the requirements of functionally oriented middle management, but the price of pushing far beyond will be stress, unless there is also strong emotional competence.

Creativity, autonomy and security anchors

The majority of Schein's small group of graduates had technical or managerial anchors. Others fitted with neither of these self-concept descriptions, but instead with one of three others.

Some men were continually involved in launching new ventures or getting new projects underway. Once these projects reached a certain stage in development they would get bored and turn to something different – another venture. Schein saw their career anchors as based on *creativity*. These men were either successful entrepreneurs, or were actively thinking of breaking out of their current jobs to found their own businesses. Schein observes that although many managers have dreams of founding their own enterprises because of the autonomy and independence that this will bring, the true entrepreneur has very different drives from the managerially anchored man. He is a person who revels in the process of creating something new. When that project reaches a mature stage, he is torn by boredom on the one hand and possessiveness on the other.

The one value that Schein's fourth group prized above all others was independence. These people were anchored by *autonomy*. They saw the constraints of organizational life as restrictive and intrusive, and they found it difficult to belong to any large and formalized group. Schein found that they had often started in business or government but had left for related occupations which provided them with more autonomy: consulting in a small firm, an academic position in a university, free-lance journalism, or running a very small business. They wished above all to work on their own, controlling their lives and work without the interference of others.

The anchor of the fifth and last group was very different from the others. These people appeared to need *security or stability* above all. Some were deeply attached to their local community or their families, where perhaps their wives had their own careers. To maintain their private life stability, they would change job or company rather than accept a transfer. Others placed a high value on stable membership of an organization and were willing to accept an organizational definition of what their work should be. Very sensitive to the expectations of other people, they corresponded in Schein's mind to the conformist 'organization man' described by William Whyte in the 1950s classic of that name.

The concept of the career anchor illustrates at a general level the types of positive fit between personality and work that emerge from the process of launching the career.*† This concept focuses of course only on the central theme of that professional identity: the skills, needs and values which, separately or in combination, are the crux of positive fit in the occupational world. Another interesting dimension of professional identity, for example, is the fit between one's cognitive style and the work one does (Kolb and Plovnick, 1977; Kolb, 1971; Keene, 1977). Obviously, a list of all the shapes of positive fit would be infinitely long. Launching the career means that each person has to explore and discover his own particular shape, and the type of organization where he may fit best.

The stabilizing gyroscope

Schein calls these professional self-concepts 'anchors' because that term denotes 'a growing area of stability within the person without, however, implying that the person ceases to change or grow' (Schein, 1978, p. 126). With this professional identity comes the career stability that permits growth and change in other areas – the turning to private life in particular. This inner gyroscope that after much tribulation has steadied now serves to guide, constrain, stabilize and integrate the person's career.

Talk with someone who has a clear sense of professional identity and you feel this in his vocal and confident description of himself. His self-confidence come across as authentic, not simply as a mask. He is capable of describing who he is, but also who he is not. He is not all things to all people. He knows what he wants to become; he tells you he would say no to opportunities that would not fit in with his life path, even though on the surface these opportunities might appear tantalizing. He is very conscious of what he likes doing, but he does not disguise his dislikes. He has learnt to manage his time by saying no to interesting challenges that would overload him; indeed he has earned the freedom to say no because what he does he does very well. He can describe his strengths, and also his weaknesses. But these weaknesses do not seem to be strong limitations on

---

* Schein certainly envisages other anchors. Discussions with people in the personnel area suggest that service may be a central career value for many of them. Power and control, and also variety may be anchors as well.

† The evidence today suggests that the technically anchored person is the most common in business, although the mission of management development has been to develop the general manager. Ansoff (1978) argues cogently that the demand for managers in the 1980s will be for 'T-shaped' managers, as opposed to the general manager prized today. The T-manager is a generalist-cum-specialist. The top of the T is his general knowledge of the various functions and activities of the firm, while the stem of the T is his area of technical speciality. The reason for this demand, says Ansoff, is the exponentially growing complexity of large organizations. This increasingly requires specialist expertise without sacrificing overall coordination.

his career because the work that he does rarely requires him to venture into areas of weakness. In short, he fits with what he is doing.

For most people, launching the career is a history of partial misfit situations where one discovers what one does well or badly, what one likes doing or dislikes doing, what one feels proud of or ashamed of. It is an exploration of oneself in the real world, and the search for a realm which fits with what one has discovered about oneself. At best, this is a process of guided trial-and-error. Unfortunately, it is often a random process – even successful people, who fit with the career paths they have found, often attribute their successful launching to luck. Later, in Chapter 7, we look at how exploration can be guided. Before this, we will assess what happens to private life during these early career years.

Chapter 6

Misfits and prisoners

> I know a little about his work, but not a lot. He doesn't talk much about it, especially in recent years. I ask him what he's doing and he just mumbles something and grunts.

> The trouble is that he is *not* happy with what he is doing. I'd prefer him to be in a more technical job where he is happier. He wanted this job, but I can't see where it will lead. It's impossible to talk with him about it. The problem is that he does each job well. But I feel this career path won't give him the satisfaction he wants. I wish that he would change, but it's useless to try to talk with him about it.

The misfit is not happy with his work, and his wife feels it. Tension spills over into private life. If one takes the comment above as an indicator of 'poor fit', then managers are having serious problems – nearly 30 per cent of the wives we interviewed wished that the job, occupation or company of their husbands were completely different. His present job brought unhappiness into his life, and thus into hers.

The private life of the misfit is a 'private life' – in inverted commas. Physically and materially it exists. A wife, several children, a house, a garden, a workshop, maybe some friends. In terms of what he values, these may be the most precious part of life, maintained with money and modest time investment. But psychologically, private life has become almost non-existent. Private life is not maintained with the type of investment that gives it meaning – the investment of attention, sensitivity and energy.

Our purpose in this chapter is to look at the private live of two types of managers. They are the people at the extremes in terms of the process of finding professional identity. One is the extreme misfit, who has been quite unable to discover any sense of professional identity and who feels blocked, or who has lost that sense of identity for some extended period of time. The other is the prisoner of success. He has a very strong sense of professional identity – his job and career path fit him like a glove. He finds such excitement and stimulation in his work that his whole identity has become wrapped up in that part of his life. There is little room in his life for any private life identity.

The misfit

The consequences of lack of fit between personality and job manifest themselves in different ways at different stages in the career cycle. We call the younger people, in their twenties and early thirties, simply misfits. In their late thirties and forties we call them strugglers. The men in their late forties and fifties who have still not found their path or who have lost it, and who begin to accept this with resignation, are called resigned plateaued managers. At this time we will only describe the problems of the misfit in launching his career.

The young misfit

The misfit is a person in his late twenties or early thirties who derives little pleasure from his work. He feels that he puts too much time and energy into it in proportion to his private life. But he has no immediate intention of changing behaviour. His problem is that his professional life does not give him any sense of achievement, enjoyment or pride. He does not fit with the demands of his job. He may have pushed himself into a particular function because he saw it as the quickest route to the top in his company – for instance, one manager was in a financial position even though his skills and interests lay in marketing. Or he may have difficulty in adjusting to a middle management job since his aptitudes match better the technical demands of a relatively junior position.

Highly invested in work but with little sense of reward, the young misfit has a low sense of self-esteem. The misfits whom we interviewed were the men among the younger managers most likely to show signs of emotional strain; they often felt moody, exhausted, irritable, restless, and unable to concentrate. Four of the 16 young managers in our interview survey were clear misfits. Their wives complained bitterly of the unhappiness that their spouses brought home with them from work. None of the men saw their marital lives as being particularly happy. And curiously enough, all but one of the men assessed their marriages as even more unsatisfactory in all respects than did their wives. This assessment is not a concern, however. Other younger managers are at least disturbed by tension in the marriage. The misfit has difficulty *even* in becoming concerned about the health and future of his family life. The sensitivity valve is practically closed, even to sadness, anger and desperation on the part of his family.

The case of Pierre

Pierre is the 33-year-old marketing manager whom we introduced on page 24. Outwardly he is very successful, but inwardly the picture is different. He feels very stressed, worries about his health, and is vaguely worried about drinking too much. Pierre has never experienced any other line of work than marketing. But it gives him no sense of satisfaction. He feels tense in his work but cannot trace this to any single feature of the job – it results from a multitude of small things. When at home, his thoughts are never far from his job. But when at work, he thinks more often of his family and leisure than any other manager in our survey.

He talks of his work as interesting and varied, but exhausting and frustrating. 'You never see the results of your efforts,' he says. 'It is competitive; you live with a constant fear of being outdone. It is fluid, you never know whether you have done well.' Yet apparently his work is appreciated by his superiors and his company – he has been promoted rapidly into a position of considerable responsibility and is seen as successful. That very success makes it difficult for him to envisage changing to any other function: he has no experience in other areas. Perhaps sales rather than marketing, he asks? But he has never experienced a sales job.

The way Pierre talks of the influence of work on family life illustrates the extreme spillover experienced by the misfit.

'Oh, it's above all the stress. One has always some worry in mind. And those worries prevent me from profiting from my family life. I suppose I rarely leave my work behind me. It is always in mind. It's OK at the moment, but will it go on? The future worries me.

'For example, if I was more firm, I'd come home much earlier than I do. But you pay the price for that later – it gives a bad impression. That's why the future worries me. I'm willing to pay the price now if I was sure of the future. ...

'If I do a balance sheet, then I suppose I don't do much which is tangible outside work. I don't paint any longer. I used to be good at the piano, but I've given that up.'

'Have you given up time with your wife and children?'

'Time, no. It's not a question of time but a question of being available. I'm not as relaxed as I'd like to be to enjoy the time I have with my wife and children. I don't *want* to be with them often. Sometimes it's sad not to want to talk with your children when you come back home. I don't feel very *useful* outside my work. It's not a problem of time. I'm just at an important stage in my career. And it's difficult to forget it when you come back home.'

Jeanette, Pierre's wife, is not sure what is wrong. He's not enough at home. Maybe it's his anxious character, she speculates? Maybe he should not stay in marketing? 'It's too risky. You don't last long. They squeeze everything out of you and then chuck you away.' She would like him to have a calmer job, but she does not know what this would be. For her, the problem has become worse with time. Earlier in their marriage, he would come home at six; now he is rarely there before the children are in bed. She comments that he seems more and more edgy – he has problems in relaxing and in falling asleep.

This growing strain has created a worrying personal dilemma for Jeanette, about which she cannot talk with her husband. She feels quite content as a mother and housewife. But in recent years she has often thought of getting a job – a prospect which previously she saw in the more distant future. Pierre does not even take her work at home for granted; he is hardly even aware of it. That for her is worse than rebuke. She suffers from coping alone not only with the two children but also with the 'eldest, eldest child', namely Pierre himself; at times, it is a relief when he is away on a trip. She feels alone; a job may give her a sense of perspective and balance, as well as contact with others. But she feels doubly trapped because every time she talks about this, Pierre becomes moody and withdraws into himself. Rather than making him suffer more, she has to keep her own frustrations to herself.

Talking of this as 'being an important stage in his career', Pierre has all the career preoccupations of the younger manager. Few younger managers are prepared to compromise their ambition until their mid-thirties. But many signs indicate that Pierre is nearing the end of a long struggle; that he is psychologically and unconsciously preparing himself for one option in the misfit struggle. To search for identity in private life alone. To turn to an instrumental existence.

Though his behaviour as seen by his wife does not bear it out, he saw the relationship between professional and private life as increasingly instrumental (work serving to maintain private life) though for the time being predominantly one of spillover. While his wife saw his family life as diminishing in importance during the last five years, judging by his behaviour, he saw his private life as having greatly increased, judging by

75

his inner values. He was one of the few managers who described his ideal job as low on challenge, pressure and competitiveness; one of his fantasies for the future was to work until 3.00 each afternoon and then return home. Yet his other hope was to be promoted, and this hope was built on a partially acknowledged myth:

> You know, what I'm going to tell you may be stupid, but I have the impression that the higher one climbs in the hierarchy, the easier things become. Up there, you can rest much more on other people. *They* do the work.

If Pierre is promoted, we believe his dilemma will be even more extreme. The interviewer described him as someone who lives on a boat in perpetual fear of being thrown in the water, and who has thus decided to sleep on the life raft.

Pierre is a misfit. He has never explored any other types of work, any other aspects of his personality, so change is difficult. It has become increasingly difficult as he has become more successful. And he *is* outwardly successful. Probably his bosses are unaware of his inner turmoil. They may even see him for the time being as an aggressive and energetic high flier. But lacking deep interest and natural skill for the work, the misfit can only make up for this with an overinvestment of energy. Even more energy is consumed in masking his feelings towards his colleagues. This *may* lead to success, but at the price of enormous internal tension reinforced by fear of failure – and the suspension of private life.

If one assumes that the launching of the career is most salient in the life of the younger manager, then the passive stance of the young misfit towards his family becomes understandable. He is deeply troubled by his work problems, the nature of which he is unable to diagnose. He is psychologically most involved in his career, but that career is giving him little return on his investment. Consequently he experiences considerable emotional strain. Paralysed by a vicious circle of anxiety in the dominant arena of his life, he has little if any constructive emotional energy to channel into his marriage. He withdraws from his marriage. From a social point of view, his situation is perhaps the most alarming among the managers at the early stage of adulthood.

The dangers for the misfit are very real and very serious. The impact of emotional spillover on private life may damage that private life irreparably. He may eventually succeed professionally and later in life regard the destruction of his family life as the price he had to pay for success. He may, on the other hand, never make it and continue through his late thirties as a struggler, eventually becoming a bitter manager on a plateau. In such cases the cost for everybody involved, the man himself, his family and the corporation, will be enormous.

The prisoner of success

At the other end of the spectrum we find the prisoner of success. This is the man who in launching his career found a perfect fit between his personality and the jobs available to him. After the sad story of the misfit you may breathe a sigh of relief and assume that since he is so happy at work he will have a wonderful private life. But unfortunately this is often not the case.

You may remember that we said that at this stage in an individual's life, having a well functioning professional life is a necessary precondition for a well-functioning private life. Necessary but not sufficient. Having a good professional life does not guarantee having a good private life. The situation of the prisoner of success illustrates this. He *has* discovered a sense of professional identity. But in a different way, his dilemma in balancing professional and private life is every bit as acute as that of the misfit. He is a hostage to the success of his career.

The prisoner of success has very definitely succeeded in launching his career. His work fits his personality like a glove. He enjoys his work, is good at it, and is very proud of his success. He is the dynamic manager who radiates self-confidence, who is the model and envy of all around him. This is true regardless of his career track, be he the general manager, the technical specialist, the academic researcher, or the entrepreneur underway building his empire of companies, The three 'prisoners' in our interview survey were all younger men, but there is no reason why a prisoner may not be in his middle years.

The prisoner is ambitious, and his situation illustrates the dangers of a strong professional identity coupled with ambition. He is on the success spiral we described in Chapter 4: an initially challenging job, mastery of that challenge leading to recognition, praise, and a feeling of psychological success, leading in turn to greater challenges in a spiral which reinforces itself. The result is a person passionately absorbed by his career. His work gives him immense satisfaction. If he feels tense, it is the positive stress of excitement and stimulation. He is on a colossal ego trip. But in one area of his life only, and this is his deep source of worry. As with the misfit and most other younger managers, private life is a blackcloth to the stage, but for different reasons. For the misfit, professional tension pervades and dulls private life. For the prisoner, professional satisfaction excludes and obliterates private life.

The prisoner may see the relationship between professional and private life as one of spillover, though more likely as one of conflict. His problem is not one of energy – it is more a feeling that there is no time for private life. His limited waking hours are consumed by the drug of professional fulfilment. When he returns home, he simply wants to relax, unwind, have his bodily needs taken care of. The spillover into private life is at the basic level of physical fatigue. Holidays are a bore to him. His conscience tells him that he owes at least this much to the family, but deep down he feels the absence of the stimulation of work. He eagerly accepts excuses to postpone, cancel or abbreviate his holidays, rationalizing this to his wife with a guilty conscience.

The prisoner is the person who is most likely to *escape* back into his career when there are family tensions. To quote the wife of a prisoner:

> When things are going badly at home, he certainly puts more emphasis on his work and career as an escape.

In contrast the misfit is paralysed by family tension – he does not have the energy to face up to it. He does not have a satisfying point of escape like the prisoner. The misfit goes down to the pub, out to the café, or turns on the television. The prisoner goes back to his work.

We want to emphasize that although the prisoner is ambitious, it is not his ambition alone which marks him as a prisoner. It is the fact that he has discovered a powerful sense of professional identity. The young misfit is also ambitious. Ambitions and aspirations help create the dilemma of professional and private life, but it is the degree of fit that leads to the way in which that dilemma is experienced. One might think that the prisoner has values which revolve around his career. This is not necessarily true. He is likely to have dual values – his private life is if anything more 'important' to him than his professional life. The dilemma that he experiences is acute, as the life of the following prisoner shows.

The case of Bill

At the age of 34, Bill is probably the most successful of all the managers we interviewed, regardless of age. At the time of interview, he was running one of four divisions of a large company and was tipped off for the presidency. (Two years later, he is indeed president.) If you ask him how come he has been so successful, his answer is 'luck'.

Luck turns out to be the fact that, with a strong but unrecognized managerial anchor, he found a first job which suited his personality ideally. He does *not* attribute success to his ambition – in fact Bill sees himself as no more ambitious and no more talented than any other man. The events that led to his success spiral were as follows.

At university, where he met his wife, he studied languages. He had no particular idea what he wanted to do with his life, and initially looked with disfavour at the idea of a career in business. The choice of this career came about more through the pressure of having to choose a job to support himself and his new wife, and by a process of eliminating other opportunities. The element of 'luck' was the fact that the first job he chose turned out to interest him. As a very junior manager, the rapid path upward on the success spiral began. Unconsciously and without searching more than any other man, Bill found himself in a line of activity which matched his personality. He short-circuited the process of discovering professional identity.

> When I look at the person that I am now, and at my wife, we are both very different persons from when we came out of university. And one of the reasons why one is very different is one's work experience and the way one reacts to that work experience. Had I not found an interesting job, or had it not just happened that way – if 'la Fortuna' hadn't played her cards that way – then I might have had a very different reaction. I might have been much more home-oriented, much more intellectually oriented than I am.

Bill is indeed the first person to recognize that his career may have been very different if this had not happened to him. His personality, the balance between professional and private life, would have been different.

Bill spends 90 per cent of his energy on his work and is often away from home. He sees his marriage as 'interesting', but full of conflict and unhappiness. And without knowing what to do about it, this plagues him with guilt and doubt.

> I *do* find the conflict between my desire to achieve in business terms and the desire to satisfy the very reasonable needs of my family creates the most difficult decisions for me. And *yes*, one does *not* do things one would like to do ...
>
> To be fair, I *often* get tired and I frequently regard my home as a place to relax in rather than to do what my wife has stored up for me to do. I've been away, for example, and it's nice to have a siesta in the afternoon, or whatever. But there are all the family demands, and I actually *understand* that. But I haven't found a solution to that.

Jane's own feelings are tinged with bitterness since she herself gave up the beginnings of a very successful career in order to have children and support her husband. It is not that she regrets the decision, for she feels the need to spend part of her life in this role as a mother and wife. Jane regards this role, in this stage of life at least, as a career, and had high aspirations for her performance. What makes her bitter at times, furious at others, is the fact she cannot perform in this career for lack of the necessary partner. She talks about her reactions to his travel and frequent lateness in coming home:

> It's not a very simple answer, obviously. To a certain extent it suits me, because I have a lot of work myself in the evening. But that only allows for I suppose about 30 per cent of his absence from home. And then I give him credit for perhaps another 20 per cent! [laughs]. The rest of it I resent. Resent? Well, perhaps that's a rather loaded word. But certainly I think it's a pity – both myself and my children lacking the kind of companionship and fathering which we would like ... And his travel is now a fairly major source of conflict. It's probably difficult to say 'conflict' because one understands why travel has to take place. It's more sadness. And of course sadness leads to conflict.

The dilemma of the marriage of the prisoner is acutely felt by both partners – Bill and Jane are different from other such couples only in the fact that the dilemma expresses itself in the open conflict of two very expressive people. With other couples, the tensions are more hidden – less voiced but equally felt. The resolution of this dilemma is uncertain, though the options are clear. Bill may turn more to his private life, especially if he reaches a plateau in his career. Jane may settle for the role as a supportive wife, turning her energies fully to the children. She may try to find her own independent life in a professional career, settling for marriage as home base. Or they may divorce, finding new partners who are more willing to accommodate to their life aspirations.

But for the time being, they live with their dilemma. According to Jane:

> I think the worst bit about being married to a business executive is that it means conflict over priorities. If he were a nine-to-five man and we knew exactly where we stood in terms of commitment and time, then everything else would fall neatly, perhaps too neatly, into place. But because it's a high pressure job and he's been unusually successful unusually young ...

> Having got used to the loneliness, its just the fact of having to be responsible for running a family and a home. And having to be totally healthy, totally responsible all the time – never being able to relax, to be drearily exhausted. To get the flu and not being able to flop down and enjoy it – just having to be superhuman, I think that's the worst part of it. Because I think if you are married to a man who has this sort of executive responsibility, then the woman has to take on many of the tasks that the man really should do at home. And therefore one has to be really superhuman – both physically and mentally!

But I suppose one should say that the good bits about being married to an executive are having the financial security. One gets slightly spoilt in not having to worry about whether my housekeeping will stretch or not. But I think he'd like these sort of things to be more important to me than they really are.

According to Bill:

My wife feels that we should accept a less high standard of living and I shouldn't travel so much. But what she doesn't realize is that I work for job satisfaction – not for money.

If the misfit's problem is that he lives with a sense of failure, the prisoner's problem is that he is too successful for his own good. When you ask him if he thinks that he is paying a price for his success he is likely to answer 'not really. If I didn't work as I do I'd be unhappy, and the price I'd pay would be more than whatever price I'm paying now.' But he is not perfectly happy. He wishes he had more time to take care of other aspects of his life. But at the end he is like a man in love with his work and loving his wife and children. This demanding love affair makes him happy and unhappy. He wishes it wouldn't hurt his wife so much but he won't give it up for anything in the world. As for his wife she is often jealous. It is not as if she dislikes his being in love with his job; it is that she misses his being equally in love with her. The prisoner lives with a dilemma which he may resolve in the next phase of his life. The misfit lives with a dual dilemma; unable to launch his career, he risks becoming a struggler still with few resources available for his private life. What could he have done different- ly? We take this up in the next chapter.

Chapter 7

Launching the career

Launching the career means finding professional identity and managin spillover, thus creating the basic preconditions for a healthy private life. In this chapter, we wish to describe the processes that this involves, and in particular that of exploration.

Exploration

As we described in Chapter 5, the professional self-concept has three components: the talents and abilities that one sees oneself as having, the motives and needs that one recognizes in oneself, the attitudes and values that one holds (Schein, 1978). This self-concept develops through experience. A man does not know whether he has good negotiating skills until he has handled several negotiations; past experience in situations of conflict may give him indications, though he may not associate these experiences with the negotiating situation until he has tried it out. He does not know whether he will like selling until he has tried that out, though again past experience in similar situations may be an indicator. And through the experience of selling, he may find out something about himself – for example, that he likes it (because it brings him into contact with people), but is not good at it (because he cannot be pushy).

A person may have certain vague attitudes about corporate responsibility or abortion. But these attitudes crystallize when one is confronted with the test of a real dilemma. One is asked to go along with a corporate conspiracy. One's wife is pregnant with an unwanted baby. Attitudes and values take solid shape at moments like these.

One side of exploration is exploring this inner world through successive experiences. The other side is exploring the outer world – the characteristics of ocupations and jobs that represent alternative scenes for a career. To find out about different roles, one often has to try out acting the different parts. A man is attracted to a consultant's job. He can explore a little by talking with some consultants. They tell him that it involves solving complex problems, and he learns something about the characteristics of certain consulting organizations. But he may not find out about the pressures and loneliness in that profession until he has tried out being a consultant. And what about a product management job? It is difficult to describe anything but the bare bones of product management, and even then only in a stereotyped way. Through direct and indirect exploration, one acquires that knowledge of jobs and occupations. The misfit feels that somewhere the ideal job for him exists. But he has no idea where since his exploration of jobs and occupations has been narrow.

Childhood and exploration

The earlier years in childhood and adolescence may have prepared a man well or badly for this process of exploration. Exploration is indeed a central process throughout childhood, and it continues into adulthood. The child pushes, tests, tries out, experiments – it explores its world. Its skills develop through this process; it becomes aware of its own likes and dislikes. Personality slowly starts to crystallize.* White (1959) calls this the competence motive and he views this as the mainspring of human development. Children play games and act out roles. The developmental psychologist Jerome Bruner calls this 'serious play': it is a vital part of learning to undertake adult roles (Bruner, 1966).

The process of exploration continues into early adulthood, with three important differences. First, 'serious play' is over. An adult is exploring in a real world where he or she will suffer or enjoy the consequences. Second, the exploration is now no longer constrained by parental figures, though, constraints may remain as a residue of parental do's and don'ts. But third, a new constraint is added which did not exist before. There is now a sense of urgency and intensity to the process that grows with age: I must find out quickly what I want to do before it is too late.

Let us be clear about one point. The fit between personality and work that leads to a career is not predetermined or measurable at an early age. Fit is discovered through experience. The young manager is attracted to a new job. But the job calls for skills which he has never proven. Will he be able to master it or not, he asks himself? Will it be a stepping stone in his development, or will it be a stumbling block? He may spend sleepless nights wrestling with such questions. But if it is one of those borderline opportunities, just within and just outside his capacities, he will never

---

* Research on handicapped children shows that physical or motor ability is essential to intellectual, psychological and personality development. If the child cannot physically explore its outside world, it becomes handicapped even in its intellectual development.

know whether it fits him or not until he tries it out. *The actual doing is the only real test.*

Exploration as career search

For may people, exploration means finding an occupational pyramid that one can climb. For others, it means attaining the freedom to pursue some satisfying activity for a few years, then branching into another activity that now looks appealing. For yet others, it means finding a satisfying job that one can pursue for the rest of one's days.

Michael Driver of the University of Southern California has shown that the idea of a career, and the type of fit that people are trying to attain, takes four different forms (Driver, 1980). These are:

The steady state career
The linear career
The spiral career
The transitory career

The *steady state career* is epitomized by the engineer, technician or government administrator who fits with his job and resists all pressures ever to move. He carries out his duties well and finds his work interesting. He is not overly ambitious, for as he rightly points out, ambition only brings stress. His career focuses on maintaining the niche that is his source of satisfaction and of income, in the face of inevitable changes and pressures. Launching the career for the steady state person thus means discovering his niche in the organizational world.

The man with a *linear career* concept, on the other hand, sees his career as a ladder, a progression up a hierarchy. Professional identity for such a man does not mean finding *the* job; it means finding some career ladder, usually technical or managerial in nature, where he has the skills, enjoys the type of work, and is proud of what he does. The linear person is particularly prone to falling into emotional misfit traps at all stages of his career. He is the most ambitious person; he desires prestige and material reward. While launching his career, he is often tempted into jobs that appeal to his ambition and that he can do well. He may not explore widely enough, tending to convince himself prematurely that he has found his career path and realizing only later that he has trapped himself by his success in a line of work that he does not enjoy or does not value.

His career after launching is also more hazardous, for career ladders are rarely if ever straight. For example, in most corporations the ladder of rewards for a technically oriented career reach a plateau fairly early. To progress further on the company ladder, he must move into general management. In a former study, Paul Evans showed how this creates a severe dilemma for some technically oriented managers. Not all such managers experience it, only those who are ambitious or linear in how they view their careers. At one time sure of their sense of fit, they become more and more uncertain of themselves as they near general management. Most of them begin dreaming of leaving to join very small enterprises in the belief (probably correct) that only there can they become top directors and also remain close to the technical action (Evans, 1975).

An increasing number of people (particularly in the United States) have begun to question the linear type of career. Driver describes these people as spirallers. The *spiral career* is one of successive and qualitatively different careers. If one reviews the career of a spiraller, one finds change every five to seven years to a different career path. A work area is found which more or less matches with personality. There is a period of professional stability for several years within that career path, as a production manager for example. But gradually the person begins to feel discontented with his choice – too immersed in the action, he finds little time for reflection. One day he seizes an opportunity or makes a break, leaving business for the academic world. He launches into a new career path and establishes a new fit. Again, some years later, he feels the itch to break out. He has many ideas that he would like to realize through an organization of his own. He leaves the university world to found his own enterprise.

The spiraller rejects the linear success values of our society. He is oriented toward self-realization and self-fulfilment. Each time he fits with a job, he satisfies one part of himself and discovers other parts of himself through that activity. He learns and changes through his work, and eventually he sees in front of himself another area of exploration. It is the process of exploration that is for him exciting. Each exploration is an opportunity to grow, develop, change, and realize himself.

All of these three types of career imply discovering some sense of fit, either of evolving or life-long duration. All three are stabilized by some form of professional self-concept which may change in the case of the spiraller, be more permanent in the cases of the linear or steady-state person. In contrast, the *transitory career* is not based on any clear professional self-concept. The transitory person does not have a sense of professional identity. He does not search for an anchor to the organizational world. He does not want to be tied down.

In the lingo of the other careerists, the transitory person is the 'drifter' or 'hippy'. The psychologists would say that he has a diffuse sense of identity. Ask him what he will be doing tomorrow, and he says he doesn't know. He is opportunistic, giving in to current whims and pressures. The idea of fit with a role and development of that fit has no meaning. There was a tendency in the past to label such people as maladjusted or immature. But Driver sees transitoriness as a viable self-concept which indeed matches the demands of certain types of organization. However, we rarely meet the transitory person in large profit-oriented business organizations, the majority of which are structured around the concept of the linear career.* Most of the managers we interviewed considered their careers in this latter way. Such people are least likely to pay adequate attention to the elements of exploration.

The elements of exploration

Obviously, one cannot try out all opportunities, and so career exploration has to be guided. If successful, it is likely to be guided by seven sub-processes. These are:

Assessment
Development
Risking
Moving out
Finding a mentor
Negotiating with the family
Choice

Assessment means using experience to arrive at conclusions about the kind of person one is, one's strengths and weaknesses, likes and dislikes. Development is the broadening of skills and abilities. Risking is the process of jumping into the unknown to assess and develop new aspects on oneself. Moving out means cutting clear and moving out into a new task without getting trapped on the way. Finding a mentor is a process which facilitates the others. Negotiating with the family means coping with the needs of the

* Many business organizations are too changeable to afford a place for steady state careers; sweeping organizational restructurings eliminate the niches with the signature of a memo. However, government bureaucracies and the smaller banking organizations do provide such environments. Rules and procedures protect against too much change. This type of organization is quite incomprehensible to many corporate managers. They rant and rave about its slowness and cumbersome form. They have little in common with the steady state careerist and little understanding for his career concept.

Driver views complex high technology organizations as an arena for spiral careers. Organizational change is so rapid that the linear manager feels uncomfortable: the corporate ladder is constantly being modified. For the spiral person, this very change and instability is an environment of opportunity for exploration and self-renewal. As for the transitory person, he feels uncomfortable in the linear or bureaucratic organization. But he is often most at home in an enterprise which is opportunistic and lives from day to day – the case of many small entrepreneurial companies (see Driver, 1980).

family during this phase. Finally, choice is the end result of exploration – easy or difficult according to how thorough it has been.

Assessment

Successful exploration is partly the result of luck; Bill, the prisoner described in Chapter 6 who is a successful general manager at age 34, talks about 'la Fortuna'. He was in the right place at the right time. But the difference between childhood and adult exploration is that time is now too urgent to leave things to fate. Opportunities can be made if one knows roughly what to look for. This involves self-assessment.

We use this word to describe the process of discovering some of one's characteristics so as to be able to choose among career opportunities: the discovery of one's skills, what one likes, one's values. The source of this self-knowledge is experience. Personality tests in books and magazines are usually no more than simulated experiences: 'What would you do if ... check a, b, c, or d.'* Even the younger manager has two-and-a-half decades of experience behind him. The problem is that people often do not use their past experience to learn about themselves.

We have developed exercises for use in our management development work to assist people in assessing themselves on the basis of their past experiences. One of our observations in using these exercises with managers is that people have most difficulty in learning about the emotional aspects of themselves. They may learn from experience what they do well and do badly, especially since this is usually confirmed by the recognition or disapproval of others. But younger managers in particular think less about what they enjoy doing and value doing. Doing a task badly is taken as an incentive to try to do better next time, not as a reason at least to ask oneself the question: 'Do I really want to have a job involving that type of work, and do I really value it?' Instead of exploring to find a career path which also fits with the emotional aspects of their personality, many people struggle with themselves to overcome 'weakness' in what they are doing. Often this struggle lasts into the forties, when they first ask themselves seriously what it is that they really enjoy, as we will show in Part Four of this book.

* Psychological tests can assist people in choosing occupations. A well-known test is the Strong-Campbell Interest Inventory (Campbell, 1977; Kotter, Faux and McArthur, 1978). This attempts to indicate the likely fit between one's personality and such occupations as farming, law, surgery, engineering and sales management. The test is based on data from people happily employed in each occupation, on their likes and dislikes, attitudes and values. But such tests only give a general indication, at best. The actual career must develop and unfold through experience.

We live in a performance culture. Great efforts and much research are devoted to developing performance guidelines and evaluation instruments. But we have no 'enjoyment-meter'. A boss, colleagues, clients can see the result of one's performance. But they cannot see what one enjoys doing, and they would usually say that this was one's own affair. For this reason, self-assessment has to be the responsibility of the individual and not that of the organization. The young manager who succeeds best in the process of self-assessment realizes that the other people can provide him with useful information about himself, but the most relevant information comes from his own assessment of his past and present experience.

One should bear in mind that it is above all enjoyment that distinguishes the misfit from the prisoner. And one does after all have an 'enjoyment-meter' – one's wife. Because of the spillover effect, her view is exactly complementary to that of the organization. She may not know much about the professional skills of her husband – what he does well. But she knows when he is doing something he does not enjoy. His lack of enjoyment spills over into private life: 'He isn't happy with what he's doing,' said a third of the wives in our survey.

Self-assessment, and thus ultimately self-awareness, depends on two qualities. The first is the richness and width of the exploration process. The person who has experienced only one type of job never knows for sure what else he is capable of and might enjoy. But second, it also depends on his capacity to learn about himself by reflecting on his experiences.

Development

One of the most important aspects of the exploratory process is the reinforcement of existing skills and the development of new ones. If the process of launching a career is one of finding a fit between personality and job, each job nevertheless develops that personality in some way. This leads to a basic question. What type of skills can a person develop, and what skills can never be developed?

If one considers the three different components of professional identity – talents and abilities, motives and needs, attitudes and values – one might say that skills are included in the first category 'talents and abilities'. But one could take a broader view and say that one really possesses a skill only when one is able to do something well, to enjoy doing it, and to be proud of doing it. In that case one would have something that could be called a 'rounded skill'.

The technical ability to do something exists independently of our liking doing it or being proud of it. This is particularly true with respect to mechanical operations or chores such as doing the dishes. But it is much less true regarding human skills because here attitudes and behaviour are intertwined. For example, it is difficult to become a good listener if one is not interested in what people have to say. One may learn the techniques but one will not develop a stable ability to listen unless one's deeper attitude is changed.

We are taking the position here that the attitudinal and emotional sides of personality are the part of our nature that changes most slowly, evolving through the experience of living or through traumatic experiences. It is difficult to learn to like doing something that one does not feel one likes. Rounded skills are those built around one's acknowledged likes and values. But awareness of the emotional side of our selves usually comes slowly, only after having tried for some considerable time to be competent at a particular activity. Confronted with a new challenge, most people feel anxious. They may realize that they enjoy it only as they learn to do it well. On the other hand, they may never feel they do it well and slowly realize that this is because they do not enjoy it. Let us give an example.

Peter Wallace took over a new sales job that would require him to undertake client negotiations. He had never proved himself as a negotiator, and, worried about this side of his work, he decided to attend a seminar on negotiations skills at our management campus outside Paris. During these three days, he felt that he learned a lot. But nine months later, he was far more worried than before, seeing himself as having failed in some important negotiations. He began to feel that he should never have accepted that job. He might have been right, but it would have been difficult for him to know for certain in advance.

Our assessment of Peter is that he is someone who dislikes conflict with other people. He avoids it, he smoothes over conflict. Yet this is one of the aspects of his personality that had led to his high reputation in the company. He was the person who could find the compromise between departments who disagreed with each other. He was known for his diplomatic skills and his ability to get on with customers. One can understand why he was a candidate for the sales manager vacancy – except that the job requires the responsibility for negotiation, and that *is* often a situation of conflict. At the seminar, Peter found that he tended to get flustered when he was in the centre of a conflict. He left full of resolve to be tough, to change his personality. A year later, he decided instead to seek a new job in the company. Although one day he might become a better negotiator, this would take too long and never lead to a sure result. He now acknowledges that he dislikes conflicts, and though he has developed some skills in handling them, he would prefer to build his future on his strengths.

Peter Wallace may not have developed negotiation skills from this experience, but he did develop something else that may be valuable. He developed *knowledge about* negotiating. When he is involved is decisions about who should negotiate for the company, he knows not only that it is not him – he also knows something about the sort of person who will negotiate well. And that is very useful knowledge.

Risking

Exploration requires taking risks. One can minimize the risks through self-assessment and by exploring around one's existing skills rather than moving far away from them. But in the earlier career years, taking the risk to move from one job to another is necessary. Furthermore, it is only at this time that one is unlikely to pay a heavy penalty for mistakes.

The risks that are worth taking are those which allow a person to explore new professional areas, to learn about the professional world; those where he can learn about his skills, needs and values, as well as developing his skills. The risks which are not worth taking are those where in return for status and salary one accepts a job, knowing that it probably lies outside one's competence and inclinations.

Being prepared to plunge into new jobs is essential to increase self-knowledge and test skills. Some jobs consolidate one's sense of professional identity and lead to the development of rounded skills. But, by definition, taking a risk means that this does not always happen. After some time, one may feel that one does not fit with the job, like Peter Wallace above.

Moving out

Risking oneself in a new job implies another process, namely being able to move out. A good indication of when to move out is continued, chronic emotional spillover. Each new line of work will start by creating considerable spillover because the people and the tasks are new; this reflects the fact that one's energy is mobilized to master the job, and is both healthy and natural. But if, after a certain time, that spillover does not decrease, it is a sign that the person has chosen a job that he cannot fully master, something that does not fit him. Many of the wives in our survey felt that their husbands had remained far too long in such jobs.

The individual less skilled in launching his career often feels that he has failed, that he must prove himself at all costs. He persists in trying to master the work, only to find out that even if he succeeds he still does not enjoy it. In contrast, the more skilled man does not feel that he has failed.

He has learnt something valuable, namely that certain types of activities do not fit him. He uses his experience to guide himself better in the future.

Negotiating with the family

One may as well recognize in advance that each new job will create spillover for some time. There is no point in pretending that men will be active, available husbands during that period. Taking risks implies another process, namely negotiating this with the family in advance.

There is a frequent failure scenario which illustrates the danger of not negotiating job changes with the family – of not mutually recognizing the spillover effect of a new job. It is the case of an assignment to a foreign country, often entailing a major promotion. Studies consistently show that one of the most important factors in the successful professional adaptation of the executive abroad is the adaptation of his family. The following pattern of events is typical. The husband has an offer of an exciting job in Latin America, a major step in his career. The wife is reluctant to move, but there is no genuine negotiation of the decision. She feels that his mind is made up and she is reluctant to hold him back. Her fears are assuaged by reassurances that life will be exciting and that he will be there to help out. They move.

What the executive does not realize is that the change for him, to a new and important job, to a new locale, and to a new culture, will create great professional tension. The spillover into private life will be intense. For a year or more, he will rarely be psychologically available to his family. If his wife expects and needs that availability, this is a formula for disaster. His physical and psychological absence may aggravate to explosion point the adaptation problems which she herself in undergoing. Tired from work, he returns home not to a haven but to a new set of problems that must be confronted. The only hope for such a transition is when the wife herself has recognized the likely spillover consequences for the husband in advance. Ideally, she sees the foreign venture as an independent challenge; at a minimum, she accepts to go with no false illusions about her husband's likely level of attention to the family, while he is aware of the adaption problems she may experience.

Finding a mentor

Having a mentor may facilitate the other processes in launching the career. Investigating the careers of 550 professionally trained people in fourteen organizations (scientists, engineers, accountants and professors), Dalton, Thompson and Price (1977), found that many individuals who were successful in their careers had had one or more mentors in their early career years. In one research organization, 65 per cent of the scientists and engineers said that this was their experience, Moreover, those who had had a former mentor were given significantly higher performance ratings than those without. (See also Levinson *et al.* (1978) who developed the original concept.)

A mentor is usually an older person, 8 to 15 years senior in age. In many cases, he is a direct boss. He is competent in the field, though not perfectionistic or excessively competent. His orientation goes beyond a purely technical and personal concern for his own career, and his attachment to the mentee goes beyond the strictly professional. Consciously or unconsciously, he is serving the organization as well as himself by taking one or a few persons under his wing. Moreover the mentee may be very helpful to him in discussing his own ideas and in assisting him beyond the bounds of duty in his work.

For the younger person, the mentor is an invaluable guide, helping him to discover his professional self. Through the mentor, he receives not only a deeper technical training but also a wider knowledge of the unspoken aspects of organizational life. He receives challenging assignments, but the mentor is more tolerant and understanding of mistakes. The apprentice can talk more freely about his personal doubts and problems with someone who has wide career experience. All this naturally facilitates and speeds up the processes of exploration, assessment, and development, while minimizing the element of risk.

Choice

After eight to ten years of exploration, most people feel that a moment has come to make a choice. This is an inner experience, not necessarily with any outward signs. Wife, friends, and colleagues may be quite unaware of the doubts and questions that come to mind at this time of choosing. Statistically, it is most likely to occur in the early thirties: between 29 and 35. Thirty-two is the average time of choice (Levinson *et al.*, 1978). This choice is as to a professional lifestyle, a career path. Exploration is over, time is felt to be too pressing. Choice brings with it the first crystallization of professional identity. The person knows more clearly what is his career anchor.

The prisoner of success never experiences this time, which is likely to span several months or several years. He has long since found his professional identity. But the necessity of choice is experienced by the majority of people. They have found *a* job, not *the* job. It gives them a certain satisfaction, but not the consuming passion which they admire in the prisoner, and which they may outwardly fake. Some parts of their work are enjoyable and lie well within their skills. Other parts are stressful, and there is a feeling that one can never develop those skills. Alternative jobs or career avenues are still tempting – one would like to explore them. Or it is clear that one's career can take different directions, all of which are appealing in different ways. But the period of choosing has come. Commitments must be made with oneself so as to release one's energies to pursue whatever path is chosen.

There may be a feeling at this time that these choices are definitive, locking one into a particular career. We want to stress that they are important but not definitive. They will indeed influence one's lifestyle and life events hereafter. But choices can be questioned and remade. Many people will question and even remake their professional choices much later – one element in the so-called midlife transition. Professional life has been launched, but not decided, and this is the reason why we talk of life phases rather than life stages.

One idea that facilitates choosing is to view the career as a spiral path rather than as a linear path. Take for example the engineer who has explored both the technical and managerial aspects of his work. He feels a deep need now to choose one path or the other. Both are tempting to different aspects of himself – he is conflicted. But he feels more and more that in order to succeed, he must commit himself to one path or the other. If he views the career as a linear path, this is a paralysing decision. Yet if he recognizes that a career can be a spiral path, the choice is less painful. He can pursue one path intently well into the future, building later on his skill and experience to turn off into the other – or to alternatives that he has not envisaged, that only opportunity will bring.

In the case of this engineer, the first part of his career has allowed him to explore in different areas, narrowing his field of choice to these two. The successful outcome of launching the career occurs when one can see clearly what choices one has. If one has explored widely and assessed oneself, then the alternatives are clear though the choice process itself may be painful. If one has not explored widely, the choice – if it is made at all – is made with a feeling of regret which may colour life afterwards.

The extreme misfit, on the other hand, does not experience the period of choice. He does not see the alternatives. All he experiences is a growing sense of urgency and desperation. He begins to struggle. He may continue to explore – he may make his choice later. He may become trapped. He may psychologically abandon his professional life, turning his search for identity and fulfilment to other areas of life.

Common mistakes in launching the career

Observing people in the process of launching the career, we found a number of common mistakes.

Being dazzled by external rewards

We all like and need money and have some healthy needs for status and recognition as well. But because in our Western society having these things implies that one is a 'good' person, we sometimes put too much value on them. As a result, many people end up doing what will bring reward rather than what fits them. They are good members of society but do not feel good about themselves.

Executives we spoke with often justified accepting jobs they didn't really want on the ground that the material rewards the jobs provided were essential to realizing a fulfilling private life. They failed to realize (except with hindsight) that no matter how much they earned, no matter how much status was attached to their position, their private lives would suffer through emotional spillover if the job did not fit them.

Inability to resist organizational pressures

When management approaches an individual to offer him a job, in most cases it does so after carefully analysing available candidates. The person chosen is usually the one deemed most competent.

But management pays little if any attention to the two other dimensions of fit – will a candidate enjoy the job and will he be proud of it? If management assesses these dimensions at all, it will usually dismiss them as problems of personal concern only. A person's capacity to do the job well is all that counts. Some managers assume that if a man does not feel he will like it or be proud of a job, then he will refuse it; some also assume that if he doesn't say no, the personal issues don't exist.

But here is a problem. When management reaches its final decision and offers a man promotion or a new job, he is no longer simply a candidate for that job. Management has made a statement that he is the best person available. To refuse is to deny management what it wants. Of course, he is free to say no on emotional grounds; but is he *really?* The pressures to accept are considerable.

Management often adopts a selling attitude that manifests itself in a variety of ways. The rewards and incentives are expressively described, the fact that this is a 'unique opportunity' is stressed, and the argument that 'this will be good for your career' is emphasized. If the individual points out that he may lack some of the necessary skills for the job, management is likely to say that this is 'an exceptional opportunity to develop such skills', expressing vague doubts about the future otherwise. At the end of the process, management often brings the ultimate pressure to bear. It makes it clear that a decision has to be reached quickly, that an answer is expected 'let's say, in 72 hours'.

By this time, many managers will have succumbed to the appeal of external rewards or to the fear of saying no or of showing hesitation. While every executive runs the risk of giving in too easily to such pressures, the risk is highest among young ambitious men who are eager to show their loyalty and advance.

Insufficient exploration

Exploration requires lateral moves. Ambition is the desire to advance *vertically* as quickly as possible. There is nothing wrong with ambition, but it leads some people to short-circuit the process of exploration. The ambitious linear person who sees his career as a ladder is in particular danger. He wants to be at the height of his ladder as quickly as possible. He wants all the external trappings of success – money, prestige, status, fame. He may spend little time on exploration, settling quickly for a career path. Since he spends little time on exploration, his is probably the most smooth and successful path through the twenties and early thirties. He is admired by all around him as the dynamo, full of energy and self-assurance, the successful model for others.

Pierre, the misfit in Chapter 6, is a case in point. Now well along his path – further than most colleagues – he starts to wonder for the first time whether marketing is really him. Trapped by his outward success, he faces a bitter battle. Deep inside, he dislikes what he does. Yet he has never explored any other area of work which would have given him a sense of alternatives, and the skills to implement those alternatives.

Jean McFarlane came up with a pertinent finding when following a group of people through their lives in order to understand the process of life development. These people, all Californians, were interviewed in the 1920s at age 18, and then at successive intervals until recently. She found that some who were seen in their teens and twenties by friends, teachers and even psychologists as the outstanding achievers, collapsed in their early thirties. At high school, they might have been nominated as 'the individual most likely to succeed in life'. They radiated confidence and success in their twenties. But by the mid-thirites, they were unsure of themselves, depressed, and doing poorly. They were now the individuals least oriented to achievement, scoring poorly on measures of mental health (reported in Jones, 1969).

For us, these findings show the consequences of lack of exploration. Life stage research indicates that people question for a 'last' time their professional choices around age 32; exploration ends and choices are made. McFarlane indeed finds that age 32 is the typical time when this collapse happens. But only further research will prove our hunch that the price of not exploring is growing doubt about narrow choices where one is both committed and trapped. In some cases these doubts lead to an early thirties collapse; in other cases they lead to the extended career struggle.

Lack of exploration traps a person because he does not have the direct experience of alternatives, nor the skills for alternative jobs. The price of exploration, on the other hand, is that real success comes much more slowly. Time is 'wasted' on the lateral moves and re-training for new careers. One is perpetually an apprentice. Salary is low, maintaining a family difficult. This looks like a very real price. The temptation to make an early choice is high, though this may later turn out to be more costly.

The outcome of launching the career

The central process in these long years of launching the career is exploration of oneself and exploration of the occupational world. The outcome of launching the career is a crystallized sense of professional identity, an ability to describe who one is and is not.

This sense of professional identity can be seen as having four interrelated elements, the results of the exploratory process. The first element is that the person has developed rounded skills. These are abilities that he likes exercising and is proud of. These are the tools of his particular trade now and in the future.

The second element is his knowledge of the real occupational world. He knows a great deal about the way in which things function, and the way in which organizations are structured. He knows the opportunities and the rules of the game. He knows of the paradoxes, traps and pitfalls in the evolution of a career. Above all, he knows something of the requirements and characteristics of different types of jobs.

The third element is a product of these two things. He is now likely to find himself in a job which fits more or less with his personality. But fourthly and more importantly, he has developed the capacity to manage the fit between himself and his environment in the future. He has the ability to assess opportunities that arise, knowing when to say yes and when to say no, knowing how to calculate trade–offs, and knowing how to open up opportunities on his own initiative. This now opens up the path to professional realization as well as material reward.

He has made a choice as to his career path, and he is capable of making sound choices for the future. Here the sense of professional identity differs between the linear person and the spiral person. The linear person sees himself as having made *the* career choice, and his professional identity rests on this. The spiraller has made a temporary choice as to a career path, but he has developed the capacity to manage an exploration process that repeats itself.

Some older people view this first part of adulthood as the most straightforward period of their lives. It is straightforward only in the sense that people appear to focus their investment behaviour on the launching of their careers. It is rarely experienced as straightforward at the time.

Nor is it experienced as straightforward by wives. How in fact do wives view their own lifestyles, their own self-development, at this time? This is the theme of the next chapter.

Chapter 8

Maintaining private life

The demands of simultaneously launching three separate careers in early adulthood are so heavy that to cope with all challenges and demands with equal success at the same time is beyond the capacities of most people. As we have seen, the young manager copes by unconsciously giving his career priority. He still retains high ideals for his private life careers as husband and father. But the gap between what is ideal and what is realistic at this time often colours private life with guilt and sadness. How does his wife cope with this?

The emotional influence of work life on private life is massive, as previous chapters document. The influence of private life on the career is very modest. It was hard to find a single example, among the 16 younger managers in our survey, of any major accommodation made for the sake of the wife. Men spoke of coming back from the Middle East because their wives were discontented, but closer scrutiny usually showed this to be only a contributing factor – they were not doing to well there in their jobs in any case.*

What struck us most was how accommodating the wives were, even though many of them had full or part-time jobs. There was no single case among the younger couples of a wife who had put her foot down and insisted. We asked each of the wives to talk about the positive or restraining influence they had had on the careers of their husbands. They had never restrained them, nor did their husbands ever talk of any restraint. This was true even for the wives who expressed the strongest

* There was one exception, a man very different from all the others in the entire survey. Aged 32, he had turned down several jobs and opportunities which would have entailed a move and which would have compromised the successful career of his wife, also a business manager. 'I will never take a decision which compromises my family life,' he said. Yet he was a very clear misfit, working – as his wife herself put it – in the marketing area when he should be like herself in finance. She felt strongly that he should change and take his career more seriously before it was too late. For the moment, it seemed, he was the one misfit who experienced no spillover. His identity was wholly wrapped up in his private life. Yet this was changing as he started to worry about whether he really meant what he said: could this contented lifestyle continue? Did it really mean that his career was endangered?

resentment, like Jane, the wife of the prisoner Bill described in Chapter 6:

> I think I had a very strong influence on his career during the first five
> to eight years, in terms backing him up with drive and ambition of my
> own. And supporting him in all the usual ways wives do. I don't think
> ever held him back from an opportunity, though I'm sure I've influenced
> the way he looks at opportunities.

It is possible that ours was a biased sample of managers in this respect.
First, because most of them were successful. And second, because
although some of the wives worked, only one of them had her own
professional career.

And what is the reward for accommodation to one's partner, the
younger manager? Material well-being, yes. Many wives mentioned
this – in passing – when talking of the positive side of being married to an
executive. Some added laughingly that their husbands would like them to
take that side of things more seriously than they actually did. Rewards in
terms of the partnership itself, in sharing time with him? Here the majority
of the wives felt ambivalent; while sharing time was the most satisfying
aspect of life for many of them, they felt its rarity rather keenly. Rewards
in terms of freedom to pursue one's own self-development? The extent to
which the wives feel free is one of the issues raised in this chapter.

I *should* spend more time at home

More than half of the 532 husbands (55 per cent) in our survey thought
that their wives were unhappy with the way they, the men, were investing
their time and energy. This is slightly higher than the proportion of
husbands who were themselves dissatisfied. There were 43 per cent of
those. And there were just as many dissatisfied men and dissatisfied wives
among the younger couples as among the older ones. However, among the
older couples, when the wife was dissatisfied with her husband's investment behaviour, the husband was likelier to be dissatisfied too. This was
far less true among the younger people. Among them we were likelier to
find just the husband or just the wife discontented.

If the wife is having problems in adapting to this lifestyle (which is
not the case for all the wives), if she talks openly about these problems
(which again is not the case of all wives) – how does her husband typically
react? At one extreme, some managers do not react at all – their wives'
words do not even penetrate their awareness. At the other extreme, some
react with feelings of guilt – though rarely with more than guilt. Short of
crisis, husbands do not change their behaviour. They may react in their
mid-thirties, at the next phase of life, but for the time being ambivalence
is bottled up and experienced as guilt.

We have a strong impression that the degree of guilt experienced between the 'should' of family attention and the 'want' of professional involvement depends on two things. First, there is the age of the manager: the further he is into his thirties, the more likely he is to feel guilty, since his level of sensitivity to his family will be heightened. Second, there is the extent to which he has discovered a sense of career fit. If he is a misfit, there is a clear overriding value which says he *should* focus on launching his career. But if he has discovered a career path, the guilt conflict becomes severe. His conscience tells him that he should pay more attention to the family. When his wife complains, this adds to his guilt; and when she supports him, that too increases his sense of obligation. But he wants to invest in his work: his work has become an immense source of satisfaction and temptation. Increasingly he has a feeling of stealing hours from his family, hiding behind a cover of alibis and excuses. 'I'm doing it all for you, dear!'

Charles, 33 years old and a manager who fits well with his career, talks about how these feelings of guilt have recently grown. His wife has accommodated to his 90 per cent investment in work. She has always had a full-time job as a market analyst; with the occasional aid of her mother, who lives nearby, she also fends for the household and children.

> I can only find positive words to describe her. Either as a wife or as a mother. And that is even more true when one bears in mind that she has her own professional life. It takes an incredible person to do this when you have to live with – let's face it – a husband who is phsysically absent [laughs], a job which after all is as absorbing as my own, and bringing up the children which takes a lot of time. She succeeds fantastically well.
>
> I'm inclined to say that she is perfect. She is a very rare women. She is quite independent. Is it because she wants to be independent? – I really can't say. She is independent and very organized because she *has* to be. What I mean to say is that I think she would like to have a closer family life and even deliberately give up some of her independence. But ... [shrugs his shoulders and laughs].
>
> As for me, I'm very reliable and hardworking in a professional sense. But I have to say that from a family point of view, I don't play my role. I feel more and more guilty about it as time goes on.
>
> With regard to the children, it's a little different. I feel guilty, that's for sure, but I'm more interested in them. I find a sense of satisfaction from creating something, from teaching them, in helping them. I spend what time I have with them, but they certainly need my attention when I'm not there to give it to them. I'm getting more and more involved with them – even here that's all of recent date....

The thing that dissatisfies me the most in life at the moment is this feeling of guilt. About the family. My wife is suffering, I know that. I don't know how to explain it. It's a feeling of not having shouldered my adult responsibilities, if I can put it that way. Having a wife and adorable children, one takes it for granted up to a certain point. I feel a bit adolescent about it all. I alternate between periods of excitement and periods of feeling guilty [laughs].

If we view adulthood in terms of life phases, then the 'successful' completion of this first phase of launching one's career will leave the person with a new task – that of balancing professional and private life. The feeling of guilt is the call to face up to this task, the lead into it. Meanwhile, the wife has to cope with her own problems of adjustment and of finding her own identity.

The wife's adjustment

It is not only the husband who is wrestling with finding his identity. The wife's struggle is also a long and protracted one, which typically comes to a head in her mid- or late thirties. In the past, society clearly prescribed how the young women should view herself. Her mission was to rear children and support her husband. She should fill in time after school or university with a job, and find herself a husband. Her identity problems were solved then, her career path was found. She could focus on realizing herself in a career as wife, housewife and mother.

Some women may fit that prescription – we say 'fit' because the model of matching personality to work of course applies equally to the woman as to the man. The research of Charles Handy, professor at the London Business School, indicates that the role of the supportive wife suits the woman who has strong needs for affiliation and nurturance (the 'caring' person), with weaker needs for achievement and dominance (Handy, 1978). If she, like her husband, has a strong need for achievement, she may find she fits this role only partially. She may tolerate it while the children are young, feeling that she has little choice. But as the children get older, her unresolved identity problems will re-emerge.

But that societal prescription is changing. The way we bring up children is changing; more and more women are attending university and the housewife role is increasingly denigrated. The housewife career is no longer the only career alternative for the younger woman.

Our view of the wife's identity problem as it confronts the younger woman appears in Figure 8.1. Two dimensions of inner conflict have to be resolved in facing up to the realities of life as a wife. The first dimension is

101

Figure 8.1 Identity of the younger wife

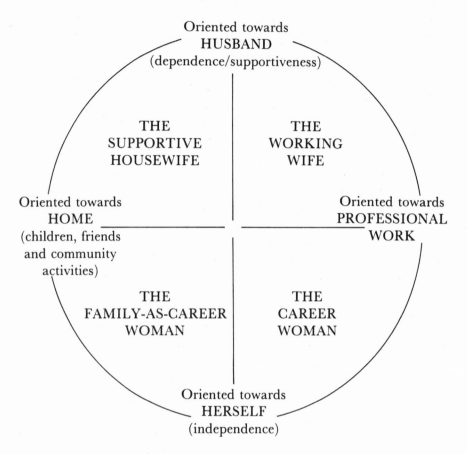

Oriented towards
HUSBAND
(dependence/supportiveness)

THE
SUPPORTIVE
HOUSEWIFE

THE
WORKING
WIFE

Oriented towards
HOME
(children, friends
and community
activities)

Oriented towards
PROFESSIONAL
WORK

THE
FAMILY-AS-CAREER
WOMAN

THE
CAREER
WOMAN

Oriented towards
HERSELF
(independence)

dependence versus independence *vis-à-vis* her husband. The dependent or supportive wife adjusts herself to her husband, becoming 'the total woman', even to the extent of accepting that she is number two in his priorities. Independence means realizing her own self-concept, and probably insisting that he accommodate to her. A young wife, who had abandoned a successful career to have children and support her husband, expressed her ambivalent feelings about these two extremes:

> There wasn't much discussion about me stopping my work. It was a tacit agreement. And I looked forward to being a mother. But what I've had to do because of *his* career is give up an ideal – an ideal of how family life should be . . . .
>
> As a wife, I'm probably difficult. I'm very *caring*, although I don't feel that way at the moment. At the moment, I'm probably very unsure about how I am, how I should be as a wife. How far should one be a wife to a job? To an occupation rather than a person?

There is of course an ideal middle state of interdependence '*Us*'! The dream of 'us-ness' crystallizes in adolescence. It is the dream of the 'ideal family'. There may be some couples who maintain it, but certainly not among our executive pairs. The will for individual achievement is too strong among the men, and among many women too. Interdependence – mutual adjustment, sensitivity and the 'us-ness' of two people – becomes one part of marital life. Moments, frequent or rare, when the couple feel truly intimate.

In the executive marriage, the difficult process of launching the career makes these moments very rare. The husband is not in control of his moods when at home – his struggle pervades family life. One of the reasons why the wives see his happiness with his work as so important is that intimacy and interdependence are more frequent when he is happy with what he is doing. Emotional spillover dulls any sense of intimacy. But spillover is so frequent, that these moments are a poor reward for a lifestyle. If his sense of professional identity is successfully found, the re-finding of intimacy and interdependence may be the key theme of the next phase in life. The struggler may never turn to this life task.

One of the 'attractions' of the role of the supportive wife to both man and woman is that if she assumes this role, moments of interdependence occur more often. The supportive wife is always available. She gears into her husband's moods. She soothes and calms him down. But the rewards are very thin. For all young managers, and especially for the misfit and the prisoner, these family moments are few and far between.

The other dimension of identity conflict for the wife, as indicated in Figure 8.1, is the choice of focusing her life on the *home* or on *professional work*. In our society, the demands of giving birth to children and bringing them up, especially while small, conflict with the demands of a full-time career. Bailyn shows that it is difficult for the dual-career mother to pursue her profession unless her husband is exceedingly accommodating (willing to sacrifice career for family). If she does persist in her career, the marriage is typically unhappy (Bailyn, 1970, 1978). Of course, there is again a middle point on this dimension: pregnancy leave, an *au pair* or day-care centre, and simply taking a job rather than pursuing a career. This 'best-of-both worlds' is unattractive to many wives because it may entail the best of none. The wife fears being left with the responsibility for both home and her own work. And she asks herself what will happen to the children if they do not have daily love and attention – that was one of the questions most frequently put at wives' seminars we have conducted.

The two dimensions of identity conflict, dependence/independence and home-orientation/professional-orientation, map out four identity roles that the wife may adopt during this first phase of life. Forces often draw her to the 'supportive housewife' role, high on dependence and with an orientation towards the home and children. Some women happily fit with the role, whereas others live with a sense of loneliness, to some extent filled by building a network of friends. From time to time, this woman may wish to talk with her husband about her loneliness. But if she does, she feels guilty – he has so many other important preoccupations; why make him more unhappy by adding to them? The dilemmas experienced by some housewives are well described by Mira, the 'heroine' in Marilyn French's novel, *The Women's Room*.

The supportive wife's sense of loneliness may be eliminated by her adopting a role as a 'working wife'. She takes a job, ideally one that is flexible and part-time, though frequently there are no part-time jobs available.* But her motivation remains essentially supportive rather than independent. She is aware of the fact that her loneliness as a housewife often leads her to feel moody, even when her husband and children are around. She takes a job so as to fill her life; her husband too may want her to work 'to keep her busy'.

Thirty-seven per cent of the wives in our questionnaire survey had full- or part-time jobs, while 12 per cent had active volunteer pursuits; 17 per cent were working full-time. Most of these women were working wives rather than career women. The most common reasons given by the husbands as to why their wives worked were: to develop her own interests (34 per cent), and to have contact with other people (25 per cent). Only 12 per cent of the husbands saw their wives as building their own careers. And judging by data from both the interview survey and the questionnaire survey, there is no evidence that the 'working couple' leads to an unhappy marriage. Where the wife works, however, there is likely to be more frequent conflict over who should do what in the household. The marriage is more tense, though not necessarily unhappy.

Many wives argue with their husbands, that the marriage of a working couple should rest on a pattern of equally shared responsibility. This means introducing segmentation into each partner's life by strengthening the boundaries between family and work (Bailyn, 1978): when one leaves the office, one leaves work behind. Life is disciplined and organized. We agree in principle yet regard the argument as utopian for the younger couple at least.

---

* For the educated woman, it is particularly difficult to find part-time professional work. However, work sharing is on the increase. One Danish pharmaceutical company has set a pattern. Demanding but challenging jobs as research chemists require full-time commitment. The company has allowed pairs of women to split jobs. One woman works for a full week, meets with her partner the following Monday morning, and passes the job on to her for the next week. They split the normal salary. This is the typical schedule. But partners are free to negotiate changes. Thus the partner of one woman was willing to work full-time for six months while she herself joined her husband for a six-month assignment abroad.

It is utopian because the phenomenon of spillover gets in the way. Until the career is truly launched, the husband will find segmentation easy to promise but difficult to deliver. And even if he finds his sense of professional identity at this stage, he will be consumed by a passion to pursue his career path. Yet the importance of segmentation rests as a valid ideal; the Rapoports show that it is one of the key characteristics of the small but growing number of successful dual career families (Rapoport and Rapoport, 1971).

The working wife role may be satisfactory if there is only one child in the family who is of school age. It becomes increasingly stressful in a larger family, if the wife cares a great deal about the upbringing of the children, and if the husband is unaccommodating because of his professional life. But far more stressful is the identity role of the 'career woman'. She is different from the working wife in the sense that she is committed to her own individual growth and development through finding a professional identity and advancing along her own career path. She chooses independence. Even if she feels supportive, her availability to provide this support is much less, not only in the sense that she has less time available, but also that she has less energy available, just like her husband. She needs that support herself.

The dual career marriage is a stressful lifestyle at this phase. The wife regards the household as a necessarily joint duty. But jointly running the home is an explosive task at this stage of heavy family demands. Both persons are suffering through the process of launching their careers, and the more committed she is to her career, the more anarchic household life becomes. Each needs a haven to recover from stress; instead, tensions aggravate that stress so that professional life suffers. The couple is rarely in phase; each member is tempted to escape back into his or her professional world. If there are children, the family tension is felt by them, and their adjustment problems worsen the situation to crisis point. It is an untenable life situation although, as we will later show, the career woman may be one of the more fulfilled people in the later life. Unless the husband is particularly accommodating, the only solution may be for her to abandon her career orientation for the time being and settle for the role as a working wife. In this way, she keeps her professional life warm while bringing her lifestyle to a more manageable level.

The outcome, of course, is unfair in the sense that it is usually the woman and not the man who lands up sacrificing her career for the time being. Later on, if she so chooses, she will face the problem of relaunching her professional life. We will talk of this problem in following chapters.

Career women are rare at this early stage in the couple's life, although researchers expect more young women to opt for this path as couples decide not to have children. But the desire for independence

105

expresses itself also in a fourth identity role, a role built around the family rather that the outside career. We call this the role of 'family-as-career'. It differs significantly from the concept of the supportive housewife. The wife has strong ambitions and ideals for how family life should be, ideals which her husband may not be able to share. The family is regarded as a professional enterprise. The wife runs that enterprise, and he is one, albeit important, member. She sees it as a creative task, the building of a home. She is likely to sympathize with the view that a housewife has an occupation like any other person – she should be paid for it, and is owed recognition and praise (a view which the supportive housewife thinks is utter nonsense). Many of the wives we interviewed had this conception of themselves, but our questionnaire survey showed that it was often a difficult role, leading to her unhappiness.

We can draw a statistical portrait of the young man who considers his wife to be unhappy with how he invests his time and energy, regardless of his own feelings about his lifestyle: he views the marital contract in a characteristic way. On the one hand, he sees his wife as attributing enormous importance to her household role, and much less importance to her role in supporting him. On the other hand, he feels that his own obligation in the marriage is above all to provide her with financial security. Relaxation in her company is far less important to him, as is supporting her in her own self-development. These younger men whose wives are unhappy tend to view marriage in a utilitarian spirit. It is almost a question of exchange, money for household services.

The overtly discontented wife, meanwhile, concentrates on her household role and he is full of admiration for her performance. Her 'career' is the house and family. But she feels frustrated because in order for her to make a career of this, the husband must play his role in the household. She needs his presence, his support, his complementary participation in household life. Without it, her household role loses much of its meaning. In the same way as her husband 'understands' her dilemma, she 'understands' his. The family-as-career woman feels trapped under these circumstances, she feels more and more uncertain of her role. To change occupation becomes very tempting – to look for a new area of fit in a role as a supportive housewife or a working wife.

Is she free to choose?

Clearly, a key aspect of identity formation is the process of experimenting with different activities and roles – finding out what one likes doing and dislikes doing, finding out what one does well and does badly. The sense of self crystalizes as the person makes choices as to a life structure after this process of experimentation. That life structure may not satisfy all aspects of one's personality; hence the sense of incompleteness that leads some people to break out into a different life structure in the mid-adulthood years. This applies equally to men and women.

For the male manager, the range of opportunities for experimentation and self-discovery are very wide. His problem is that inertia, low risk-taking and pressures may prevent him from taking advantage of these opportunities. He may remain within a narrow career path which does not suit him. He does not experiment, he stays too long in jobs which do not fit him. He has difficulty in making personal choices. His wife rarely ever constrains him at this life phase. If he wants to change job or company and this entails a relocation, research indicates that at this point she will hardly ever hold him back.*

In the not so distant past few women experienced any dilemma. A role was expected of them, the role of wife and mother. Only this role was available to most, and most of them accepted it as natural and desirable. The only question seemed to be to find the adequate partner. During the last two decades some things have changed radically, even though others have remained the same. In many countries today, women raised within the old model have found as adults that new models have been invented and real choices opened to them. They are often conflicted between old ways of thinking about themselves and the new options they see. Compounding the inner conflict are pressures from the outside world, with contradictory judgements from the feminist and from the old guard. Many of the younger wives in our sample belong squarely to this highly conflicted group.

The conflicted young wives we interviewed often felt constrained by their lack of freedom to experiment with different roles. While we devoted a whole chapter to the choices that confront younger managers, it was easy to boil down the choices of the young wives to four, one of which (the career woman choice) hardly exists for these wives of aspiring managers. And even among the remaining three choices most women feel that forces

---

* A study by Glueck (1974) shows that early relocations are generally accepted by the wife, but that after the first few moves attitudes may polarize in pro-relocation or anti-relocation directions. After living for years with a misfit, the non-supportive wife puts her foot down. There has been no reward for the difficulties of relocation in the past – why pay the personal price again? We ourselves have indirect support of this finding (Evans, 1974).

The one husband who is constrained is the man married to a career woman. This is a further source of stress in this type of marriage. The marriage can only last if one or the other partner will compromise career, or where neither partners ever have strong pressure to relocate. For this reason, we would expect to find dual career couples more frequently in the civil service and professions than in business (see Rapoport and Rapoport, 1971).

and pressures outside themselves pull them strongly towards the supportive housewife role. Unless their personalities fit this role (and they will not know until they have tried it), this phase of their lives is likely to be coloured by a perpetual question: Who am I?

We can summarize the four principle constraints on the young wife.

1. *Societal values and prescriptions*: Today, this is the most talked of and least serious of the constraints. In the past, a women who did anything else after marriage but become a supportive wife was a deviant. Having children while working was labelled as irresponsible. Companies had no tolerance for anything but the supportive wife: 'That's *your* problem,' they would say.

Although discussion and research have begun to change this, the heritage of old values is still influential. The supportive mother brings up her daughter to regard the supportive role as the only viable lifestyle for her. If she is to go to university, it is to find a husband who is likely to be worth supporting, abandoning her studies unquestioningly to get married. We found painful problems of adaption in the early years of marriage among some couples interviewed.

> We seriously considered getting divorced after the first two years of marriage. It was hell. I met him while I was still at university. I gave up my studies to get married – I never even thought about it at the time. And that is the one thing that I really regret now. He was always busy, and I would get mad at him. I wanted to go out and work, but I didn't have any qualifications. We couldn't afford for me to go back to university. So we decided to have a baby instead.

2. *The husband's work*: In reality, a far more serious constraint is the effect of the husband's launching his career. Despite his good intentions, spillover and physical fatigue make him often an absent partner. We need not elaborate. In effect, the viable identity choices are reduced from four to two – supportive wife and working wife. The price of the other two is intense stress, and unhappiness in the marriage.

3. *Pressure brought to bear by the husband*: The choice between the supportive and the working roles may not be constrained in any absolute sense by the husband, but he may have strong views and exercise a powerful influence in one direction or the other. The sterotype is that executive husbands do not want their wives to work, but in fact our survey contradicts this. Twice as many men were in favour of married women working than were against. Fifty-one per cent of the group, however, had mixed or neutral feelings.

We found that the husband of a woman who is espoused to a family-as-career concept, but who is frustrated in this role by his absence as her partner, is quite likely to push her into work to fill her life. One woman instead 'discovered' (her word) the supportive housewife role in this way:

> No, I'm not happy with his time and energy. Well, I suppose I don't mind the amount of work if he is happy with what he is doing. What I resent is the unhappiness he brings home with him . . . .
> He's dying for me to get back to my career. He doesn't understand what the fulfilled housewife is [laughs]! He's pushed me to go out to work, but I'd rather be a housewife. I don't envy him leaving in the morning. I'd rather have my free time, my children, my husband. Once he forced me to go out and work in a shop. I stuck it out for six months. The only sort of work I would think of now would be part-time work. What I suppose I'd really like to do would be to work with him in his own firm if he ever starts that. But he thinks that is a bad idea.

4. *The effect of children*: For the young couple, the choice of roles may be narrowed by children to the single possibility of supportiveness. Contrary to what some people still believe, there is no evidence that the upbringing of the children *necessarily* suffers if the wife is working (Rapoport and Rapoport, 1978). But each additional child increases more than proportionately the task of running the household. Simply distributing the chores between husband and wife becomes a major problem. Struggling with his career, the husband hardly concerns himself with housework. The wife complains: 'Even if he does what I ask him to do, I'm the one who has to bear all the *responsibility*. In order to get anything done, I always have to *ask* him – he never thinks of anything himself'.

In theory, one solution is to hire a professional housekeeper – the full-time servant or more likely the *au pair*. In reality, this solution is more problematic. The chores will be done. But unless one is exceptionally lucky in the choice of the *au pair* (as well as able to overexploit the standard five-hour-day *au pair* contract), the 'responsibility' still rests with the wife. After some years of struggling with 'good *au pair* girls' and 'bad *au pair* girls', the working wife may feel that settling for the role of the supportive wife may, after all, be an easier way out.

Children may on the other hand fill something missing in the marriage, at least temporarily. Two of the couples interviewed spoke of serious relationship problems early in the marriage; one of them seriously discussed divorce. In both cases, the crisis was 'resolved' by deciding to have another child . . . By keeping her busy, the relationship problem can be put off until later. It is a risky strategy.* If the husband finds his sense of career identity, it has at least a chance of paying off. If he remains wrapped up in his career problems, the option of separation is constrained by the presence of the children.

How adjusted are the wives?

The majority of the 16 younger women interviewed had reached some form of adjustment. Three of the wives were fully content – two supportive wives and one working wife. The largest group, eight of them, were more or less adjusted: marginally satisfied or dissatisfied with their husband's investment behaviour. They accepted the fact that their lifestyles were constrained by their husbands. All without exception made one of two comments:

He behaves like that because it makes him happy.

He has to do this, and I understand that.

For many of these women, whether housewives or working wives, their identity problems were only temporarily resolved. Their misgivings were hidden, but still remained to surface later in life. In the words of one wife, 'I'm contented – but not fulfilled.'

Five of the 16 wives were less adjusted. Two of them worked, two of them did not, and one had a family-as-career concept. All were dissatisfied with the behaviour of their husbands, and the discontent went deep. There were two common denominators among these five women. The first was that all five husbands were either extreme misfits or extreme prisoners. The second was that four of the five women had serious problems about their own identities. 'I'm probably very unsure about how I am, how I should be as a wife,' said one. 'He threatens my sense of independence, and I don't know what to do,' said another. 'I'm afraid that I'm not a particularly interesting person,' said a third.

This is too small a sample of people to provide any definite conclusion. But we feel that there is a link between the career situation of

---

* Some couples believe that children will bring them closer. This belief is reportedly held by most newlyweds (Lowenthal *et al.*, 1975). Research indicates absolutely the contrary.

Hicks and Platt (1970) reviewed research studies on marital happiness. They state that the single most unambigous and surprising finding is that children *detract* from it. In one study, 440 couples were observed in public places. The couples with children touched each other less, talked less, smiled less than those without children (Rosenblatt, 1974). Ryder (1973) analyses a series of studies that indicate frequent marital crisis or dissatisfaction after having children. This is true only for the wives. His conclusion is that this is not only the result of post-partum depression; it also reflects 'lovesickness'. The husband's limited attention is channelled toward the children at the expense of the wife.

the husband on the one hand, and the uncertain identity of the unadjusted wife on the other hand. Her strong feelings express her uncertainty as to who she is. And her uncertainty originates partly from the fact that any freedom of identity choice is foreclosed by the husband's physical or emotional absorption in his work. Both the misfit and the prisoner are 'absent partners', for different reasons and in different ways. The only viable marital role with an absent partner is that of the supportive wife, but to play supportive wife to a misfit or prisoner is an empty and thankless role. If this situation lasts for any time, the choice for her is narrowed down to two extremes. She can settle for this cheerless life, or she can leave her husband. Rejecting for the time being these unacceptable extremes, she muddles through – with a confused sense of who she is, bitter feelings of resentment, and, in the miserable case of marriage to the perpetual misfit, a sense of guilt at aggravating his problems by expressing her own feelings.

The children: the one chink in his armour

There is little if any evidence that the younger manager is willing to accommodate to his wife ('capable of accommodating her' might be a better way of putting it). But there is a chink in his armour, a point of particular sensitivity. And that is the children.

Many of the wives reluctantly adjust to his coming home late, working week-ends at the office, and the days or weeks spent away from home travelling. They can understand the reasons for this. But this is not so for the children. When the husband is frequently away, the children are 'fatherless'. It may not trouble the father initially, but it invariably disturbs the mother. She becomes the advocate for their welfare. It is particularly the time demands of the job that are at issue here; energy spillover is in second place unless the husband vents his tension on the children. Two-thirds of all wives who complained about travel and late hours commented on this.

Yes, he comes back home late – he's rarely here before 7.30. Or else he comes back at 11 o'clock. Then he doesn't even see the children, and that can go on for weeks at a time. He gets back after they have gone to bed, and leaves in the morning before they get up. That means that he isn't there for them, he doesn't exist ...

It was a big problem when they were very small. When he used to travel abroad when Jacques was smaller – well, Jacques would forget him! He'd completely wipe his father out of his mind! Finally I found a solution. I found a photo and he'd sleep with a photo of his father

111

under the pillow [laughs]. But the first time he left for three weeks away, Jacques refused to talk of his father. He was lost. He refused to talk about him. He was sullen and would sulk whenever his father's name was mentioned.

That's the most annoying thing. He brings a certain way of ... Well, when I'm with the children all the time, I'm less amusing, less tolerant. Him – he tells them stories, and especially with the boys he creates make-believe worlds [laughs]. He really has a gift for telling stories about fantastic things. And that's important for the children."

This is a sensitive point for the wife,* and it is also the point of maximum sensitivity for the husband – even for the misfit and the prisoner. We saw in Chapter 4, when discussing life phases, how the younger manager tends to feel dissatisfied with his lifestyle if he feels upset about his relationship with the children. When we asked the managers whether their family life had increased or decreased in importance during the last five years, three-quarters of the young managers said that family life was more important now than in the past. Almost all spontaneously added that this was because of the children.

When asked whether their family lives had influenced job behaviour or job decisions, the younger managers generally mentioned vague positive influences when they talked of their wives: 'She gives me a lot of moral support,' 'She helps me relax by talking with me about my job.' Where the wife's influence was negative, it was an influence on his feelings but not his behaviour: "I feel very dissatisfied with how I use my time and energy because of the consequences for her."

The only specific instances of the influence of family on job behaviour were connected with the children. Here, examples of 'trying to ...' were frequently mentioned:

Yes, my travel does upset my wife. But the primary consideration is continuity for the children. So on the whole I try not to be away for more than two or three days at a time.

The husband would say that he tried to come home early from the office to see the children before they went to bed. There was no clear example in our interview survey of anyone having turned down a move

* Pahl and Pahl (1971) studied the concerns of British wives when their husbands were asked to relocate. They report that although pay and job characteristics are of greatest importance, it is striking how much emphasis is laid on the children's educational opportunities. Links with family and friends, and the influence on the wife's own career and interests, are of quite subsidiary importance. A quarter of the wives in this survey of 86 couples viewed the educational facilities of an area as the deciding factor.

because of the children. But in seminar discussions since the survey, we have heard of such decisions. In almost every case, the deciding factor turned out to be the interests of the children, not of the wife.

As we reported in Chapter 4, the husband is most sensitive to the *difficulties* in his relationships with the children and in their upbringing. He regrets his short-temperedness with them after a frustrating day at the office; he worries about their fussing and whining, or their problems at school. He is less sensitive to the positive aspects of his relationship with them: that he may be missing the opportunity to play with them or share pleasures with them. A troubled frown appears on his face when we confront him on this. But then he says, 'Well, I'm at a particularly important stage in my career now, and that will have to wait.'

That will have to wait. He makes what we call the 'assumption of equivalent time': one day invested three years from now is equivalent to one day invested today. Maybe he is a financial analyst and recognizes that time has a discount factor: so he says, *two* days invested in three years' time is equivalent to one day invested now. 'I'll make up for it later.' This assumption is false. A son who was three years old becomes now six. If he learnt to swim during those three years, his father will *never again* share with him the experience of teaching him how to swim. If a daughter learnt how to read, he will *never* have the opportunity to participate in teaching her. The opportunity is gone and never returns.

This is one of the most painful realities of adulthood. One may try to catch up later with another child. But with one of one's offspring, an irrecoverable pleasure is lost. Unless it is pointed out in black-and-white, this reality rarely penetrates the awareness threshold of the younger man. Yet, as we shall see, it becomes a point of maximum sensitivity for the man in his forties and fifties. He is aware not only of the pain in bringing up a child, but also of the pleasure. Usually, his awareness is coloured by regret. His awareness comes too late.

What is far more arguable is whether one's child will be different as a result of this three-year absence of a father (or for that matter, a working mother). Research here is based on broken homes, and even so the results are contradictory (Furstenburg, 1974, p. 342; Mussen, Conger and Kagen, 1969; Rapoport and Rapoport, 1978, p. 179). They may or may not be different.

There is some evidence that an important factor in child-rearing is consistent behaviour. For the child to develop in a healthy way, its environment must be predictable. From this perspective, emotional spillover may be most harmful to the child. On some occasions, Daddy is happy and attentive. On other occasions, he is irritable, exploding at things which the night before made him laugh. For the small child, the rights and wrongs of behaviour become uncertain. He withdraws or becomes rebellious. What the child cannot understand (though the wife can) is that his father's behaviour depends on random events at the office.

The Rapoports cite a French study which reinforces the idea that the most harmful effect of professional life on the children is spillover. This French research team found that within reasonable limits it is not so much what the parents do to their children that effects them as *how* they do it (Rapoport and Rapoport, 1978). Children want their parents to be happy and to feel personally fulfilled. What disturbs them is if the parents conflict, or feel guilty and discontent in their domestic or occupational roles.

The psychological adjustment of the children is one issue, but the effect on their personalities is another. Bronfenbrenner (1970) has contrasted how American and Russian families raise their children. American families bring up their children to be independent and competitive. Russians raise warm and cooperative children. The children of the executive may be more 'American' in nature – independent achievers rather than outgoing human beings who enjoy doing things. Although the wife may compensate, the husband at least is likely to pay most attention to success or failure (particularly success) – drawing good pictures, sporting accomplishments, good or bad results at school. He may participate less in the day-to-day activities of play and fun and chatting, thus giving no reinforcement for such pursuits. Winterbottom (1958) shows this to be an important element in the development of the high achieving child – a child who for better or worse may be the image of the father's outward behaviour.

But private life will change ...

The typical couple ends the phase of young adulthood in an uneasy state, carrying much unfinished business along. The wife has perhaps adjusted ... but is not fulfilled. The husband usually has a sense that his career is launched ... but feels guilty.

Such feelings announce the arrival of the next phase. It is to be hoped that the manager has found his professional identity and has not irreparably damaged his private life in the process. He can now turn to consolidate and develop his private life. Issues resolved leave place for unresolved issues. This leads us to the next part of our book.

Part 3

Private Life

In literature, new lives, second chances, lead to visions of the City of God. But I have been suspecting for a while now that everything I ever read was lies. You can believe the first four acts, but not the fifth. Lear really turned into a babbling old fool drooling over his oatmeal and happy for a place by the fire in Regan's house in Scarsdale. Hamlet took over the corporation by bribing the board and ousting Claudius, and then took to wearing a black leather jacket and German Army boots and sending out proclamations that everyone would refrain from fornication upon pain of death. He wrote letters to his cousin Angelo and together they decided to purify the whole East Coast, so they have joined with the Mafia, the Marines, and the CIA to outlaw sex. Romeo and Juliet marry and have some kids, then seperate when she wants to go back to graduate school and he wants to go live on a commune in New Mexico. She is on welfare now and has long hair and an Indian headband and says *Oooom* a lot . . .

Tristan and Isolde got married after Issy got a divorce from Mark, who was anyhow turned on to a groupie at that point. And they discovered the joys of comfortable marriage can't hold a candle to the thrill of taboo, so they have placed an ad in the Boston *Phoenix* asking for a third, fourth, or even fifth party of any gender to join them in tasting taboo joys. They will smoke, they will even snort a little coke, just to assure a degree of fear about being intruded upon by the local police. Don't judge: they, at least, are trying to hold their marriage together. Are you?

The problem with the great literature of the past is that it doesn't tell you how to live with real endings. In the great literature of the past you either get married and live happily ever after, or you die. But the fact is, neither is what actually happens. Oh, you do die, but never at the right time, never with great language floating all around you, and a whole theater of witnesses to your agony. What actually happens is that you do get married or you don't, and you don't live happily ever after, but you do live. And that's the problem. I mean,

115

think about it. Suppose Antigone had lived. An Antigone who goes on being Antigone year after year would be not only ludicrous but a bore. The cave and the rope are essential.

It isn't just the endings. In real life, how can you tell when you're in Book I or Book II, or Act II or Act V? No stagehands come charging in to haul down the curtains at an appropriate moment. So how do I know whether I'm living in the middle of Act III and heading toward a great climax, or at the end of Act V and finished? I don't even know who I am.

from *The Women's Room*, by Marilyn French, pp. 191–3.

Chapter 9

Rebalancing private and professional life

Tomorrow will be different, says the young manager to his family and to himself. His intentions are sincere; he means well. He has lived a life of increasing guilt, of inconsistency with his values. Gradually tomorrow comes – for some. But Act II does not begin with a clash of cymbals; one act merges with the next. Statistics, though, say that the centre point of transition falls around age 34 or 35.

Act II does have a hidden overture for those who can pick up the melody. This overture is the professional choice that has been made – whether or not this is accompanied by a sense of professional identity. We showed earlier how people cope with multiple life commitments and the accompanying stresses by limiting their focus of attention to one or a few areas of life investment. They lower their sensitivity to other areas, doing little more than maintain them. Now, sensitivity to private life increases. Having made professional choices facilitates this – energies are released to turn to other areas of life. One becomes aware of things that only dimly penetrated consciousness beforehand: the feelings of one's wife, the fact that she too is a human being, the rich or poor quality of one's relationship with her, the way in which one uses free time.

Awareness is one matter. Liking is another. Behaviour is still a third matter. Being sensitive does not mean that one behaves any differently from before. The quality and quantity of investment behaviour does not necessarily change. Professional life itself is no less important than before – it is just that now that choices have been made, the career enters a qualitatively different phase of realization and performance. This releases sensitivity towards private life, not the drive to action. What the person does with his awareness depends on himself and others.

Five paths

Different people appear to experience these years of rebalancing professional and private life in different ways. So far, we have been able to identify five paths through the late thirties and early forties.

1. Confirmation

First, there is the manager who has successfully launched his three careers – as a professional, husband, and father. His work career may indeed have been his major preoccupation in the past, but he has simultaneously found the time and energy to build a gratifying private life. He is most likely to experience a sense of confirmation of himself at this phase in life.

None of the couples we interviewed at this stage of life were clearly on this first path, though several couples indicated that their late thirties had been years of fulfilment and confirmation. This confirmation may turn out to be illusory, or temporary, since the wife's development path may become a source of disequilibrium. She may previously have actively supported her husband in launching his career, finding her own sense of purpose in that and in her role as a mother. Now that the children are starting to grow up, she may begin to feel the need for a new purpose in life (the so-called 'empty nest' crisis). Her self-questioning and her anxiety, latent or manifest, coupled with her husband's desire to maintain their existing lifestyle, may provoke a crisis at this point.

The manager most likely to experience a sense of confirmation is the one who fits his job well and has a clear sense of professional identity. But confirmation also depends on his wife. If she has developed a clear sense of *her* identity, if she has not simply adjusted, accommodated and put off this issue until tomorrow, she may reinforce his stability of lifestyle. But if she feels no inner fulfilment, if there is no zest and colour to the marriage, stability will become monotonous routine. It will be more 'his' marriage than 'her' marriage, to use Jessie Bernard's distinction (Bernard, 1972). But she does not voice her doubts for fear of rocking the boat – his boat. She suppresses her doubts with the thought that 'after all, isn't this what life is all about?'

In this way, the path of confirmation may lead in later years to the so-called traditional marriage, perhaps still the most frequent among executive couples. The husband works while the wife looks after the home or works part-time. She wants him to be happy, supporting him in his professional development. Her task, as Handy (1978) describes it, is to absorb family problems and not to burden her husband. At home, conversations are ritualized ('how was the office today?') or logistic ('who is going to take the children to the party tomorrow?'). There are few deep discussions, but the couple pride themselves on their happy marriage because there are few conflicts. When they feel tense or anxious, they withdraw from each other. They suffer in silence or channel their tension into other activities. The pattern is stable, dull, ritualized – accepted. Today, it is a much criticized form of marriage, but under certain conditions (as we will see in the two subsequent chapters) it can be the basis for a fulfilling lifestyle.

In this traditional marriage, the couple are rarely expressive towards each other. They hide their feelings, doubts, guilt and resentment. Expressiveness may change the arrangement by rocking the boat.

2. Marital and lifestyle renegotiation

Among those we interviewed, it was the managers in their mid-thirties and early forties who were most likely to talk of having worked through, or being in the middle of, periods of marital adjustment. Two 40-year-old managers and their wives were now very satisfied with their relationships, and with their lifestyles. They mentioned periods of turmoil lasting a year or more: stormy rows and bitter arguments triggered in one case by a mutual feeling of having grown apart and in the other case by mutual recognition of the husband's lack of family involvement. Having come through this, both couples felt strengthened as individuals and as partners. We believe that a period of accounting for one's marital behaviour and lifestyle, however stormy it may be, may have great value for a couple in and beyond this phase of life.

There are two major issues in renegotiation; sometimes they are fused together, sometimes one is suppressed. The first is the quality of private life. The second is the wife's own identity. Of course, other feelings may be expressed also, including those of incompatibility or dislike ('you are too passive', 'you are not sociable', 'nothing interests you except work'). The first element, the quality of private life (or the consequences of the husband's career for the marriage) is a continuation of an earlier dialogue, but now with a tone of urgency or ultimatum. The successful manager begins to feel that he has indeed sacrificed the quality of his marriage and private life on the altar of career. But now he responds actively to his worries, sparking off an often painful period of renegotiation. One wife talked about what had happened:

> 'He should participate much more in family life, even if there are constant work demands. But it has changed a lot in the last six years. Earlier on, it was terrible! He was the husband who comes home from his work and who picks up his newspaper at the same time as he switches on the television. We had a talkative little boy who he totally

ignored. And me – everything, but *everything* fell on my shoulders. He was physically there, but that's all.'

'What led to the change over the last years?'

'Well, we had some very violent arguments. We had long, long discussions which at times didn't seem to get anywhere. We fought about it! And slowly things seemed to get better. I'm still not satisfied, but he's more attentive than he was before.'

The second element in renegotiation is often the wife's own identity. In Chapter 8, we showed how recognition of that is often postponed or suppressed. An uneasy accommodation is reached, pressured by lack of a sense of real choice. When the children grow up, a wife may resent her husband's lifestyle if it prevents her from exploring what she would like to do with her own independent life. This important issue will be the topic of Chapter 12.

When discussing the relationship between professional life and private life, we observed that family has very little day-to-day influence on work life, except where the most important life decisions are concerned. However, there were instances of accommodating career to family considerations among men in their late thirties and early forties. The wife puts her foot down and refuses yet another move. The husband questions whether a promotion will be worth the spillover consequences for the family. The tensions that career involvement has built up in private life now express themselves in career decisions. This willingness to accommodate is a necessary part of renegotiation of the marriage. Confrontation leads to deadlock if the partners are unwilling to question their positions.

For this reason, it is clear that the successful manager who has found his professional identity is more willing to negotiate rather than hide behind the small talk of household routine. His career options are open and he feels sure of his professional qualities. In turning down a move abroad, he is not sabotaging his entire career – if his company holds this decision against him, he can leave for another company. Not so for the struggler. He has still no sense of his career path, his attitude is still defensive. Turning down that move may be turning down the opportunity which would make his life different. He is less likely to be willing to rebalance his life except on minor issues (helping more with household chores).

The essence of renegotiation is communication – the expression of feelings, conflicts, joys, pleasures, doubts and resentments. We call it expressiveness, to contrast it with withdrawing into the self, putting on an outer mask, or trying to work things out alone. Expressiveness is only a first step, and the outcome is not necessarily the happily renegotiated reconciliation. Nicholas Monserrat tells the story of a middle aged man in his collection of short stories, *The Ship that Died of Shame*. The man's life is peaceful but dull. His wife is perfect, but boring. He reaches the point where he can no longer hide his feelings from her. He tells her. Far from exploding, she asks him gently if he wants her to leave. At his 'Yes,' she calmly packs her bags and leaves.

The weeks go by, and his life has not changed despite a brief affair. He begins to wonder what his wife is doing, and hires a detective to find out. The report is a revelation. She is living a life of luxury and pleasure, accompanied by one famous playboy after the other. And so his torment begins. Since this is a story, the outcome is predictable. He contacts her, the reconciliation is made. Although what they each did during the time of separation is by tacit agreement never mentioned, from that day onwards he sees his wife in a different way. Outwardly, nothing has changed in their lifestyle; inside, a humdrum marriage has become an exciting marriage.

The outcomes of expressiveness and renegotiation in real life are often not the storybook endings. They may be separation and divorce. Issues now painfully brought out into the open may not be resolved. But the path of renegotiation should be contrasted with the next path, of no renegotiation.

3. Uneasy acceptance of *status quo*

This is a path experienced by some managers who feel dissatisfied and tense in their marriages. At this stage, they are also likely to feel dissatisfied with their lifestyles – with the way in which their career-oriented behaviour affects a marriage that is still important to them. But this man is afraid to unleash the storm of a marital renegotiation, preferring to let mutual tensions express themselves through petty bickering. At a deeper level, however, he prefers to live with his dissatisfaction in his private life because he is fundamentally unwilling to change his career-oriented behaviour. Renegotiation of the marriage will not get past the first point of spasmodic quarrelling, self-justification, and efforts to persuade the other partner to adapt to one's own preferences.

Why should some managers be unwilling to change their lifestyle even though discontented? In talking of how the manager turns inwardly towards his private life, one should not forget that the career (even though launched) remains very important to the man. Some managers are more mesmerized by their careers than others. Drawing upon Michael Driver's research, we suggest that the men least ready to change are those who have experienced *partial success* in their careers – enough of a taste to whet their appetites, but not enough to satiate them (Driver, 1980). Driver suggested that a high degree of success in one's career may lead to openness toward broadening and reorienting career and other interests. The highly successful manager, his sense of competence and self-esteem as a professional well reinforced, is quite likely to feel the urge to turn his talents to another activity – to politics, or to setting up his own business for example. But he may also be the person who is most receptive to renegotiating his marriage if he feels dissatisfied here. On the other hand, the person who feels that he has failed in his career may be equally willing to turn to developing his family life. But what about the large number of managers who have been partially successful? They have some of the outward trappings of success – a certain level of authority and responsibility, a large office, and a fancy house. The play of success on their egos has nurtured in them the desire for success. But they do not, deep down, feel an inner success and security. W. H. Whyte characterized these people twenty years ago in *The Organization Man*. They are people so mesmerized by their careers that they do not respond to any other call. They are hypnotized by the desire to 'feel successful' as well as be successful. We will see the consequence of this when we talk of the older manager.

It is, in part, the behaviour of the wife of this 'partially successful' manager that determines the path he will take through the late thirties and early forties. One of her earlier aspirations may have been to realize herself through the family and marriage itself. Consequently, in the earlier years of the marriage, when her husband was intent on launching his career, she may have complained about his long hours of work, his travel, and the worries he brought home. She may have tried to make him understand the consequences of his behaviour for her. Since the family will have been important to him, she probably will have met with enough understanding to encourage her, though she may not have succeeded in changing his behaviour. He may well have said, like the young manager previously quoted: 'I understand her problems – but I haven't found solutions to them.'

Now, in her mid- and late thirties, his wife may be on the verge of giving up in frustration. Resigned, she may be ready to adapt herself to the *status quo*. This adaptation may take several forms. Some will reconcile themselves to finding gratification in supporting their husbands in their careers. Others will try to establish their own separate and independent lives by, for example, going back to work. For a few wives, this adaptation may take the form of separation and divorce. But the paradox is that many women are ready to give up their efforts to renovate their marriages and family lives precisely at the same time when their husbands start becoming more concerned with the quality of their private lives, and especially of their marriages.

4. The turning point for the misfit

The early thirties have been a particulary trying time for the misfit, who has been coping with feelings of frustration, tension, and failure. This has extracted a heavy toll in his private life. Now he risks losing both domains of life, one of his options is to turn his energies to invest in private life. In various studies of men early in their careers, Hall and others have found that success reinforces the drive to be more successful (the success spiral). But they do not find that failure has the opposite effect in early adulthood. Failure does not result in giving up, but in renewed perseverance (Hall, 1971; Schneider and Hall, 1972; Faunce and Dubin, 1975). We believe, however, that if this sense of failure endures into the mid- to late thirties, the manager adapts at this next phase, compensating for lack of success in one life domain by reinvesting in another.* His values shift entirely to private life. He comes to regard his professional life more in terms of 'work' than 'career'. The relationship between professional and private life becomes instrumental, or perhaps independent. Where failure has been marked, it may even be explicitly compensatory.

We found that among managers there was no difference between the work involvement of 'dominantly family-oriented' managers and the work involvement of managers with dual or career-oriented values (see Chapter 1, page 9). But at this middle and later life phases, family-oriented managers invest on average 10 per cent less energy in their work than their more career-oriented counterparts. In a previous study of the trade-offs people make it their careers, one if the authors found that this process of reorientation was seen as one of 'broadening horizons', 'getting a more balanced attitude to life', 'maturing', or 'becoming more realistic' about self prospects (Evans, 1974). These are all very sound rationalizations to describe such a turning point in life. Such a manager is likely to believe that success exacts a price – he does not wish to pay that price.

> I suppose like everyone else I've always wanted to be the company president. But the price that one has to pay is too high. I've seen those guys up on the sixth floor, and the strain that they are under. God help them – I certainly don't envy them any longer. So I made a decision a few years back to pay more attention to my family, and I don't regret it. I suppose that you could say that I've matured, become more realistic about my chances, if you like.

* Faunce and Dubin (1975) argue on the basis of various studies that this applies to workers and lower level employees. Despite having routine jobs, they have aspirations for their professional development while in their twenties and early thirties. They change jobs and companies at this stage in search of opportunity. If they have not progressed by the early or mid-thirties, resignation to their fate sets in. They adopt an instrumental attitude to work, where job security and money are all that count.

5. The dilemma of the late-success spiral

Not all people may be strongly career-oriented as young adults, though our survey has focused on such men. Launching the career comes late to some. Contrast the above statement with the views of a manager whose aspirations have recently gone up. He was a 37-year-old product line manager, who had moved into his present job eighteen months before.

> I've always been in a technical marketing job with some manage-rial responsibility until just a few years ago. I had a balanced life there, but the work started to get boring. I decided that I couldn't just drift through life in that sort of capacity, as I had originally intended. So I got the offer of this job in a new field with a lot more managerial responsibility. A *lot* more! I knew the family would be affected, but I didn't realize how much.
>
> I think I can say I've done my job well so far, but that means that everyone wants me. Manufacturing, R and D, clients – everyone! So I've shifted into a 24-hour working schedule, and now I find that I even feel guilty if I'm not working! I'm getting pretty ambitious because I like it. And I tend to rationalize away the cost to my home life by saying that I'm on a steep learning curve at the moment, that this is just a few years' investment. (In Evans, 1974, p. 129.)

This manager was not particularly fulfilled in his earlier work in technical marketing, but he could not have been described as a misfit. He was not particularly ambitious; he saw his job as work rather than as a step in a career. His earlier family-orientation insulated his private life from the spillover effect. Now in mid-career, he showed all the characteristics of the career prisoner.

This last path is that of the person who is neither successful nor career oriented until his mid-thirties. Typically he is an engineer in a technically oriented company who is only moderatedly involved with his work. His main interest in life is his family. However, although he does not realize it at the time, he is, as an engineer, somewhat of a misfit. His latent inclinations lie in the direction of the management of people and tasks rather than as a technical contributor to the company. He is offered – often by chance – a management position. In the first years in this position he feels a zest and verve for his work that he never experienced before. His investment in his work escalates, in the way described by the success spiral syndrome. Yet he feels acutely conscious of the sacrifices that he is now making in his private life where he has also such a high stake.

Dilemmas in leisure time

Leisure life as opposed to family life was not a major theme in our questionnaire inquiry,* although the comments of the managers we interviewed revealed both the importance of leisure activities to them and their frequent dilemmas in using leisure time. This was particularly true for men at this mid-thirties to early-forties phase of life (confirmed by Rapoport and Rapoport, 1975). At this point, people begin to become sensitive as to how they use their leisure time; previously, such activities have been taken for granted, if undertaken at all.

In *The Symmetrical Family*, Michael Young and Peter Wilmott show how leisure time means different things to different people.† Leisure is often viewed as the opposite of work; it is one of those words which makes most sense as an antonym. An intuitive definition is that work is what you have to do, while leisure is what you want to do, and this idea makes sense for some people. But a postman in the Young and Wilmott survey commented that, 'I get more leisure at work that I do at home.' This is certainly true for many of the managers in our own survey, particularly for the prisoners. Leisure is obligation, while work is pleasure – even for those who use a more puritanical word such as 'sense of commitment' to describe their enjoyment in professional activity.

From the comments of managers, we can distinguish four different concepts of leisure. We will show how these concepts are conditioned by professional life. Both of the first two leisure concepts reflect the influence of spillover tension on family life – leisure as recovery, and leisure as a release from tension. These are two very different ways of viewing relaxation.

1. Leisure as recovery – passing time

Studies show that watching television is the most common leisure activity

---

* The questionnaire results show that the two main private life activities are 'being a companion to one's wife' (talking or doing things with her) and simple relaxation (light reading, TV, a siesta, a relaxing hobby). In third and fourth place are playing with the children, and going out with the wife and family (excursions, cinema, sports events). Active hobbies, sports and pastimes, as well as self-development activities such as reading or studying, are less common.

† Young and Wilmott cite Kaplan's definition of leisure: "The essential elements of leisure, as we shall interpret it, are (a) an antithesis to 'work' as an economic function, (b) a pleasant expectation and recollection, (c) a minimum of involuntary social-role obligations, (d) a psychological perception of freedom, (e) a close relation to values of the culture, (f) the inclusion of an entire range from inconsequence and insignificance to weightiness and importance, and (g) often, but not necessarily, an activity characterized by the element of play. Leisure is none of these by itself but all together in one emphasis or another." They add that leisure can also be a state of non-activity. (Young and Wilmott, p. 206)

among all social classes, though least so among managerial and professional people (Young and Wilmott, 1973; Robinson and Converse, 1972). Although some people may hide behind an alibi of 'wanting to catch up on world events', the most popular programmes are those of pure entertainment. The routine is predictable: the manager returns home from the office, says five words to his wife, pours himself a stiff whisky, switches on the television and settles into his comfortable armchair. If the programme is boring, he may read the newspaper or snooze. Mummy protects him from the children. 'Don't bother Daddy, he's tired.'

Watching television is one form of leisure as recovery. Others are similiar non-activities, like snoozing, drinking and chatting at the pub or café, or mild activities like gardening or doing jobs around the house. Most of these activities are solitary, though other people may be nearby. Conversation appears to inhibit recovery. Recovery is probably the dominant use of leisure time when spillover is strong. Leisure is absorbed by spillover, particularly emotional spillover. The misfit says that he would like more time for private life; but he cannot actively profit from the time that he has available.

2. Leisure as relaxation – venting tensions

In comparison with other occupational groups, managers and professional people spend a high proportion of their time on sports and very active hobbies. This is particularly true for managing directors and top executives (Young and Wilmott, 1973). Their activities are active and demanding – tennis, golf, swimming, and sailing on the one hand, building a boat, renovating a house on the other. Two newer sports, often called 'executive sports', are skiing and squash. Both are intense and demanding. 'In squash, I find total relaxation,' says a manager. 'When I'm playing I can't think of anything else, and I feel invigorated afterwards – especially if I've won!'

The essence of these activities is that they go beyond simple recovery – they are enjoyable and relaxing. But why in particular for the manager and executive? One reason is that they are a satisfying outlet for tensions and aggressions. In the family setting, a man does not have an outlet for such aggression. They are competitive or achieving activities which have two properties work does not have – they are physically demanding, and offer immediate results for one's efforts.

Hans Selye, the stress researcher, points out the sound biological foundation of this type of relaxation. The body cannot take too much stress on one part, for example that most used in work. Stress research shows that when one is tense or blocked in one activity, a voluntary change of activity is frequently more relaxing than simple rest. The answer to the problem which you have been struggling for days to solve often comes when you are doing something completely different. In other words, stress on the one system helps to relax another (Selye, 1975). Corporations these days are investing less in Transcendental Meditation programmes for their executives, and more in gymnasiums and squash courts.

3. Leisure as private life investment – building the family

The National Recreation Association in the United States pioneered the slogan, 'The family that plays together, stays together.' Lowenthal *et al.* (1975) observe that in leisure, men emphasize play while women emphasize sociability. Building the family is 'sociable play'.

The difference between this concept and the previous two is pointed out by Orthnor (1975). He distinguishes between individual, parallel and joint leisure activities. The husband goes off fishing while the wife meets with friends: these are individual activities where nothing is shared. The husband and wife both work in the garden, he planting vegetables while she weeds the flowers; or they go to the cinema together. These are parallel activities: the presence of the other partner is not indispensable to the activity. If the wife leaves the garden or the husband goes to the cinema alone, the activity is still relaxing, enjoyable and meaningful. But imagine an excursion or picnic in the country without the other members of the family. Remove them from the garden football match and the evening barbeque. These activities lose their meaning. They are joint leisure activities. They have the element of sociable play.

Joint activities are both an investment in the family and a return on that investment (that is, if they *are* enjoyable). Orthner found in his study of how 220 couples use their leisure that the frequency of joint activities was positively related to marital satisfaction; the frequency of individual activities was negatively related (though the correlations were in both cases low). There is probably a 'success spiral' at work here. The more one invests in joint activities, the more fun and exciting they become. If one invests little, the family moves apart – there is less gratification from being sociable with the family.

4. Leisure as personal development – the substitute or second career

Some people choose hobbies or interests which fit none of the previous concepts. These pursuits have a paraprofessional quality – they are

127

consuming passions which demand skill or expertise. They are seen more as development than relaxing. For one person, this may be participating in local politics. For another, it may be painting or sculpting, studying for an evening school degree, playing a musical instrument in a trio.

These activities have a 'substance' to them which is not found in those of other leisure concepts. The person's sense of identity is partly wrapped up in them. Each could be an alternative career and it is sometimes the person's dream that they might become one. They are often as jealously regarded as invasions of the family's right to the man's time as is professional work itself. This is paraprofessional leisure – the only difference is that the hours of leisure are self-determined and there is no payment. Even these two differences do not always apply.

We will talk more about this leisure concept in Part Four of this book, for generativity is sometimes the product of the paraprofessional career. Among managers in their twenties and thirties, we found few instances of this particular leisure concept. The professional career at this time allows ample room for self-development and personal purpose, except for those few who explicitly saw themselves as compensating in their private lives for lack of fulfilment in their work careers. Others had hobbies such as painting or music (very few), but these clearly served a relaxation function. That they *could* later become paraprofessional activities is quite conceivable.

Conflicts between leisure concepts

More than half of the managers we interviewed in their thirties and forties saw leisure as an area of conflict within the family. Just as the younger manager saw himself as having to make choices between work and non-work (and then looking back later and seeing these choices as sacrifices), so the mid-life manager sees himself as having to make private life choices between time spent with his wife, with his children, and on other pursuits. As Young and Wilmott (1973) put it, 'leisure was sometimes a duel rather than a duet'. They point out that most people do not consider the demands of the family as interfering with things they like to do in leisure – but managers and professional people are most likely to feel that they do.

Some managers in our survey had chosen to give priority to building the family:

> I took up golf about four years ago. But the last time I played was six months ago. And I suppose that in an ideal sense I feel that this has been sacrificing something. I feel that I should be able to play golf

or have time to swim and so on. But then these aren't very sociable sports as far as the family is concerned. So if there is a choice, I feel I should do something that is more *shared*.

The leisure lives of other husbands centred on relaxation. We interviewed the wife, in her mid-forties, of a marketing director who was very involved and satisfied with his work. His wife had fully accepted a supportive role, and was content bringing up their three children. The only time during the interview when bitterness and resentment showed through was when she talked of his tennis. He had taken up tennis six years ago and had become a prominent member of the local club. His wife could accept that his career was a legitimate call on his time and energy, but tennis certainly was not. When asked how he used his leisure time, she said, with an edge to her voice:

His favourite occupation is TV. And now he's taken up tennis as well, which is something I can't share with him.

This is the cruellest blow for the supportive wife – even the little free time he has cannot be shared.

If one can talk about the most 'natural' shape of managerial leisure, one has the impression from our study and others that it is relaxation (tension release) – with recovery in second place at times of high spillover, and family investment at times of low spillover. Why should this be?

Our map of the four leisure concepts is shown in Figure 9.1 The adjoining concepts overlap. Sports and hobbies express relaxation, but assist in recovery as well as creating their own need for recovery. Some of these sports may be part of family life, as when the tennis or sailing partner is one's wife. On the other hand, recovery (watching the TV) is the opposite to joint family activity. Relaxation is shown as the opposite to self-development.

The different relationships between professional and private life mirror themselves in different leisure concepts. When spillover pervades the lifestyle, as is the case for the struggling misfit, recovery dominates leisure time. Investment in the family is a distant preoccupation. However, when the manager is at ease and fulfilled in his job, relaxation and the family will be the keynotes. But notice that the more he is involved in his work, the more he will be drawn to relaxation alone – this is the situation of the mid- or late career prisoner described by Young and Wilmott, the managing director who spends most of his leisure on sport and active hobbies. If the wife and children happen to share these interests, well and good for them.

The resigned misfit, the person who has turned away from his

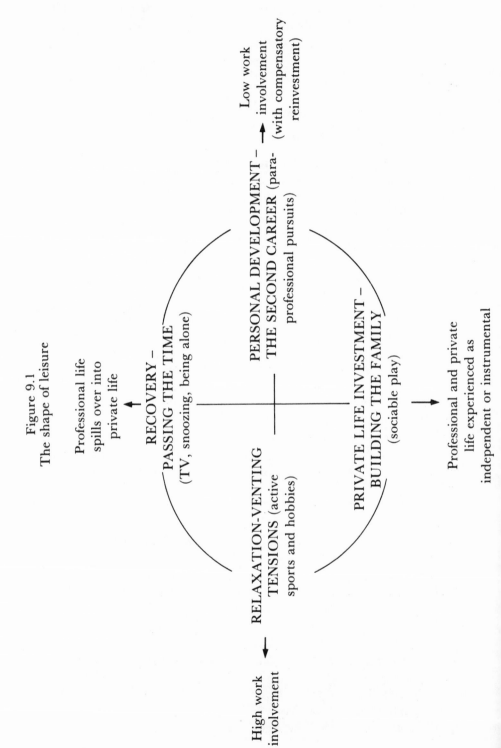

Figure 9.1
The shape of leisure

career, has little sense of fulfilment provided by work. Work is instrumental, and he seeks this fulfilment in family activities. If he is still very oriented toward personal achievement, he may compensate by investing in paraprofessional pursuits. If taken very seriously, for instance when a person is trying to find professional identity in private life, these create their own spillover and need for recovery.

Leisure life is thus a point of sensitivity and concern for the manager at this phase of life. The men talk of choices here in the same way as they talked earlier of choices between professional and private life. Now they face choices within the private life arena – because private life is becoming a more differentiated concept. But we have the impression that these choices are influenced, if not constrained, by the course of events in professional life. For the person who is still struggling with professional identity, the choices are limited – the failure to accomplish one life task satisfactorily renders the other more difficult. The overall level of stress that the person experiences is heightened, and these years may be experienced as tense and difficult. Leisure choices are most real for the person who has found his sense of professional identity.

Of course, other processes are shaping the marriage at about this time, and we turn in the next chapters to discuss these.

Chapter 10

The shapes of marriage

What is the formula for a successful marriage? Probably even more research has been devoted to this question than to exploring the formula for career success. Yet it is still as difficult to describe what constitutes a successful marriage as it is to describe a successful career. Some researchers view a successful marriage as one where the couple declare themselves happy with it, while others measure success by the duration and stability of the relationship. Still others take as indicators such factors as what the husband and wife do together, the strength of their sexual relationship, or whether they are able to share with each other their deeper feelings and thoughts.

Indeed, there is nothing in human nature that prescribes the form that a partnership of a man and a woman should take. Jessie Bernard, the eminent American sociologist, who has spent a lifetime studying marriage, is quite blunt on this point.

> The variety of ways in which husbands and wives can relate to each other in marriage, and have, is so staggering as to boggle the imagination. Human beings can accept almost any kind of relationship if they are properly socialized into it. Just as people learn to accept fasts, painful rites, scarification, sacrifices of the most difficult kinds as a matter of course, so also can they accept lifelong celibacy or lifelong virginity – and they do – if that is defined as their lot. Girls accept doddering old men as husbands if that is what their parents tell them to. Wretched, miserable, quarrelling spouses remain together no matter how destructive the relationship if that is what their community prescribes. Almost every kind of relationship has occurred somewhere, sometime – monogamy, polygyny, polyandry, exogamy, endogamy, matrilocal residence, neolocal residence, arranged marriages, self-selection of mates, parental selection of mates, marriage for love, marriage for convenience. . . . There is literally nothing about marriage that anyone can imagine that has not in fact taken place, whether prescribed, proscribed, or optional. All these variations

seemed quite natural to those who lived with them. If any of them offends our 'human nature', we have to remind ourselves that 'human nature' as we know it this moment in this country is only one kind of human nature. (Bernard, 1973, pp. 284–5)

In fact, if there is one thing that is surprising to the researcher of marriage, it is the fact that the vast majority of marriages are seen as successful – that is if one accepts happiness as reported in a survey as a measure of success. Statistics consistently show that some four out of five people see their marriages as happy (Leslie, 1976), and our own survey is no exception – this is shown in Figure 10.1. Few people report their

Figure 10.1
How the men feel about their marriages

	Percentage*
Very happy	41
Pretty happy	39
Sometimes happy, sometimes unhappy	16
Not very happy	3
Unhappy	1
	——
	100

* $N = 482$

marriages as unhappy. Unhappiness is rarely a good predictor of separation and divorce; although a separating couple usually see their marriage as unhappy, that couple will report that the marriage is at least 'pretty happy' until the day of open discussion about separation.

The development of marriage can be seen as an exploratory process like the professional one – exploring how to share one's life with another person.* The developmental path is visible in statistics. Marital happiness, as it is reported in surveys, peaks in the early years of marriage (even though there are more divorces in the first year than at any other time). It declines thereafter, to reach a low ebb in the thirties and early forties,

---

* Yet in today's society at least, people do not explore, risk, move out in the marital career in the same active way as they do in the work career. The predominant social view (though less and less) is that to experiment with marriage is irresponsible.

climbing gradually after this point. The pattern is observable in most data on marriage, including our own. This low ebb in the thirties does not necessarily represent particular difficulties that the marriage faces at that time. It can also be interpreted as the time when people are most aware of their lives as partners and the shape that their marriage is taking. Is this the life that I envisaged for myself in marriage? Do I want to change the shape my marriage is settling into ... and can I? Even if I am less than fulfilled in my marriage, is the price of breaking out not too high? Can I even talk about these doubts and questions with my partner – won't the very act of posing them openly create a problem in our relationship?

For couples who stay together, reported marital happiness rises thereafter. The marriage may be no different, but what has changed is acceptance of one's lot. Faced with conflicting feelings, most people come to terms with their conflict. The marriage has taken its shape.

The shapes that marriages take

Compare the comments of these two people. Both of them are in their mid-forties. Both of them live in reportedly happy marriages – we will not say whether they are men or women, for it does not really matter. They each describe their marriages.

> *A*: I view our marriage as very happy. The best side of it is having someone to talk to, to share things with. When I am worried, then I can always get it off my chest. And when I feel excited, I have someone to share that with too. Even though we've been married for twenty years, I think he/she is the most interesting person I know. We don't always agree about things, we can spend hours arguing. And it is fun having someone to do things with. And then there are the two children – I'm very proud of them. They are both growing up now and beginning to lead their own lives, but we still have a lot of fun together.
>
> On the negative side, I'd say we don't spend enough time together. It's a source of sadness, and we've never been able to resolve the issue. There are periods when we seem to grow apart, each doing our own thing. Something small sparks off a mad quarrel, and we don't speak to each other for days. But finally, one or the other of us breaks in, and we'll spend a whole weekend talking it through. And then of course we have disagreements about the family budget and who should collect the children from a party, but that's less serious.
>
> *B*: I view our marriage as very happy. We're very proud of our two

children. They are a source of a lot of fun and excitement, and I'm delighted with their achievements at school – especially the eldest. The home that we have now is everything that we dreamed of, and we've put a lot of work and thought into it, which has been fun. The community around here is an interesting one, and we've made a lot of friends over the years – we're always popping into each other's houses, and I like that informality. We never have any serious conflicts with each other, we've been able to resolve most of those over the years. We understand each other, we fit in with each other's moods.

You could say we don't spend all that much time together. But then, frankly, I suppose we don't have all that much to say to each other. That's probably the biggest negative thing that I can think of. Things are best when other people are around, and in any case we each have our own activities. Sometimes, I feel we're in a bit of a rut – settled, if you like. You feel staid in your ways. Our relationship with each other is still good, don't get me wrong about that, even our sex life and so on, but – well, it is not like it used to be. But I suppose that's natural. After all, we've been married for eighteen years. But, I don't know, from time to time you feel that something else could be more exciting.

Despite similarities, despite the fact that both are considered as happy, these two marriages represent opposite extremes in the shape of marriage. In the first marriage, what are emphasized are the aspects of life *together*. The emotional aspects of the relationship are sources of both satisfaction and tension. It is a marriage based on expressiveness, representing one element of marriage, namely *companionship*. In the second marriage, these aspects are played down, especially when talking of the positive side. What marriage provides is more emphasized than is the relationship itself: children, home, social life. Marriage is a provider of many things other than companionship. This second marriage, equally happy in the eyes of the partner just quoted, captures the second element of marriage, namely *instrumentality*.

A fundamental difference in these two marriages is the degree of expressiveness. The companionship marriage is an expressive marriage, where the husband and wife openly share their thoughts and feelings. They also confront grievances and conflicts – in a way it is a conflictual marriage. But then, any partnership between two persons is a situation of potential conflict – the difference here is that this conflict is openly expressed and negotiated. The couple do not allow themselves to drift apart into settled ways, onto separate islands.

The husband and wife in the instrumental marriage have arrived at a more stable way of accommodating to each other. They share a common lifestyle, but their discussions are limited to the routine dialogue of life together. Neither person rocks the boat by talking of personal feelings – neither of joys, which might make the other person jealous, nor of doubts and worries, which might upset the other. There is little open conflict. The partners have learnt to control themselves. If they feel angry, moody or upset, they have learnt to withdraw or to sublimate their moods – by venting frustrations on the tennis court or by busying themselves with the children. Or by redoubling energy at the office.

Traditionally, marriages have been evaluated in terms of their intimacy, happiness signifying happiness with each other. But family researchers during the last 30 years have been struck by the fact that couples stay together despite an absence of close personal contact. They may even regard their marriages as happy. Marital stability is a different concept from happiness in the relationship. It depends more on the structure of what marriage provides, and on the difficulties of dissolving that marriage, as well as on the belief that things would not be much different in another relationship. Children hold the couple together. The marriage provides financial security for the wife, as well as a certain standing in society. Within limits, it provides her with the resources for what she wants to do as an independent person. It provides the husband with a stable home base, with a haven away from pressures, with a leisure life where he is free within tacit limits to do what he wants to do.

The instrumental marriage is more often than not structured on traditional lines, with the husband and wife having distinctly different roles (Hicks and Platt, 1970). Its stability depends on an unspoken role contract that has evolved over the years, established during the early period of marriage (see Chapter 8). The huband's obligation is to provide for the family. He is the source of income and status; this suits him well, especially if he enjoys the work that provides him with the means to provide for the family. Beyond this, his obligations are few, except to spend a minimum amount of time at the house. His wife's obligation is the responsibility for running the household – children, home maintenance, and the social life of the family. If this is not a full-time task, what she does with her remaining time is largely up to her.

This role structure was clearly visible in our own survey. A third of the 532 men could be described as 'passive providers'. In their relationship with their wives, they saw two roles as being important: providing financial security for her, and providing social status for her. Figure 10.2 shows that these passive providers were very likely to attribute great importance to the wife's role as the person who looks after the household. This was not so for husbands who simply took for granted their role as a provider. Their expectations of their wives lay in other

Figure 10.2
What 'passive providers' expect from their wives

| | | Extent to which the wife is expected to look after the household and children | | |
		High*	Moderate-low	
Extent to which husband sees himself as a passive provider in his relationship to his wife	High†	61%	39%	100% (N = 93)
	Low	29%	71%	100% (N = 107)

† The high passive providers saw themselves 'essentially' or 'very much' as providing both financial security and social status to their wives. The low passive providers saw both these roles as important only 'to a certain extent' or as 'not really important'.

* 'High' indicates that looking after the house and children is seen as an essential or very important part of the wife's role, whereas 'Low' indicates that this is important only 'to a large extent', 'to a certain extent' or 'not really'.

directions: they expected them to share times of relaxation and leisure, and assist in the self-development of both.

This traditional role contract has come under heavy fire in recent years, not only from feminists but also from researchers (Gavron, 1966; Bernard, 1973; Gowler and Legge, 1975; Bailyn, 1978). It is often a marriage of unequals, supposedly favouring the husband, and we will talk more about this critique in the pages and chapters ahead. The marriage it underlies, though, should not be seen as unhappy, though research shows that it is rarely vital. Gurin (1960) asked people to describe the happiness of their lives together. He found that in 'very happy' marriages, people were likely to talk of their relationships as the source of happiness as well as unhappiness. The 'happy' or 'pretty happy' couple were likely to focus on the situational aspects of life together (home, children, social life) as sources of happiness; the relationship itself was mentioned as a source of unhappiness.

The instrumental marriage is far more common among couples over 35 than is the companionship marriage – in society in general, and certainly among successful people. Two sociologists, John Cuber and Peggy Harroff, reached this conclusion in their study of *Sex and the Significant Americans* (1966). They interviewed 437 men and women who had distinguished themselves in various professions, such as business, teaching, law and the military. The relationships of these people with their partners were of five types, each named for its predominant theme.

Three of these were 'utilitarian' marriages (as Cuber and Harroff call the instrumental type) – the 'conflict-habituated relationship', the 'devitalized relationship', and the 'passive-congenial relationship'. Two of them were 'intrinsic' or companionship types – the 'vital relationship' and the 'total relationship'.

The conflict-habituated relationship: Conflict, nagging, quarrelling are a way of life for this couple. They are constantly at each other, playing barely concealed games which express hostility and tension and also a sense of togetherness. At best, the couple hide this when in the company of others, though not from the children. The children may become instruments in the conflict, as the film *Family Life* portrays (the daughter in this film becomes schizophrenic as a result of being caught in a never-ending battle between mother and father). The couple regard themselves as incompatible but chained together – this expresses itself in an active way by the perpetual conflict that permeates the home. Some psychiatrists have gone so far as to suggest that it is the deep need to do psychological battle which is the cohesive glue ensuring the stability of the marriage. Some such marriages do last a whole life time. The couple in *Who's Afraid of Virginia Woolf?* is an example of this type of relationship.

The devitalized relationship: This couple have settled for what they regard as the 'reality' of life together, once you have been married for a number of years. In their early years together, they were close, intimate, and shared much with each other. Now all that is past. The relationship is numb, void of any zest, ritualistic. They are habituated to each other, and there is little tension. The couple is held together by activities with the children, by habit, by joint entertaining, by participation in community events. The past is 'recaptured' at ritual dinners out on anniversary occasions; otherwise they lead separate lives.

They regard each other positively – 'He's a good husband,' 'She's a fine mother.' But there is no substance behind this view. Their lives outside the relationship may be active, but the relationship itself is stale. This is accepted as the inevitability of marriage. Separation is not considered – it would be too disturbing, and there is an absence of other alternatives. They compare themselves with other couples and feel that, in any case, their lot is not so bad after all.

The passive-congenial relationship: This, together with the devitalized relationship, is found to be the most widespread type of marriage among successful people after the mid-life years. There are many similarities with the devitalized relationship. The couple share certain interests and there is little conflict. They each have their separate lives. Their relationship is congenial but not intimate – they invest little in it and have no particular expectations for it. The difference from the devitalized couple is that they never expected marriage to be much different. They entered marriage with a logical, 'calm and sensible' attitude – often at a later age. They had no particular dreams or marital ideals, and thus they do not look back on 'the good old days'. Cuber and Harroff find many dual career marriages to be of this type. The energies of both man and woman are invested elsewhere, and they have never wished for any intense emotional involvement. The marriage satisfies a certain need for a peaceful home and children, yet allows them both to pursue what is really important, namely professional interests. It is a stable marriage, with no great demands placed on it, and possibly a very egalitarian marriage. There are few hidden resentments and misgivings, as with the devitalized couple – if there are disagreements, they can be discussed on an adult basis by two rational human beings.

These are pure types of utilitarian or instrumental marriages, and a particular marriage may have characteristics of all three. Cuber and Harroff note however that these marriages are distinctly different from the two intrinsic marriages. There is rarely ever any doubt in the observer's mind whether a marriage is utilitarian or intrinsic, no matter how much the couple may delude themselves. The companionship marriage is always characterized by three things: a high degree of mutual expressiveness, intense feelings about the other person, and the importance of the spouse's welfare in each person's scale of values.

The vital relationship: This is the stereotypical relationship of two newlyweds that is still found in some couples in the later years of life together. Their life together is vital, vibrant, and exciting – each invests heavily in it. What is important is sharing and togetherness. What matters is not what one does (picnics, theatre, holidays, tennis, hobbies, home rebuilding) as long as one does it *together*. The man feels that travelling to exotic places on business trips is a bore if he does it alone; it is exciting if his wife accompanies him. The woman feels that chatting with friends is just passing the time; it becomes fun if he is there as well. They may have their own separate lives, but these are less important than the part of life that they share.

Such a relationship is less free of conflict than the instrumental relationships, for the partners nevertheless have their own identities. They disagree on issues from time to time. The difference is that their disagreements are openly expressed – they do not hide what is important to them. They will compromise on unimportant issues, but battle it through on important convictions and problems. But unlike the conflict-habituated couple, they genuinely search for a solution. They seek to resolve issues rather than to score points in family warfare. They avoid solutions where there will be a winner or loser. Conflict brings the couple ultimately closer together rather than maintaining distance.

The total relationship: The total relationship is similar to the vital relationship, though more rare. It is even more expressive. There are no areas hidden from each other, there are no pretences. The marriage is the mainspring of life. That part of self-identity which lies beyond the couple is unimportant – the relationship is total in that each defines himself or herself in terms of the relationship with the other. A promotion which will entail frequent travel will never be seriously considered, and turning it down is not felt as a sacrifice. It is a multi-faceted relationship in that everything that either person does is shared – either by doing it together or by talking about it. There is no feeling of separateness.

Marital adjustment

One should not interpret the total relationship as being more happy than other relationships. People are happy and adjusted in each of these five types of marriage – they represent different meanings that marriage acquires. The couple in the passive-congenial marriage may regard the total couple with scorn as leading insular lives in a romantic cloud. The total couple spurns the passive-congenial lifestyle as one without pleasure or excitement.

There is no single best marriage, and the point must be stressed. Marriage entails *adjustment*, and researchers agree that marital happiness depends on the degree of mutual adjustment (Leslie, 1976; Bernard, 1973; Hicks and Platt, 1970). The typology concerns relationships, not personalities. A wife may be committed to an ideal of the 'family-as-a-career' and search for a vital relationship. Her husband understands this, but, intent on his career, he seeks a passive-congenial relationship. There is little adjustment and frequent conflict, which neither partner likes. The marriage is maintained for many years in a state of uneasy flux. Neither partner feels happy. Years later, it has settled into a clear mould as a devitalized relationship. Both have adjusted to this as the inevitable shape of life together. They look back on the old days, which certainly were more intense. But both now see their marriage as more happy than they saw it at that time. The couple has adjusted.

The years between the mid-thirties and early forties appear as particularly important in the shaping of the marriage. These are the years of adjustment. In our interviews, we felt we could quite easily type the marriage relationships of the couples in their forties and fifties. There were many devitalized relationships, some passive-congenial relationships, and some vital relationships. It was much more difficult to classify the relationships of the young couples. Typically we sensed elements of all three, as well as the conflict-habituated. Varying with the degree of spillover, there were vital moments alternating with long periods of simple congeniality or conflict. Private life, as we would expect, was maintained.

Gradually, as the wife adjusts to her husband's behaviour, a dominant pattern begins to emerge. Usually it is an instrumental relationship of one type or the other, for it takes two to be companions. But the younger couple denies this crystallization of the relationship. 'Tomorrow will be different,' each one says.

In the same way as forces press the young wife of the manager in the direction of a dependent or supportive role, so these forces press in the direction of the instrumental marriage unless something disturbs them. Cuber and Harroff concluded this as follows:

> The overriding inference from our inquiry is that the Utilitarian Marriage is shaped for most Significant Americans by a series of related, often unconscious, yet impelling choices. Once one sets his personal sights primarily on goals which lie outside the pair, once he thus devalues the private sphere in deference to some other, he commits himself, whether he realizes it or not, to an almost inexorable sequence of actions which culminate sooner or later in a full-fledged Utilitarian Marriage. For the passive-congenials it all comes quite undramatically and naturally; for the devitalized it seems about the only sensible way 'at this time of life'; and for the conflict-habituated its serves about as well as any conceivable arrangement to contain the contest. Once set up, the valences are mutually reinforcing and the tide is therefore very hard to reverse. Chiefly, they do not want to reverse it; they are content with the current order of things, whether or not in other compartments of their minds they might like it otherwise.' (Cuber and Harroff, 1966, pp. 130–31)

For the many couples who have as an ideal the vital relationship, this is a very pessimistic view, but our survey supports that it is a justified view ... *if* the couple allow choices to be inexorably and unconsciously made for them, if they continue to put off and off until tomorrow, until there is no tomorrow. Some couples do face up to choices explicitly in the process that we have called the renegotiation of the marriage. In all cases in our survey where this had happened, the shape of the marriage had changed. In one example, a devitalized couple spent two years confronting themselves and rediscovered the vitality of their relationship. In another example, they opted for the passive-congenial path.

The essence of renegotiation of the marriage is recapturing the vital part of the relationship, namely expressiveness. This is the theme of our next chapter.

Chapter 11

Expressiveness

While there is, objectively, no 'best' marriage, what Cuber and Harroff call the vital relationship probably comes close to representing the ideal for a majority of people in our society. The fact that people declare themselves happy in other types of relationship does not necessarily mean that they do not hold the vital relationship as an ideal. We, and others, find that a human quality we call expressiveness plays a fundamental role in maintaining that vitality. This is a quality that is also important in personal self-development.

What is expressiveness? It is what holds a marriage vitally together. Of course, expressiveness has something to do with sharing, though it is more than simply sharing four walls, a bed, and various activities. It is the sharing of feelings and thoughts about all the dimensions, professional and private, of one's life; it is being able to explore ideas and emotions with one's spouse at greater depth and with more honesty than with anybody else.

What we mean by expressiveness has little to do with the romantic cliché of perfect bliss and fusion of two people. It has to do with sharing who one is with the other. This of course means sharing the good and the bad, authentically living and honestly fighting, exploring positive and negative feelings, sharing answers but also unsolved questions, acknowledging even the most uncomfortable feelings of one's own ambivalence.

Humanistic psychologists, those psychologists most concerned with the quality of relationships between people, almost unanimously agree that expressiveness (or self-disclosure) is the essential characteristic of the intimate relationship (Jourard, 1971; Rogers, 1961; Maslow, 1971). Many people, particularly men, rarely disclose their inner thoughts, feelings and problems to anyone – not even to their wives and families. They may be skilled at small talk – or at discussing professional activities, sports events or intellectual issues. But whenever the conversation turns to their personal feelings or to the problems and feelings of others, they feel uncomfortable. They make a joke to deflect the conversation, or become silent. No-one is sure what they are really like.

The men in our interview survey often found it difficult to describe themselves as human beings. They were more at ease in describing their wives, but in terms of performance rather than qualities. Few of them spontaneously talked about their feelings towards their wives. "She's a good mother," "She's a good wife," were typical reactions. One of the men asked to describe his wife said that he would rather skip the question – he did not know what to say. When asked to describe himself, he would rather not answer that either. 'I'm a good husband, and that's as far as I'll go,' he said. He refused to discuss his current preoccupations and worries. His wife said of her husband:

> He is lovable, kind and very much the businessman. Conscientious, reliable, takes his work very seriously. He loves his job, it's very important in his life. He is calm and human outwardly, but he keeps most of his feelings to himself. I *think* he retains a lot inside himself, but he never talks about it, so I don't know. During the weekends, he is always *busy* doing something alone. He doesn't spend much time with us. But he has a good sense of humour, which makes it easy to forgive him. He'd be an ideal husband if he wasn't always so busy. I suppose he is just selfish, like any man with a woman ...
>
> I'm proud of what he does, but just sorry that we are never really *together*. We never really talk. Sometimes I tell him, 'I can live with you all of my life, but we spend so little time together that I will never find out about all your faults.' He just shrugs his shoulders. We've been married for so many years, and yet sometimes I feel I don't know him at all.

Humanistic psychologists regard such a man as 'normal'. He can function autonomously. But they distinguish between the 'normal' and the 'healthy' personality. The healthy personality is one that is capable of growing and developing, of relating to other human beings as separate persons. Self-disclosure is necessary for this.

This does not mean that all expressiveness is healthy. Research shows that healthy people are expressive, but in a discriminating way. One study looked at the way in which people who were judged as neurotic related to others, in comparison with people who were evaluated as healthy. The neurotic would either disclose his feelings to anyone (boss, colleagues, wife, friends, acquaintances), or to no-one; he did not distinguish between different types of relationship. The healthy person would be reserved in his expressiveness towards people who were not open towards him (business colleagues, for example), but would disclose his feelings towards people with whom he was more intimate (wife and close friends) (Chaikin *et al.*, 1976).

The prior research of Fernando Bartolomé focused on the difficulties that executives have in being aware of their feelings and in expressing them openly. The executive risks being caught by a stereotype of how he should behave. As a manager, he should be super-masculine, super-tough, super-strong. He should be decisive, and never show signs of wavering. He should either express his ideas boldly or not at all, and never hint at doubt. Where there is undeniable uncertainty, he should express this in the cold and logical terms of probabilities (Bartolomé, 1972).*

What is striking is that the manager comes to define not just his professional self but his whole nature in this stereotypical way. It is not only fatigue and emotion that spill over into private life – it is also a way of relating to other people. 'Even my secretary can do that,' says the man in scorn at his wife's clumsy behaviour. 'Well, why don't you damn well marry her!' retorts the wife in anger.

When Bartolomé studied 40 executives (average age 37) and their wives, he looked at the men's feelings of dependence and tenderness. Very few acknowledged these feelings in themselves, and even fewer revealed them at home. Such feelings were denied – they were considered 'bad', 'unmasculine', 'weak'.

WIFE: My husband is very self-reliant, secure, self-sufficient. He never expresses his needs.

HUSBAND: At work one gets accustomed not to express dependence and one does the same at home. As a matter of fact, at work I never think in terms of asking for help or expressing my needs but rather in terms of making good use of the available human resources. When I get home, I don't want to talk about any big problem; I just want to rest.

For example, in our own study, one divorced manager had a six-year old daughter from his first marriage. Now happily remarried, his greatest source of worry and stress was what he should do to bring up his daughter, who lived with his former wife. How often to visit her? How to relate to her? Whether to integrate her into his new family? How to confront his former wife, whom he saw as attempting to turn the child's affections against him? These were issues about which he never spoke to his present wife. Yet she was aware of them from his behaviour – from his moodiness and irritability after every visit to his daughter. She wanted to

* We do not wish to debate whether the executive should or should not act out this sterotypical role in his professional life. Some researchers have pointed out the dysfunctions of playing such executive roles (Argyris, 1962, 1971), while others have stressed the individual price that the person pays (Levinson, 1964). But on the other hand, proponents of assertiveness training and the self-help school of 'If-you-think-big, then-you-become-big' argue that by putting on an outward mask, you may make it reality.

help, feeling that for the better or worse the issue was part of her life. But he denied any need for help.

It is above all the labelling of one's feelings as good or bad that blocks acknowledgement or exploration of those feelings, as well as their expression. We only disclose the 'good' sides of ourselves; we deny the bad. Take the younger mother, for example; she feels angry and upset with her infant child who is always crying and fussing. A 'good' mother is never angry with her child; a 'good' mother is always calm and loving. So she learns to control herself, to hide or deny her feelings of anger. But in blunting the edge of her anger, she blunts the edge of her love – control blunts all feelings. In training herself not to be spontaneous, she distances herself psychologically from her child. The child feels this, and fusses more – it could tolerate moments of anger, but it needs moments of intense love.

The emotional reality is that parents have deeply positive feelings for their children at times, and deeply negative feelings at others. Both feelings express caring. A relationship can be defined in terms of the depth of the feelings, both positive and negative – not in terms of positive feelings alone. It is the same with married couples. They tend to hide, deny or avoid conflict, rather than recognizing that conflict is one side of an intimate relationship. The research of Bartolomé and others shows that male executives find it even more difficult to express deep positive feelings – praise is more difficult to express than criticism, tenderness than aggression.

Let us look at three aspects of expressiveness. The first is its relationship to marital happiness. The second is its role in shaping the marriage, in adjustment and renegotiation. The third is its relationship to self-development.

Marital happiness

Companionship and vitality in the husband-wife relationship are not essential ingredients in the stable marriage. But here we will discuss only the vital marriage. Studies consistently show that happily married couples differ from couples who turn to counselling in terms of their degree of expressiveness (Hicks and Platt, 1970). Happily married couples talk more to each other, disclose their feelings more often, convey the feeling that they understand what is being said to them, have a wider range of subjects which they talk about, show more sensitivity to each other's feelings, use a more personal form of language rather than talking in abstractions, and make more use of non-verbal communication such as facial expression and touching. Sum these up, and you have expressiveness.

The relationship between expressiveness and the quality of the marital relationship was obvious in findings from our study. How did we measure expressiveness? We measured it in the questionnaire by asking the men to say how they viewed themselves in their relationship with their wives (see the questionnaire in Appendix 1): as providing financial security, social status and affection; as helping her take care of the house and children; as assisting her in her self-development, and so forth. Two of these self-descriptions were closely related, and were taken as indicators of how far a man saw expressiveness as being an important element in his marriage – namely how far he was someone with whom she could talk about herself, her interests and problems, and how far he was someone who provided affection for her. Some husbands saw these aspects of the relationship as particularly important, while others saw them as far less so.*

Expressiveness, measured in this way, is very closely associated with marital happiness, so closely that one is almost tempted to describe the association as tautological. It is revealed Figure 11.1. The results there

Figure 11.1
Expressiveness and marital happiness

Expressiveness	Marital happiness		
	Very happy	Pretty happy	Sometimes happy, sometimes unhappy/ Unhappy
An important element of the marriage	63%	33%	4%	100% (N = 179)
An unimportant element of the marriage	17%	49%	34%	100% (N = 145)

can be put in another way. In eight out of ten marriages that are very happy, expressiveness is seen as a very important part of the relationship; and in eight out of ten of the less happy managers, expressiveness is seen as unimportant to the relationship.

The significance of believing expressiveness to be important in marriage becomes even clearer if one looks at its association with those aspects of marital behaviour shown in Figure 11.2. Marital behaviour of

* Further details on how expressiveness was measured are given in Appendix 3, Note 2. Other marital role concepts that result from the statistical analysis are also explained there.

these sorts is closely associated with the belief in the importance of expressiveness – so closely that we suggest it is simply a behavioural

Figure 11.2
Expressiveness and marital behaviour

`ommunicating openly how you feel towards each other*

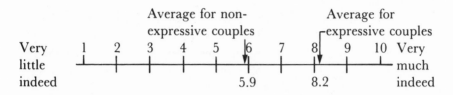

Being able to bring out and openly explore conflicts between you

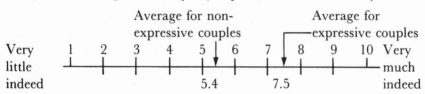

Adapting to the changing needs and expectations of your wife

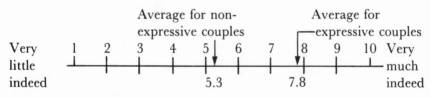

* Respondents were asked to describe their marital behaviour by checking an appropriate point on 10-point scales such as these. (See Appendix 1, Question 3g).

indicator of expressiveness.* Figure 11.2 shows how, on average, express-ive and non-expressive men evaluate their relationship.

The belief in the importance of expressiveness, the actual behaviour of expressing one's feelings, and the feeling of marital happiness, we call the 'expressiveness syndrome', though we could equally well call them the

* All correlations between expressiveness and marital behaviour were greater than 0.60. The only exception was the correlation with 'allowing each other the freedom each one desires'. This behavioural aspect of the marriage has also the lowest correlation with marital happiness.

happiness-in-marriage syndrome. If one does not see expressiveness as important in the relationship with one's partner, marital behaviour will be distant, and the relationship will be less intimate. As a result a marriage may never be vital (the case of the passive-congenial couple). On the other hand some marriages which start as vital and expressive may meet with difficult confrontations or encounter deep and complex problems. The couple may retreat from each other and as a consequence the marriage will then become devitalized.

It is worth noting how the norms regarding expressiveness seem to vary from culture to culture. The stereotype of Latin Europeans is that they are highly expressive, 'wearing their feeling on their shirt sleeves'. Northern Europeans in contrast are cool and controlled. The volatile Italian marriage is a favorite cinema theme, as also is the controlled, Bergmanesque Swedish version.

Our data partly support these stereotypes. Contrast the managers of four cultures (those where we had at least 60 respondents in our survey): the French, the British, the Scandinavians, and the Germans. The British men are most likely to see expressiveness as important in their relationships with their wives, despite the stereotype of the phlegmatic Briton. The French are also expressive, though less so. Far, far less importance is attached to expressiveness by the Germans, and at the bottom of the scale come the Scandinavians (mostly Swedes and Danes). The Scandinavians attached the least importance to expressiveness of any national group in our survey. Nordic people appear very reserved when it comes to intimate relationships.

One should not jump to the conclusion that Scandinavian marriages are necessarily unhappy! There were no differences in marital behaviour or in marital happiness between the different cultural groups. But if one takes each national group separately, one finds the expressiveness syndrome represented statistically even more strongly than for the survey overall. What this implies is that each culture has its own norms regarding expressiveness and self-disclosure. The Scandinavian norms are very different from the Latin ones, but no matter what the standard of desirable expressiveness is in any particular culture, those who within their culture standards are more expressive tend to have happier marriages than those who are less expressive.

Interestingly, one source of marital tension which couples interviewed often spoke of, was the clash between the open, spontaneous and emotional temperament of one partner and the introspective, closed and controlled nature of the other. The expressiveness of one partner is not enough to satisfy the depth of intimacy desired by the other. In most cases, it was the less expressive partner who felt guilty about his or her lack of openness.

Renegotiating the marriage

The expressiveness syndrome is the most apparent among people in the second life phase, between the ages of 35 and 42. It applies to younger couples, though to a less significant degree, but it applies least of all to people above the age of 45. The older men see their marriages as happy even though they do not attribute much importance to expressiveness. This indicates again that marriages are taking shape in the first phase of life, acquire their definite form in the critical second phase, and are relatively fixed by the third phase.

In the mid-thirties, marriage often begins to settle into a routine (statistically, the proverbial seven-year itch and the fourteen-itch are borne out by minor peaks in divorce statistics for the seventh and thirteenth years of marriage). Now, with the establishment of the career, the husband takes stock of his marital life. Often he feels there is a discrepancy between his ideal relationship and reality.

My marriage is happy – but am I really happy with it?

Our marital behaviour is close and intimate, we have a good relationship with each other – but how often? And do I really feel close and intimate with her?

Investing in my marriage is very important to me – but how much do I do it? When my actions lag so far behind my intentions, can it be that I don't really want to invest in it?

The wife, who is also taking stock, thinks these thoughts too. Each knows that the other is thinking them, but neither voices them aloud. Each treads warily around what they both suspect is the flawed but unchangeable reality of life together. The husband says to himself, 'Something may be missing but things aren't so bad after all. My job is going well. Why disturb this balance? Talking about my feelings can only risk everything I have. Anyway, I would not know how to do it.' The wife says to herself, 'Well, I am getting used to it. Maybe this is the way things have to be. He cannot change his behaviour. God knows, I've tried. That is simply the way he is. I should be thankful that at least he is happy with what he is doing. Everything turns to hell when he is unhappy, and if I start rocking the boat now, maybe things will just get worse.'

The eventual shape that the marriage will take depends on the answers given to these inner questions. There are only three final outcomes. The first is separation or divorce, catalysed by one person's conscious or unconscious decision to seek vitality and intimacy in a relationship elsewhere. This will be a rare outcome, since the instrumental bonds in the marriage are strong. The second is that each person individually comes to the conclusion that marriage is a take-it-or-leave-it proposition, and decides to take it. Each learns to accept distance and lack of vitality as the inevitable price to be paid for the stability and security provided by marriage.

Both of these outcomes result from individual decision-making about a joint issue. The third outcome is joint renegotiation of the relationships. Renegotiation begins with some expression of personal feelings, moves through an often stormy phase of venting and exploring those feelings, first to a phase where each person acquires a greater understanding of the other, and then into a phase of search for a new equilibrium in the marriage.

The expression of personal feelings often marks the start of a violent period in the relationship. One 40-year-old wife put her experience of this in this way:

> Every marriage goes through a bad patch. And we did a few years back. That really rose out of us having both been very independent. We were living in a small box with four small children who were terribly demanding on me, and his job was very demanding on him. I think we just simply stopped communicating for a number of years. Our exchanges were restricted to the banalities of life together. I forgot what he was like for a while, really. And then we started to have terrible rows.
>
> We gradually started communicating again. It was either that, or we'd have split up. No, I don't think we'd have ever split up, because of the children. But we didn't like each other very much for a year or so. We'd drink too much and yell at each other. I thought it was all me at the time, but I look back on it and part of it was him. He's a very self-controlled person. He tended to retreat into himself or leave the house if I got angry about something. And that would make me more angry. But gradually he started being more open, and we began talking again. Really talking. And now I can say that our marriage has never been so good as it is at the moment.

The frequent violence of this process is quite understandable. Life as a couple is full of frustrations and annoyances, occasionally important but more often petty. At the time, it does not seem worth confronting one's partner with one's irritation, risking a quarrel. So one hides these feelings, learning to live with them. But the feelings themselves do not go away. They remain there as a growing sense of resentment or hostility, even though one can no longer remember what particular incidents were originally responsible. This produces distance in the relationship. One day, some small 'typical' incident sparks off an explosion of these hidden resentments. Hostility expresses itself as a desire to hurt the other person – and naturally the quarrel escalates.

The important point is that negative feelings do not go away. If they are not expressed at once they still remain, dislocated from the incident that created them. The wife feels distant, angry and resentful towards her husband, but she cannot justify her feelings except in terms of the most recent, probably trivial incidents. To the outsider, these incidents may indeed seem petty; but they have to be seen in the context of many other such incidents, now forgotten. In order to be able to renegotiate a relationship, to talk about one's own views, to understand the views of the others and work towards some common resolution, feelings have first to be released. It is a cathartic process; negative feelings block any genuine discussion. This is the essence of the stormy rows that often precede and accompany the process of renegotiation.

Some couples learn to deal with their feelings through psychological or physical withdrawal. They learn to lead independent lives, even when together. They learn how not to get upset by not caring for the each other person and each other's behaviour. They learn to sublimate their feelings by releasing tension in other ways – by physically attacking something else in a socially legitimate way – the tennis partner, the golf ball, the vegetable patch. Or they may rechannel tension back into even more aggressive actions in professional life.

In one way or another, people adjust. They learn to deal with their feelings in direct or indirect ways.* Direct adaptation, in the form of a full renegotiation of the marriage and a rediscovery of its vitality, is probably rare. We noted in the last chapter how the majority of marriages, at least those of successful people, appeared to take an instrumental or utilitarian shape. There are in fact a number of psychological barriers to renegotiation.

The first barrier pertains in particular to the husband. He may feel dissatisfied with the investment behaviour, but nevertheless recognize his

---

* One cannot pronounce value judgements here, for many of these indirect ways of rechannelling emotional tension have socially desirable consequences. George Vaillant shows this in his *Adaptation to Life* study, where 120 university graduates were followed through their lives between the ages of 23 and 50. He shows how the men who had successfully adapted to life had learnt to rechannel or sublimate their aggressions, if they had been blocked in resolving emotional issues. The men who had adapted less well to life denied their feelings, or expressed them in fantasies.

Vaillant would view the rechannelling of marital tension into sport or work as an active or healthy form of adaptation. An unhealthy form of adaptation would be saying with unrockable conviction that one has a superbly happy marriage, while in reality spending most of one's private life watching soap operas on the television and reading crime-thrillers about husbands who murder their wives! People adapt in all cases – whether that adaptation is healthy or not depends on whether it is growth inducing or growth inhibiting.

151

unwillingness to change it. The partially successful husband is attracted to his work, despite the unhappiness that it creates in his private life. Work gives him a lot of satisfaction and he hopes to be even more successful. He would *like* to rebalance his life, but acknowledges that he would be unwilling to pay what he sees as the price. He deals with his concerns in the same logical way as he confronts professional problems. 'Why bother to express my concerns and doubts about our marriage?' he says. 'I'm basically unwilling to do anything about it, so I should shut up and keep going.'

This barrier is partly real, partly illusory. It is real in the sense that a full renegotiation of the relationship may require re-allocating time, and this may involve real sacrifice. But it is illusory in that the most important aspect of the relationship is its *quality*, not its quantity. Restablishing the capacity to talk through significant and intimate issues involves changing the quality of the relationship, not just its quantity. One issue in renegotiation is discovering how to use one's available time in constructive ways, not only making more time available.

The wife is likely to suppress her doubts because of the second barrier. This is the assumption that 'I can't change his behaviour in any case – that's simply the way he is.' This assumption may be valid in the early stage of the career. But the assumption needs retesting now – the husband may be willing to question his behaviour, may indeed *be* questioning his behaviour for the first time. The past is an imperfect guide to the present. One thing is certain, and that is that this assumption is self-fulfilling. If a wife believes that her husband cannot change his behaviour, she will never initiate any discussion which might lead to that change. If she believes that he can – well, he may or he may not.

The item on our questionnaire most strongly associated with a husband's feeling about his investment behaviour is his perception of his wife's feelings about that behaviour; and this is particularly true at this second phase of adulthood. Where the wife is either satisfied or does not clearly express her dissatisfaction, the husband is likely to be content with his lifestyle. Where the wife expresses her discontent, he is likely to question it.* This self-questioning is a minimum condition for any form of renegotiation; translating that questioning into any change is the substance of that negotiation.

The third barrier to marital renegotiation is that of risk. Each person has some ideal for a lifestyle. For the husband it may centre on the image of an involving and satisfying professional life together with a vital and engaging private life. For the wife, it may focus on a family that is intimately together and on the discovery of her own independent identity.

---

* Except in the case of the younger manager, see Chapter 8.

What initiates renegotiation is the recognition that reality is far from this ideal. The relationship is distant and devitalized. Family life is passive. The career is not as satisfying as one would like it to be. The wife has no real sense of who she is. Now the children are growing she worries that she is becoming a less interesting person than her husband.

The risks of confronting these realities are real. In voicing such feelings directly or indirectly, one risks confronting oneself as well as another with an emotional reality that is difficult to bear. This may precipitate a crisis in the relationship. And who can say what will be the outcome of that crisis?

The probable pain of confrontation, the misery of crisis, the risk of uncertain outcomes – the more the couple has grown apart, the greater these are. It is not surprising that people often prefer the distancing path of self-control that is the antithesis of intimacy. 'Let me be content with what at least I have, what *is*, rather than what could be.' 'Part of my life is not how I would like it to be; but isn't life all about choices? Let me learn to be happy with what I have.'

Marriage is two people who are committed to live together. They can live together jointly, or live together in parallel.

Self-development

If expressiveness is functional in dealing with marital and family development, it also performs other functions. Most importantly it favours individual health and development through emotional disclosure. Expressiveness leads to emotional self-development and may enhance professional development (Bartolomé, 1972).

Feelings influence all our moods, our behaviour and our decisions. Much of this happens unconsciously, and this is particularly true of our 'bad' feelings. When bad feelings are openly expressed, put into words and acknowledged, they have a curious tendency to disappear. Expressiveness is a cathartic process. Some husbands unwind at the end of the day by talking for half-an-hour about the trials and tribulations, frustrations and irritations of the day at the office. He talks of these while his wife is busy preparing dinner – only half aware of what he is saying. This does not matter, for one needs someone to talk at, not talk to. Soon, he feels relaxed and unwound. Acknowledging his own feelings has made them go away.

For some couples, this cathartic unwinding becomes a healthy daily ritual – healthy that is for the husband but often trying for the wife. She too has her frustrations and irritations created by her working day. She

153

too needs to unwind in the same way. Catharsis has only a temporary day-to-day effect. Expressiveness can lead further if the listener reacts with sensitivity to what one is saying. That other person can act as a mirror in which one can see, explore and amplify one's feelings.

'I feel moody and frustrated tonight,' says the husband. 'That's the way you have felt for the last six months,' says his wife, not in a tone of recrimination but as a sympathetic statement of fact. 'Yes, I guess so,' he says, recognizing in himself the way in which his wife amplifies his feelings. 'It must be something to do with this job; it's getting me down.' She expresses something that he recognizes but has not dared to express himself. With her assistance, he begins to explore the possibility that this is indeed not his sort of job, and that it may be in the best interests of all to ask for a reassignment.

The wife plays the role of a therapist, and since all of us face emotional dilemmas as part of our adult development, this is a crucial marital role. Some wives (and husbands for that matter) play this role with skill and sensitivity. At a minimum. it requires genuine caring for the other person's welfare (what Carl Rogers calls 'unconditional positive regard'). Often this caring for the other is absent at all but a superficial level (the younger manager is sensitive only to his career concerns, not to his wife's concerns). Often the person struggles alone with his or her emotional dilemmas, perhaps turning to professional therapy or psychoanalysis if the dilemma turns to crisis.

In the expressive dialogue with another person, an individual is often forced to confront his or her emotional nature, painfully growing in the process. This is the constructive side of marital conflict, where feelings may be expressed more openly – if with violence at times. For example, people have idealized images of themselves; they protect themselves with 'little fictions'. Both partners play this game. The husband is depressed because he cannot understand why he has been turned down for a promotion for the third time. 'It's so unfair,' says his wife supportively. 'You work so hard at your job. You are so talented and get on so well with people.'

His continued irritability produces a quarrel. And in the quarrel, this little fiction is destroyed. The wife confronts her husband with the reality everyone recognizes but he. He is so talented and gets on so well with people because he always agrees with everything that everyone says. He always says 'yes' to his wife but never follows through. He is regarded as a pleasant conformist. For a split second, he sees himself and his promotional failures mirrored in her words. This sight of himself is so frightening that he defends himself in an explosion of anger and denial. Precisely for this reason, no-one but his wife has ever dared confront him with this image. Yet if he works through that self-insight, it is likely to be valuable. Left alone, he would never have dared. He would rather have spent his life bitterly complaining about the injustices of corporate life.

The deep, intimate relationship with a person who cares is a precious resource in times of personal stress and emotional crisis. This is an almost universal finding of research (Vaillant, 1977; Lowenthal *et al.* 1975). The intimate relationship serves both as a buffer against that stress and as a means to resolve the crisis. First, intimacy allows one to cope with stress through cathartic expression. Second, it may allow one to recognize the nature of a dilemma. Third, intimacy brings with it the emotional support for difficult decisions to break out of the crisis.

There is a limit to the amount of stress than any person can live with (Holmes and Rahe, 1967). But research shows that some people break down at a stress level that others can readily tolerate. People who break down easily are found to have a low capacity for interpersonal relationships. People who are stimulated by stress or who have very high breakdown thresholds tend to have a number of close interpersonal relationships, a high capacity for intimacy, and deep exchange of feeling within their families (Lowenthal *et al.*, 1975).

Indeed Vaillant (1977) believes that this is why he finds company presidents and very successful people to have enduring marriages and close personal friendships. Without these relationships, the eustress of such responsibility quickly becomes distress. Indeed Schein (1978) agrees that the distinguishing characteristic of a top level executive is not his skill or ability but his emotional competence: 'the capacity to be stimulated by emotional and interpersonal crises rather than exhausted or debilitated by them'. Describing men who appeared to be *en route* to these positions, he wrote that they were ...

> ... as or more emotional than any other group, but [they] did not feel crippled or bothered by certain of their emotions; rather there seemed to be an ability to express these emotions and discharge tensions so that they would not simmer under the surface. For example, a person who had the difficult job of firing someone would recognize the difficulty, face up to it, do it as humanely and sensibly as possible, feel badly about it, talk it out with a friend or spouse, and then feel some relief at having done the job ...
>
> The emotionally competent manager would be less likely to develop psychosomatic or other symptoms of health and emotional problems. The emotionally less competent manager might look calm on the surface, but might well be developing ulcers or hypertension, which would ultimately interfere with work performance. In listening to these managerially anchored [people], I got the impression that the

155

ones who came across as emotionally competent were more 'realistic' about life and more willing to confront whatever was happening, including their own tensions. For example, several of the successful managers reported that they had at one or another time faced personal and family crises, had gone to psychiatrists, and had worked out their problems. What distinguished them was not the absence of such crises, but rather their willingness to face them and do something about them. (Schein, 1978, p. 137)

In contrast, the less successful people whose lives were studied by Vaillant, as well as those who at the age of 50 appeared least adapted to life, were those who had few or no friendships, who had never married or who lived in unstable marriages. They lacked both the expressiveness and the interpersonal, private and personal life. Usually they had adapted to life by avoiding emotional stress, and thus by avoiding responsibility and challenge. Lacking the resources to cope with the stress of life, they led stable but emotionally impoverished lives.

Conclusion

The emotional demands of a successful career do not diminish with the launching of the career. Hand in hand with professional success goes increasing responsibility. This responsibility can be a source of emotional stimulation for some but a source of emotional distress for others. The difference lies in emotional maturity, the capacity to cope with one's feelings and lead an emotionally rich life. The key to emotional maturity is expressiveness, and here the intimate relationship with one's wife is particularly precious.

The storm and pain of the renegotiation of the marriage has three possible consequences. It may lead to a more vital and intimate marriage. It will probably develop one's capacity to handle one's own emotions. And it will certainly reinforce one's ability to cope with the stresses of life that lie ahead.

We begin to see how professional life and private life are intertwined, how one reinforces the other or how one handicaps the other. We begin to see how the alternative paths in the third life phase are taking shape. In the full or generative lifestyle, the successful career and the successful marriage go hand in hand. In the maintenance lifestyle, it has proved impossible to cope with either the stresses of the career or the distance in the marriage; all that is possible is to maintain a fragmented way of life.

The adage says that 'behind every great man stands a great woman'.

We would rather express this by saying that 'behind every great man stands a great relationship'. For the great woman idea often signifies a supportive wife who has dedicated herself to his realization. This is not necessarily the case. What the marriage must provide is the expressive and supportive relationship. This does not mean sacrificing everything to the executive's development. The wife too is coping with her own developmental needs, and the expressive marriage is unlikely to develop unless she resolves them. This leads us to our next chapter: the woman as a martyr or as a chooser.

Chapter 12

Martyrs and choosers

Despite changing values in society, most women who choose to marry and have children are destined to enter adulthood as housewives. In the twenties and early thirties, this housewife role may be combined with outside work, but at the price of some tension. Some women adjust easily to the role of housewife and mother, and for them these are years of fulfilment. Others adjust with difficulty.

By their mid to late thirties, things may look different. The household tasks have long since become humbrum. The children are growing up and becoming more independent. Beforehand, the presence of the young children was a major obstacle to an independent lifestyle. Now the children *can* remain a centre of life interest for years ahead, but there is no longer the same imperative. The 'contented but unfulfilled' lifestyle of before becomes less contented and less fulfilled. It becomes especially frustrating if the husband is a career prisoner or struggler, or if the marriage is acquiring an instrumental shape.

These are years of professional realization for many husbands, but where the questions of personal identity resurges for many wives. Men have spent the first decade-and-a-half of adulthood wrestling with the issue. Many women have put it aside, adjusting to the housewife role with a feeling that the question 'What do I want to do with my life?' must wait. For some women, this question waits and waits . . . until it is too late. At the point when it is too late to launch any new lifestyle, a lifestyle choice has been made without ever being chosen. We call these women *martyrs*, perhaps a loaded word but one that seems justified.

A martyr is a person who sacrifices himself or herself on the altar of some cause, a very selfless person. We found that some women in their middle years have difficulty in describing themselves as people, except in stereotypical terms as a 'good mother' and a 'helpful wife'. Many wives around the age of 38 told us 'I try not to think of myself too often.' It is a very significant statement: they deliberately suppress all thoughts of themselves.

The younger housewife puts off until tomorrow her thoughts about herself. Some housewives around the age of 40 suppress those thoughts:

A YOUNGER HOUSEWIFE: I hope that the family will become more important to him, especially as the children grow older. But I'm concerned about what happens when the kids go off and get married. The oldest is still only three. One feels that the best part of life will soon be over. . . . Would I ever like to work? Yes and no. I'd like to, but it's difficult because of the children and the family. I don't feel very fulfilled as a housewife, but I want to be there when the children need me. I suppose I'd like to take a university course later on so as to go out and work. But not now. Life is too comfortable right now – I don't have to make the effort.

A HOUSEWIFE IN HER EARLY FORTIES: Have I ever thought of working? The ideal would be to have a part-time job as well as the home. That would be the best of both worlds. [pause] I don't know. I'm really not sure. I don't spend much time thinking about myself, about what is going on. I'd like to become closer to him and offer him a bit more. But this is more a negative way of putting it rather than a positive way. I mean, it is a reason for not thinking about it. . . . I'm very easy-going as a person. Most things just go over my head. I've got so many things to do that I leave worrying about me up to my husband. [laughs].

Worries go over my head. I never think of myself. Psychoanalysts call this psychological defense. Thinking about oneself is painful and disturbing, so one fills time with other things to do. It is not time that is lacking. It is something else that leads to this selflessness: the difficulty of choice.

Societal opinion and research has a lot to say about these choices. Before contrasting martyrs with choosers, let's look at what is said about two different life paths for women – the path of the housewife and the path of the working woman.

Who is the liberated woman?

Jessie Bernard argues in *The Future of Marriage* that marriage is a very uneven contract. 'His marriage' provides him with a wide range of opportunities for satisfaction and growth, while 'her marriage' provides her with a limited range. There is nothing wrong with marriage itself, says Bernard; what is wrong is the frequent relegation of the women to an impoverished housewife role. Bernard marshals an impressive array of statistics to show how this role contributes to poor mental and emotional health among married women.

A US national survey assessed psychological well-being using various indicators of mental health – whether or not people had had a nervous breakdown, felt a sense of inertia, had trembling or perspiring hands, suffered from insomnia or headaches, and so forth. Consider men first. Both married men and never-married men are slightly better off than the average for either sex. Bachelors appear marginally better off, though other studies show that bachelors are more prone to mental problems such as depression.

In terms of psychological well-being, marriage favours the men rather than the women, since married women are above the average for mental distress. Of all groups, the person least likely to experience psychological distress is the never-married woman. Other statistics show that this is particularly true for women after the age of 40, rather than for younger women.

That seems to present a pessimistic view of marriage. Men should marry if they wish to; women risk their well-being. But as Bernard emphasizes, this would be a false conclusion. It is not being married that endangers mental health and happiness – it is the fact that marriage often relegates the woman to a life role that has little meaning: that of the housewife. Working women (60 per cent of whom are married) score very well on psychological health. On the other hand, housewives (all of whom can be presumed to be married) are the single group that is most prone to mental distress. As Bernard says, these statistics constitute one of the most cogent critiques of marriage as it is traditionally structured (Bernard, 1973).

Men sometimes simulate envy for the housewife's role. They talk of the freedom and the leisure, but they talk as people who have challenging jobs and little leisure time. Stop to appraise it as a job. Much of the work is menial labour. Being a housewife is a low-status occupation. There is no relationship between performance and financial reward. There is no opportunity for promotion.

The wives in our interview survey evaluated the satisfaction that they obtained from five aspects of the housewife's role: running the household, bringing up their children, sharing time and activities with their husbands, social activities, and leisure. Their responses showed how some people find fulfilment in this lifestyle while many do not; they also showed the dependence of the role on the presence of an often absent partner.

They generally saw household work as the most frustrating aspect. Reactions varied considerably to the satisfaction from bringing up the children. The largest group saw it as the most interesting part of their lives. Their attitudes towards time with their husbands tended to be ambivalent – they almost unanimously saw it as the most satisfying part of a wife's role *when it occurred*, but they expressed dissatisfaction that it occurred so rarely. As for leisure and social activities, attitudes were polarized on them. Some saw one or the other as very satisfying; others complained of having too much leisure or social time to fill in meaningless ways because their husbands were absent.

These statistics seem to support the feminist view. The liberated woman is a working woman. The housewife role is a path to mental and emotional disturbance. The trouble with statistics is that they lie when averages are interpreted as truths. The statements may be true as descriptions of the 'average woman', but they are not true of *every* woman. What is striking in our own survey is that although household work is generally seen as frustrating, a few women find it fulfilling. Although most women found it satisfying to bring up their children, a few found this to be a very unsatisfying task. Are you the 'average woman'? The important personal issue is your own feelings about who you are as a person.

The issue is not whether the working wife is better off than the housewife. The issue is one of making a *personal choice*. The chooser weighs the trade-offs between these and other life options, and she commits herself one way or the other. Obviously, this is not a simple process. It is as complex as launching a career. The choice process may take a decade to work through, new life ventures will lead to a process of exploration that will continue long into the future. On the other hand, the martyr – in executive marriages often a housewife who feels unfulfilled as a housewife – feels that she has no choice. She never explores other options. She commits herself behaviourally, but not psychologically.

The importance of choice in the lives of women was show in a now classic study by Bradburn and Orden (1969). They investigated the marital happiness of 965 wives in four communities in the state of Illinois. There were three types of wives: (a) wives who were working, but out of necessity (usually for financial reasons); (b) wives who were working by choice; and (c) housewives.

When there were young children of preschool age in the family, the woman's decision to work was a strain on the marriage. This was their first finding, and we argued this in Chapter 8 when talking of how the younger couple maintains private life. But at all other later stages in the life cycle, there is little difference in marital happiness between couples where the wife works and couples where she stays at home.* Once children are

* This applied to marital happiness as assessed by the 781 husbands in the survey, as well by the 957 wives.

older, whether the wife works or does not work makes little difference to the marriage. What *does* make a clear difference is if she works out of economic necessity rather than choice, regardless of the type of job she has. In this case all aspects of marital life suffer – people are less happy with their marriages, both husband and wife experience more tension in the relationship, and there is less mutual companionship. This is true for people of all educational levels, regardless of whether they have full-time or part-time jobs. The conclusion of Orden and Bradburn was clear. *A woman's freedom to choose among alternative life styles* is an important predictor of happiness in marriage – happiness for the wife *and* for the husband.

Men versus women. Housewives versus working wives. Let us now push the debate one notch further. Martyrs versus choosers. The liberated woman is a chooser. She may be a housewife, she may be a working wife, she may be some other type of person. One way or the other, she is more of a *person* than is the martyr.

The martyr

Let us look at the world of the martyr, as she perceives it. It is a busy world, with little time to think of oneself. It is a word of contradictory perceptions of self and others. It is a world where choices are seen as having happened without there having been any choosing. There is half-hidden resentment of that lifestyle.

The world of *Mrs Solomon* will serve as an example. She is 44 years old, married for 20 years. Her husband is a successful production director in an international company. They have three children, two in their mid-teens and one latecomer aged seven. Mrs Solomon was trained as a pharmacist, but has not worked since her first pregnancy. During the ten years before the birth of her third child, she often thought of going back to work, though not as a pharmacist. She was not sure about the type of job, though it would be something to do with other people. In any case, the birth of the latecomer simplified that choice.

> Seven years ago, before the last one was born, it would have been different. And I suppose in some ways I'd still like to. In any case, it is too late now. I'll be sixty when he is grown up. And then it would be too late to start work.

This latecomer provides her with the rationale for continuing her life style – at least until she is 60. A quick calculation shows that this child will not be considered 'grown up', able to do without her help, until the age of 23.

Another rationale for her lifestyle is her husband, though here some resentment shows. She is satisfied with his investment behaviour, seeing the marriage as more happy than in fact he does.

In one way or another it is my choice that we live for him. [note the impersonal 'we']. When he is at home, he is relaxed and a good family man. That is to say, *when* he is at home!

She is critical, yet does not admit to being critical. It shows in side remarks and the way in which she expresses herself. She described their marriage as very happy, then paused, and said after a moment of deep thought:

When people live together for 20 years, one gets moulded together. You learn to like some things which you may not have liked at first. You learn to like doing things which you didn't like doing, but did because the other wants you to.

Can one learn to deny one's own feelings, to like what you do not like doing? Is it liking – or tolerating? One suspects the latter, and Mrs Solomon's description in the questionnaire of their marital behaviour is one indication. Whereas her husband checked most items at a moderate level (communication, sensitivity, expressing affection, and so forth), Mrs Solomon gave a maximum ten points to every one of ten aspects of marital behaviour. With one exception. Next door to the aspect of 'allowing each other the freedom each one desires', she placed the minimum score of one point.

Her way of describing her husband was flattering; her way of describing herself was self-deprecating.

We are two very different people. He's ambitious and always doing things, I'm a typical cabbage [laughs]. I'm just a housewife. I look after the children and enjoy being a mother to a family. And I sometimes do work with handicapped children, and other volunteer activities. As a wife, I suppose I am just average, though he would say I'm good. I feel I spend too much time in the house.

She talks about her worries and preoccupations. All of these concern other people, and most of them concern problems of health. The problems seem real, but to the outsider it is as if she fears that their ill health may undermine the meaning in her world. The major stress is her teenage daughter's health; also the latecomer son (who is to be the focus of her life until 60) apparently is not growing up in the successful and adapted way of the two older children. She worries about a heart ailment of her mother, and she worries about her husband's health, even though he has no current problems. 'He works too hard,' she says. 'How long can he keep up the pressure?' Curious, the interviewer asked if she ever worried about her own self?

> I leave that to my husband to worry about [laughs]. I worry too much about the children, and I haven't got time to worry about myself.

The life of the martyr should not be seen as intolerable. She adjusts to it, as has Mrs Solomon. But it is a bland lifestyle, low on stress but low on satisfaction. The stresses are there, half hidden as doubts and resentment. One prefers not to think of these things – not to think of oneself.

Why does a woman find it difficult to choose to remould her lifestyle? Why does she settle for continuing the present into the future rather than exploring new life options? There are *four impediments to choice*. The first, lack of husband support, is the most general. The other three are impediments to one particular choice, namely to launch a career or to go out to work now that the mother career is ending: the educational barrier; the risk of career exploration; and limited opportunities.

The first impediment – lack of husband support

The stereotype would have it that executives are the stalwart opponents of the working wife concept, the line of last defence in a battle that they have already lost. Popular essays delight in citing extreme quotations as the views of 'the typical executive'. We have no doubt that some managers have extreme views, but rigid opposition is in fact far from typical.

In our questionnaire, we asked the 532 managers the extreme question: not simply whether they favoured the idea of working women, but whether they favoured married women engaging in a career with a long-term occupational commitment. Twice as many husbands were in favour of career wives as were against – one-third as opposed to 15 per cent. The majority (52 per cent) expressed mixed or neutral feelings.*

* In another question, husbands whose wives had worked in the past or were now working were asked to assess the influence that her working had on the quality of marital and family life. Their responses were as follows:

A clearly negative influence			A balance of positive and negative		A clearly positive influence	
1%	2%	6%	21%	26%	32%	12%
1	2	3	4	5	6	7

The interviews showed that few managers were set against their wives working. They constrain the development of their wives in a more subtle way. It is through an absence of active support for their self-development. Wives are left to struggle with the reorientation of their lives on their own. Their husbands have little time to encourage them, and may not be sensitive to the depth of their self-doubts.

At times of self-doubt, the husband's behaviour aggravates his wife's dilemma in subtle ways. On the surface, he may be open to her return to the labour market. But his behaviour contradicts these verbal cues, showing his attachment to a full-time housewife role for her. He tells her that she should take courses and look for a job, but in the next breath he praises her cooking and help with the children. He reassures her that the house will take care of itself, and then reproaches her for its untidiness. Quite unconsciously and unintentionally, his demands may lead her to doubt that she has any skills worthy of use in the competitive world outside:

> He's so terribly demanding, he has such terribly high standards. He expects such incredible efficiency from me. I can *never* make him understand that you can't run the house like you run the office! There are a number of things that have to be done. So he leaves little messages for me – you know, 'Ring up the repairman,' 'Fix the roof', 'Do this', 'Do that.' He comes home and expects it all to have been done. And if it hasn't. ... I mean, I might have rung someone up to do something about it, but he might not have turned up. And if he hasn't, well this all reflects on me. I get it!! Somehow, *I* have failed!! And this is a bone of contention, continually. He makes me feel I don't do my job properly. It irritates me. He expects from me as he expects from his *staff*! So of course I rebel. It makes me worse. I'll almost pointedly not do something! [laughs] Childish, isn't it?

A wife's self-development ranks low in the husband's priorities, as the questionnaire showed, not to speak of his actual behaviour. Among the eight marital roles, that of being 'an active support in her self-development, assisting her to develop her capacities in the work or interests she herself chooses' ranks an average second last in importance, next to providing her with an interesting leisure or social life. The husband assesses his performance on this role as the least adequate aspect of his behaviour in the relationship. Moreover, although he has moderately high

---

The majority see working as having both positive and negative influences, though clearly tending in the positive direction.

expectations that his wife would be responsible for her own self-development (as judged by how he viewed her role) he assesses this as one of the poorer areas of her own performance. He may not act as an active block to her self-realization, but as the central figure in her life he does little to support her, instead churning up the waters in which she is trying to swim.

The second impediment – the educational barrier

Few of the managerial wives who dream of going out to work think in terms of factory, shop or other manual work. In any case, their husbands would veto such an idea. The jobs to which they aspire are interesting, professional, and social in nature. Some wives see these opportunties as closed for lack of educational qualifications.

At an earlier age, the wife had typically intended one day to go back to university. But the university system is built for the young. Now in her mid- to late-thirties, the image of the middle-aged, affluent housewife socializing with younger students of a very different generation is intimidating. 'They are so terribly immature,' she says. 'I have nothing whatsoever in common with them.' If she willingly abandoned her studies in order to get married at the age of 23, she now forgets her earlier willingness and reproaches her husband for having led her into a trap. Her lack of the education necessary to open the doors of escape feeds her feelings of martyred resentment.

The importance of education should not be underemphasized. Whether a degree in reality opens professional doors varies from country to country (it is important in the more ascriptive Latin countries – France for example). The degree certainly eases the transition into the professional world. A universal finding is that the most significant difference between housewives and working wives is that the working wives are better educated, and this was also the most significant difference in our own survey.

The third impediment – exploration and risk in launching the career

The woman wants her first post-child sortie into the world of work to be right first time. She wants the launching of her career to follow a rapid trajectory towards fulfilment. On the one hand, she is unsure of what she can do well and likes doing; this is particularly true if she has led a sheltered life and has had no opportunity to test herself by working before or by exploring herself in a prior education. On the other hand, she is unsure what opportunities there are available to her. The husband, forgetting the painful decade of exploration and risk in launching his own career, becomes angry at her self-doubts. 'Heavens above, stop moaning,' he says. 'If you want to work, go out and work.' But she is unsure where she wants to plunge.

The elements of launching a career, which we outlined in Chapter 7, are as applicable to the return-to-work wife as they are to the young manager. Her launch will be a long exporatory process, and the years ahead will often be tense and painful. The obstacle for her is most often that of risk – the paralysis of doubt that prevents the first plunge. That plunge may be inelegant, but there can be no forward movement if it is not taken.

For the wife as well as the husband, work involves discovering a sense of fit. We have cited many husbands on this path, so why not now cite one working housewife who is well down this road.

I suppose as a general principle, I believe that everyone should work. I have always hated to see wasted potential, especially in women. In a curious way, I think nobody has the right not to work.

But having said that, my personal answer to why I work is somewhat different. I suppose I work because otherwise I'd be bored. I'm a family mum, but I'm not the through-and-through domestic sort of woman. I enjoy work. I even enjoy *hating* work, if you know what I mean. There are many times when I hate work, but I'd still rather be hating it than not doing it. And I suppose last of all, I know that I'm quite good at what I do, and so I've not been discouraged by it. I got into the right line of work for me. I suppose that if I'd not been so good at it, I might have abandoned all those ground premises.

The fourth impediment – limited opportunities

The wrath of feminists in the last decade has been directed to the unequal structure of professional opportunity, a structure seen as favouring men and discriminating against women. This may be true, and while legislation is changing it slowly, the limited focus of attack masks the other impediments. Assessing that bastion of male domination, Henning and Jardim (1976) show in *The Managerial Woman* how some of the obstacles ascribed to the closed doors of opportunity in fact reflect the problems of launching a career, in particular that of transition into management. The woman supervisor tends to view her role in technical terms, often showing a misunderstanding of the different and less structured world of management. She is viewed as very efficient but at her Peter Principle level of competence; in fury, she blames this chauvinist world. Nevertheless, the study of Henning and Jardim shows how the few women who rise to executive heights are those who have never broken their careers. They made a choice, and a clear choice, very early in life: come-what-may, the career would take priority over all other interests.

The martyr is someone who is impeded from making her own choice. She settles uneasily for second best. The price of martyrdom, for the time being, should not be seen as a high one. It is one that grows with the years as her lifestyle becomes increasingly shallow and as alternative options close their doors. In fact, the lifestyle of the chooser who launches into a new life style will in all likelihood be more tense and stressful in these midlife years. What are the dimensions of her choice?

The chooser

The characteristic of the chooser is not that she has a professional career. It is that she thinks of herself; she takes her self-development in her hands; she is responsible for herself rather than entrusting that responsibility to another person. In the typical case, after years of dependence (him-centeredness), she creates her own independence. Whether the marriage is vital or instrumental, this has favourable outcomes for the couple.

One woman put it in the following way:

> To be married to a business executive like him, you have to take your own life in charge sooner or later. You have to make a life of your own, and thus become a more interesting person. You have to discuss things and give each other freedom. You have to pursue your own interests without feeling guilty at not complying with your husband's wishes. . . . I have friends at work and I have freedom. It's an escape from home and it allows me to develop my own interests. And so it has had quite a positive effect on the marriage. It has made me more outward looking, more interesting as a person. And I understand his career and work pressures better.

Studies show that the quality of life of the career woman begins to bloom for the first time now in her late thirties, especially if she also has had children. The earlier years of the dual career couple were sorely marked by tension and stress, now relieved by the fact that the children are growing up. The early investment is beginning to bear fruit, but the price that has been paid is heavy. For the former housewife, those earlier years were more contented, if not fulfilling. If she now chooses to go back to work, this choice will not yield instant gratification. It is the beginning of the stressful road toward finding a professional avenue.

The Orden and Bradburn (1969) study showed that women who choose to work have more happy marriages than those who work by necessity. A study by Hall and Gordon (1973) similarly verified that housewives who prefer to be housewives are more satisfied than those who do not. Their study of 378 women also showed, as one would expect, that the work-oriented married woman has more difficulty in implementing her choice than does the housewife. It is a path of high risk but high return. Working women experienced a higher degree of satisfaction with their lifestyles than the housewives, but also a higher degree of inner conflict.

We found that the woman who now launches a career tends to have a positive but conflicted view of herself. She lives with this conflict, since she has made a choice; if she were not working, the conflict would be less, but her image of herself would be more negative. One woman, quoted above, expressed this by talking about sometimes hating her work, but preferring to hate it rather than not work at all. Another woman, relaunching her career as a researcher, spoke of her ambivalent feelings, though her choice had been irrevocably made.

We're probably at the time now when the family unit is at its strongest. I worry about the future, because I think I'm going to need them more than they need me. Because I've consciously given up a lot of my career time for them. Perhaps I expect more of them than I should? I don't know whether that makes sense or not. I sort of *expect* them to be fulfilling! [laughs] I say to them, 'You know, you've *got* to be fulfilling!' I'm very ambivalent about it really. In one way I resent the time they take up, and in another way John [the eldest child] is growing away from me. That's the way is should be, but I think it's a bit sad.

As evaluated by the questionnaire, this woman experienced a very high degree of emotional stress. This is not exceptional. She had made a choice and she was working through the consequences of that choice.

As with men, the expressiveness of the marriage may constitute a significant buffer to this stress. If the relationship is expressive, we would expect stress to be visible but not severe. Where the relationship is less expressive, the woman is left to work through the consequences of her choice in isolation, and this may cause emotional and even physical problems (Holahan and Gilbert, 1979).

Faced with a seemingly black-and-white choice between work and the home, the appeal of the *part-time job* is evident. Is this indeed the best of all worlds? Research suggests that it is not. The appeal of the part-time job was demonstrated in 'Career choices of married women' by Hall and Gordon, referred to above. Nearly half of the full-time housewives and full-time workers would prefer a different role to the one they have – they are uneasy about their present choice. Only 19 per cent of the part-time woman would prefer to change. They are indeed the most committed to their way of life. However, the part-time working women were significantly less satisfied with their work than the full-time working women. And of all groups, they reported the most home conflict. Whereas full-time workers complained of problems of time, the part-time women complained of pressures from a maximum number of roles.

Overall, the balance sheet of the part-time working woman seems unfavourable. She tries to do everything, with the result that she fails to find great fulfilment in anything. She lives with perpetual conflict in her priorities. For Hall and Gordon, the appealing part-time role appears not as the best of all worlds but as a poor compromise. 'For some women it represents an incomplete resolution of the internal conflict about a career, a compromise between working full-time and not being employed at all.' (Hall and Gordon, 1973, p. 47). The part-time job may represent a transitional step in the process of identity exploration.

Both part-time and full-time working women are trying to do everything at the same time: manage a professional life and a private life. Yet the full-time working women appear better off. This can be explained by the fact that they have made a clear choice, just as some housewives make the opposite clear choice. The decision is certainly stressful, but ultimately it is more functional.

Professional work versus being a housewife – the balance sheet

Some housewives never feel any desire to go out to work, and so the period of choice is easy for them. Put in terms of simplified polarities (Handy, 1978): some women are by nature oriented towards *caring*. Their needs for affiliation and nurturance are stronger. Throughout their lives, they seek a family role or a similar role in a teaching or service activity. Others find family life to be a trap. They have stronger needs for achievement and power; these *achievers* (or 'thrusters' as Handy calls them) always seek a career. Some women are *involved*, having needs for both affiliation and achievement. So saying, let us look at whether life appears to favour the caring housewife or the achieving career woman. The answer from research seems clear. It favours both, but at different times of life.

In *early adulthood*, the balance sheet of potential satisfactions and potential stresses favours the housewife by a clear margin over the career

woman, *unless* (and there is always an unless) the career woman chooses
not to have children or better still not to marry (again, we stress the aspect
of choice). This does not mean that a life as career mother is unviable at
this time. It simply means that the stresses outweigh the satisfactions. Nor
does it mean that there are no exceptions to this general rule. It may well
be that these exceptions are more frequent where neither person is a
business manager. Certainly our young managers are very unaccommodating. Launching one career as well as holding a marriage together is a
difficult enough task. Launching two careers may be even more difficult,
but possible. Launching two careers and bringing up children at the same
time pushes these difficulties to the limit.

In *late adulthood*, the balance sheet is reversed. It favours the career
woman, and particularly the career woman with a family and children.
This is apparent not only in the statistics on the mental health of
housewives and other results that we have mentioned, but in an assessment of the lives of 95 Californian women now in their late sixties and
seventies, written up in *From Thirty to Seventy* (Maas and Kuypers, 1974).*
Some of these women at age 70 appeared to be adjusted to life, scoring
high on indices of mental and physical health, while others seemed less
adjusted. What was striking to Maas and Kuypers was that the adjusted
women had a clear single focus to their lives – either their husbands, their
children and friends, community activities, or their work. One of these
areas was central, while others were peripheral. The women whose lives
centred on their work were those who were the most happy with their
lives. They had the most balanced lifestyle of any group. Although their
lives centred on their work they were also more involved with their
families than any of the other women, despite what one might expect.

One third of these 70-year-old women had no centre to their lives. It
was difficult to see what held their lives together – nothing really interested them. Everything was a source of dissatisfaction, nothing gave
them fulfilment. They appeared never to have made choices, never to have
committed themselves. Or else a narrow commitment had been lost, as
was the case for a formerly husband-centred woman whose partner had
died, leaving her without a focus in her life. These unfocused women were
the least adjusted of all.

Thus the lifestyle balance sheet of satisfactions and sorrows is tipped
in favour of the family-centred housewife in the early adult years. It leans
towards the actively working woman in late adulthood. Between the two lie

* These women (along with a parallel group of men) were first interviewed at the age 30 in
1929 at the California Institute of Human Development. The study thus presented a rare
opportunity to find out what happens during a span of 40 years in the lives of now elderly
people.

the years in the thirties and forties, the years of dilemma, choice and transition. And the price of not choosing seems to be high.

The traditional marriage, where the wife supports the husband and children throughout her life, is becoming obsolete. The egalitarian marriage is still something in the future – and it may prove to be a Utopian dream. The typical marriage is becoming the evolving marriage – known variously as the symmetrical family, the negotiated couple, the neo-conventional marriage. It is one where the wife spends the early years of adulthood in the housewife role, turning progressively in later adulthood to an active working role.

But of course there is nothing that tells you that you are or should be the 'typical' person living in a typical marriage. Each individual has to discover what sort of person she or he is, and make personal choices. If we are to single out the elements that, linked together and inseparable from each other, make a marriage work and an help an individual to grow through that marriage, they are three: negotiation ... expressiveness ... and choice.

Part Four

Lifestyles

The years of life investments that span the period from twenties to forties are characterized by sequenced preoccupations and life investments. This process is like building a tower out of building blocks. From a pile of blocks of various shapes and sizes, you have to find the first block, the career block, and position it on the floor. You only have one hand free to do this because the other is unsteadily holding a second block chosen from another pile, the private life block. Then one is positioned on top of the first and after re-alignment you have your tower.

In this fourth part of the book, we turn to look at these towers and what they signify to people. The towers in life are of course lifestyles. Lifestyles are emerging out of life investments. Some of these towers are very satisfying to the people who constructed them: we call these generative lifestyles. Other towers are unsatisfactory to their builders, who may nonetheless have enjoyed the process of building: we call these maintenance lifestyles. Some of these latter people spend considerable time readjusting the tower they have made; others give up with a sense of resignation. Meanwhile the generative individuals are enjoying their towers. For in reality these towers are not just building blocks; they are blocks that have been created to live in. Creation of the tower is one process; living in it is another. Making life investments and ... well, perhaps there is no better expression for it than simply saying, living in one's life.

We start off by exploring what happens in that intangible period, most clearly seen in retrospect, that people call mid-life. Chapter 13 looks at the mood of mid-life and outlines the enjoyment test that is becoming the most important principle in life. Chapter 14 shows how some people adjust 'flawed lifestyles' in the years ahead, and how the lifestyles that emerge from mid-life continue beyond retirement into old age.

Chapter 13

The enjoyment test

The widely held belief that the early forties herald a different era in adult life is documented by our own statistics – or rather absence of statistics. For a researcher whose diet consists of statistically significant 'three-star' correlations, the investigation of either the professional lives or the private lives of the younger men is a treat. His diet becomes more frugal when he turns to the older managers. Many statistical findings remain the same, but the significance of the correlations and tabulations decreases. There are few distinctively different results that indicate new patterns to this phase in life. The further one takes the survey managers into the late forties and fifties, the more shapeless the phenomenon of professional and private life seems to become. Seen with a statistical eye, this is a grey and colourless world.

We have the same reaction when presenting and discussing our findings at management seminars. It is exciting to do this with managers in their thirties and early forties. The men are visibly moved. But one never knows how the men in their late forties and fifties will react. Their reactions vary widely. Some are cynical, some are touched. Some are enlightened, some are depressed. Many are simply indifferent.

What both the absence of statistical patterns and the variety in reactions are expressing is that people are becoming very different. What we now observe are the different people, the different personalities, the different lifestyles, that emerge from the process of making life investments. The most exciting way of researching the lives of these older men is not through statistics or seminar discussions. It is through discussions with them individually – accepting each as unique.

The early years of adulthood are years of exploration and development of the self through experience. The qualities most valued by society in young adults are qualities such as dynamism, optimism, enthusiasm, risk-taking, persistence, dedication. All connote a sense of energy – a young adult *invests* himself. And by investing himself, his self-concept crystallizes. The answer to the question 'Who am I?' becomes clearer and clearer.

The older men whom we interviewed talked of themselves very expressively. What was striking was their attitude towards themselves. Whereas the younger men's views of themselves tend to be ambivalent, the older men divide into the very positive and the very negative. There are some who radiate self-confidence, self-assurance and self-respect. And then there are others who may outwardly feign that self-confidence, but who describe themselves in negative, self-deprecating terms. These two attitudes towards the self indicate the two different lifestyles that now are emerging from the making of life investments, the generative lifestyle and the maintenance lifestyle.

For the men on a generative life path, this will be a fulfilling time. They enjoy their work, having found and maintained a career that fits well. They have vital marriages and friendships; their relationships with their children are satisfying. Leisure is full of exciting activities. If they complain of anything, it is that they do not have time to do everything they want to do. But this is not a deep complaint – it simply expresses the demands of many vital interests. Theirs is a stressful but full lifestyle.

For the men on a maintenance life path, this is a depressing time of life. They have everything and yet nothing. They have invested in many parts of life, but they begin to realize that they do not derive enjoyment from any of them.

These two lifestyles are easier to understand when seen through the eyes of the people in question. So let us allow two men to describe themselves. In some ways, both Charles Dupres and Ivan Robinson are similar. Both are marketing directors. Charles is 45 years old, Ivan is 43. Each married young, and both have three teenage children. But they describe their lifestyles in different ways.

A portrait of generativity

When asked to describe himself as a person, the first thing that Charles Dupres said was, 'I love life, and I love living it.' The world 'love' and 'enjoy' were very frequent throughout the interview, even though his wife described him as having a pessimistic streak in his nature.

Nevertheless, Charles's life is not one of bliss, nor has it been in the past. He failed to obtain his degree in economics, and his career progress for the first 12 years (mostly inside sales) was slow. It got underway only when he moved into marketing ten years ago, and since then his progression has been more and more rapid. Only half of the French managers had a clear expectation for the height of their careers, and

Charles was the only person who expected to be company president, though he felt it would not be a bitter blow if he did not make it.

His marriage passed through a stormy renegotiation following a time when his wife had a breakdown. Charles concedes that he was so preoccupied by his work that he had not realized how upset his wife had been by a move and by various other events. But this led to a renewal and stabilization of their relationship. His wife went back to work; now, as she put it, 'If I didn't work, I'd feel I was only half living.'

Both Charles and his wife are discontented with his investment behaviour. His present job is very demanding, and he still tries to cope with spillover. (He sees the relationship between professional and private life as one of alternating spillover and independence). His wife complains that they only really talk with each other at weekends; but note that even after 22 years of marriage, she still wants more time to talk.

This is how Charles describes his lifestyle:

> If my wife were here, she would tell you that I love my work and that it is difficult to imagine me any other way than I am. And I think that is true. I love what I'm doing, that is certainly the case. And so it is difficult for me to imagine myself doing anything else – I mean doing anything else at the same time, that's what I'm getting at. Either it is *this* lifestyle or something completely different. And with this way of life, it is difficult to do all the other things I'd like to do. I don't want to change things, but in this job it is particularly difficult since I'm spending 80 per cent of my effort on my work. There is only 20 per cent left for the rest, and that is not logical.
>
> The fact of being happy as a couple and as a family has a lot to do with the success I've had – professional success, I mean. Perhaps that wasn't so before, but it becomes more and more so now. I don't think I'd have ambitions for the future if my family life were not so happy. The two are very related.
>
> The best time in our marriage? That's today. Yes, that is certainly now. We are much closer than we were at the beginning of our marriage. You become more open and more sensitive to each other. We have built up something together, and today we are seeing its realization. And we have sufficient mutual understanding to want to continue in the future. It is difficult to imagine being more happy together.
>
> I spend a lot of time with the children during the weekend. A lot. And it has always been that way. One is always too busy during the week. During the weekends we put all our cards on the table and talk through whatever has happened during the week. Of course they are growing up now. From time to time I feel a little excluded from their

lives. You can't get angry at them for that. It's natural even though it is a shame. My dream for them is that each of them will be able to do what they really want to do with their lives.

The life investments that Charles has made seem to be paying off. His life is very full. Having asked him about his satisfactions and dissatisfactions, the interviewer had to eventually cut him off – the list of both went on and on. His is a lifestyle full of satisfactions and also of dissatisfactions – but certainly full.

In contrast, Ivan Robinson could think of few satisfactions. Nor did he have any specific complaints – the stress that he experienced was more of a general nature. He had invested as much time and energy in the past, but these investments did not appear to be paying off.

A portrait of maintenance

Ivan Robinson was dissatisfied with most aspects of his life. As judged by the questionnaire, he showed more signs of emotional stress than anyone else we interviewed. He saw the first part of his career as absorbing and interesting. But a take-over of his small company by a multinational corporation and successive promotions had left him now with a job he found boring. While he described the present as the best time in his marriage, that was only because he had become sensitive to that part of his life in recent years. He described the relationship between professional and private life as being one of spillover in the past, but now in the process of becoming instrumental. The absence of any enjoyment, any meaning in his life, was most apparent when Ivan talked about his worries:

> What worries me about my work is a growing feeling of lassitude during these recent years. Work is becoming more and more monotonous. And I'm concerned about that for several reasons. First, I've always been very involved in my professional life, and that is important to me. And second, the people who work with me, who know me well, they feel it. I get irritable about little things, I explode and yell at someone. I had a major bust-up with someone the other day, and I don't know what I'm going to do about it. It's stupid, it is unnecessary, but I can't help it. I just don't control myself as well as I used to. This is one of my biggest preoccupations.
>
> With regard to my wife, I think that is my fault. I feel distant and detached. We don't talk much together. I hide behind my shell, and I think she does the same. She feels that something is wrong and so she too withdraws. It isn't worth saying anything. I'll tell you frankly,

177

what concerns me is that if I let it go on like that, we'll land up in a state of total indifference to each other. It's up to me. Things drift on, and I don't know whether to accept this or do something about it.

As for the children, well, it's very complicated. In certain respects, I feel quite helpless with regard to adolescent children. They are very upsetting – yes, they upset me a lot. I have tried to open doors for them. But when I disagree about something, then I put my foot down. I'm not against punishment, you know! [laughs] I suppose that's difficult to understand and doesn't fit with things I've said before, but then *I'm* difficult to understand.'

As Ivan puts it, he does not know whether to accept things as they are or do something about them. He feels that he is simply maintaining life at present, and he feels frustrated with this. What should he do about it?

The maintenance path takes three forms in these years. Ivan may decide that he wants to do something about his lifestyle. He may change line of work, he may belatedly renegotiate the shape of his private life. The first path is to *reshape one's lifestyle in a more generative direction*. But this is particularly difficult for the maintainer. He has tried to do that in the past and the reason why he finds himself in his present situation is because he has not succeeded. Moreover, he finds himself now in an all-or-nothing situation. If he chooses to relaunch his career, his already unsteady family life may suffer. If he chooses to focus on his family, that may aggravate his career problems. Perhaps his present lot is the best he can expect?

This is the second path for the maintainer. He learns to accept what he has rather than to yearn for what he has not. He *learns to resign himself*. He accepts that his life task now is to hold together a somewhat fragmented way of life. His life has its moments of joy and sorrow, but in general it is relatively free of major distress (though also of major satisfactions). He looks forward to reitrement as the day when the maintenance struggle will be over.

The third path characterizes the person who can neither break out of his lifestyle nor resign himself to it. He is the *embittered, frustrated maintainer* who either blames the outside world for treating him so badly or who blames himself for making so many mistakes. This is the person who sees himself in the most negative way. One of our managers, 55 years old, was asked to describe himself as a person:

[after a long pause] This is going to be very black. [pause] A question I ask myself from time to time, for quite a long time now, is what interests me in life. And *that*! . . . That I find difficult to answer.

The frustrated maintainer is probably the person who shows the most signs of mental illness or psychiatric disturbance. He feels intensely bitter and angry. That anger is vented towards the outside world, or turned inward towards himself.

The moods of mid-life

Generativity and maintenance as we have portrayed them are extreme portraits. The generative person is content with all aspects of his life, and his lifestyle is very full. The maintainer is not content with any aspect of his life, and his lifestyle is very empty. Among the people above the age of 43 who we interviewed, only Charles Dupres was on a clearly generative life path (though one other person aged 39 had a similar lifestyle). There were more maintainers, either frustrated or resigned, particularly among the men in their fifties. But the majority of people in their mid-forties seemed to be in a questioning mood.

The characteristic of mid-life is that the sensitivity valve is open to *all* aspects of life. What is at issue is not simply the shape of professional life or private life, as at previous times, but the shape of life in total.

The period of life around age 40 is identified with the mid-life crisis. The stories told of people at this age make dramatic reading – the depressed and despondent, the suicides, the executives who break out of the rat race to join hippy communes, and the shy clerks who break out to found industrial kingdoms. Gail Sheehy's story of the *Passages* in life centres on a collection of semi-tragic vignettes of people caught in this 'deadline decade'.

While the idea that life changes in quality goes back to research early this century, the label of the mid-life crisis owes much to another biographical study, that of the British psychologist Elliot Jacques (1965). He examined the relationship between creativity and middle age among 310 famous painters, composers, poets, writers and sculptors. Jacques found that creativity often ceased at this point in life, and that there was a jump in the death rate among artists in the late thirties. Creativity sometimes re-emerged with a changed quality in the late forties. Men such as Freud, Jung, Eugene O'Neill, Frank Lloyd Wright and Ghandi went through a profound crisis at around 40, and became more creative afterwards. Other artists like Dylan Thomas and F. Scott Fitzgerald experienced a crisis and never managed to pull through.

We found no evidence in our study of crisis or breakdown occurring in these years, and thus the cliché of the mid-life crisis strikes us as extreme.* Nor do we find any evidence of a clearly defined 'mid-life period'.† What we do find is a steady increase in awareness, and a questioning of oneself that reaches a statistical peak in the early forties. The questioning of oneself begins for some in the mid-thirties, or even before. The misfits who 'mature' and turn to private life undergo in their early thirties a similar 'crisis' to the strugglers who give up in their early forties. The way in which some managers question their marriages in their late thirties is similar to the way in which others do in their mid-forties, only now with a more intense sense of urgency.

The three themes most commonly identified with mid-life are introspection, depression, and crisis or breakdown.

Introspection does increase – that we can certainly say. The people we interviewed have more awareness of themselves, and this awareness grows. They are more willing to talk of themselves as individuals rather than simply describing what they do. Indeed the only unequivocal finding of research on mid-life is that introspection increases with age in the second half of life (Neugarten, 1977).

Depression is common – that is also true. The person most suscepti-ble to depression is the man who has invested in many parts of his life, but who begins to realize that he does not derive enjoyment from any of them. They begin to lose their meaning. Outwardly, he may describe his career as successful, his marriage as happy; he has many friends, and he keeps himself busy in his leisure time. But if he assesses his life in terms of the pleasure that he derives from it, the picture is different:

> Career and work are settling into a routine. Sure, some aspects of the work are exciting – occasionally – but much of the work is a hectic, dull struggle with petty issues. Even a promotion would probably mean simply more of the same.
> Marriage is frankly dull. The relationship with my wife is comfort-able enough, we get on alright with each other. But she has her interests and I have mine, and we don't have much to say to each other. It's comfortable, but something is lacking.

---

* An early study, often quoted to indicate the extent of the mid-life crisis, was carried out by the California Institute of Technology, which surveyed 1,000 professional and managerial people around the age of 40. Five out of six of these people were reported as feeling depressed at this age, and one out of six was reported as never recovering from this depression. But other studies contradict this extreme view. On the basis of longitudinal studies of people's lives underway in the United States, it is estimated that between a quarter and a third of the male population experience some crisis or change in personality at this time in their lives (McGill, 1977; Brim, 1976).

† Some people say that mid-life lies between 35 and 40, others find evidence suggesting it is between 40 and 45. Take all estimates together, and one can say that some form of life transition occurs for some people between the ages of 35 and 55.

The children are growing up. We get on fine, and occasionally do things together. But basically they lead their own independent lives. I don't share much with them either.

Friends? I play tennis with some. We have others round to dinner or go to the theatre with them. We talk business and politics and gripe about the price of living together. But I don't feel I really know them, and nor do we have much to say to each other.

Leisure, sport and hobbies – yes, I keep myself busy. But they seem like ways of just passing the time. I have a feeling at the end of a weekend that I have not *done* anything. Time passes pleasantly enough, but it feels empty.

Outwardly, life is full and rosy. Inwardly, it seems empty – settling into a depressively comfortable routine.

However, depression is not a phenomenon that is unique to this mid-life period. In terms of our statistics, the men in their twenties and thirties were just as likely to feel depressed as those who were in their early forties. There were individuals in their forties who were happy and buoyant, like Charles Dupres, just as there were fulfilled people at the age of 30. What seems characteristic of the mid-life depression is not that it occurs more often but that it is more intense. What is significant is not the quantity or frequency of depression at this phase but its quality.

At earlier phases in life, depression was a localized phenomenon. It was experienced with respect to one part of life at a time. The younger manager who felt depressed was someone who was having problems in launching his career, as we will show later in this chapter. Emotional spillover was one manifestation of this mood. The manager in his mid- to late thirties who felt depressed was someone wrestling with the shape of his marriage. Now at the introspective mid-life period, all sensitivity valves are open. The man who still has not succeeded in launching his career beings to feel that it may be too late. Time is running out. The person whose family life is settling into a devitalized shape begins also to feel that it may be too late. The person who enjoys neither his professional life nor his private life experiences the greatest depths of depression. He questions the whole of his lifestyle. It is not just one aspect of life that is a preoccupation, it is the meaning of life itself. In Chapter 2, we called this phenomenon 'existential spillover'.

Call this a crisis if you wish. Most often the mood is contained, controlled, barely visible to the outsider. We found no evidence in our study that the third theme of mid-life – crisis leading to breakdown – occurs often. When it does, it is probably because there are multiple preoccupations together with some specific trigger (McGill, 1977). Most people question at some point or other all the issues associated with the mid-life crisis: their family lives, their careers, their bodies, their deaths in the future, their sense of purpose in the present. The crisis, when it occurs, is brought on by awareness of all these aspects of one's existence at one and the same time:

> The hormone production levels are dropping, the head is balding, the sexual vigour is diminishing, the stress is unending, the children are leaving, the parents are dying, the job horizons are narrowing, the friends are having their first heart attacks; the past floats by in a fog of hopes not realized, opportunities not grasped, women not bedded, potentials not fulfilled, and the future is a confrontation with one's own mortality. (M. W. Lear, quoted by Brim, 1976)

The open crisis is precipitated by an extreme event – being fired by the company, the death of a close family member, separation from one's wife. This event triggers depression into crisis.

On the other hand, for the individual with a generative lifestyle, this is the most happy time of his life. He has succeeded in the earlier life tasks. His concern at this time is only that there is so much he wants to do, but so little time left in which to realize all his life projects. Even if some tragic event occurs in his life, he can easily withstand the blow. His life is multifaceted, and he can reinvest his energy from one life area to another.

As so what is the characteristic of mid-life? Increasing introspection? Yes. Depression? Sometimes. Crisis and breakdown? This seems rare among the people whose lives we have studied.

The enjoyment test

Introspection means looking inward at oneself. Our research shows that this introspection has a focus. Instead of evaluating their lives in terms of outward success (have a secure, well-paid job and being seen as successful in one's career; having a house and home, and a stable family life that is seen by others as happy), people come more and more to evaluate their lives in terms of inner success: whether or not they derive enjoyment from these various aspects of their lives.

Over the years acknowledgement of the importance of the enjoyment of life increases steadily until it peaks in this mid-life period. Enjoyment (which we call vitality when talking of relationships) becomes the test of the meaning of life. Depression is its counterpart. The people who are most susceptible to depression are those who have been outwardly successful in building a life structure, but who have never focused on creating an enjoyable lifestyle.

Though people are equally likely to feel depressed at all phases of adulthood, we find that those who do feel depressed are those who are not deriving any enjoyment from the area of life that is their current preoccupation. This was clear from our statistical analysis: the young adults who felt depressed were those who felt their career and work to be unenjoyable. The people in their late thirties and early forties who were depressed were those who found their marriages to be unenjoyable. The mid-life people who feel depressed are those who find their lives unenjoyable.

These findings are important and summarize much of what we have said, so it is worth reporting them in more detail. The depressive individuals were singled out using the questionnaire responses. The depressives were people who were worried about the possibility of a nervous breakdown, who had difficulty in concentrating on things, and who indicated in the questionnaire that they often felt depressed.

In order to find out what is associated with depression at different phases in life, we looked at the correlations between depressiveness and feelings about different aspects of life for people at these life phases. What we were interested in was whether the depressives found their careers, their relationships with their wives, their relationships with their children, and their lives to be enjoyable or unenjoyable, tense or relaxed. This information reveals what lies behind the feelings of depression of people at different life phases. We can see whether our thesis that people are sensitive to different aspects of life at different phases is a real phenomenon, or whether it really reflects something else.

The younger depressives are distinguished by a feeling that their careers, while not necessarily tense, are unenjoyable. Lack of enjoyment in the career is a more important concern for them than for the people who are not depressed. This spills over into their feelings about their lives, which they see above all as unsuccessful (the third most significant correlation with depressiveness). The spillover phenomenon is evident in their attitude to their families. These depressed managers are insensitive to enjoyment of family life, and they tend to feel that their relationships with their wives and children are tense. They rarely listen to what their wives say to them (the most important correlate of depressiveness, clearly embodying spillover), and feel an absence of supportiveness in that their wives do not help them to relax. The picture of the younger depressive is that of the extreme misfit.

This is not the case at the next phase in life. The world of the depressive in his late thirties is different. It reflects a higher level of preoccupation with the marital relationship. While the career is still not particularly enjoyable, it is above all the lack of enjoyment in the relationship with the wife that is characteristic. The single most significant correlation with depressiveness (among all the hundreds that we tested) is now the absence of playing, joking and friendly teasing in the marriage. This absence in the relationship is what concerns the depressed person more than anything else. The relationship is tense; there is frequent resentment after marital arguments. The couple have not succeeded in getting beyond the early stages of renegotiation of the marriage. And depression is now less associated with a feeling that life is unsuccessful, but more with a growing feeling that it is unenjoyable.

The pattern up until this point is exactly what one would expect from our assessment in previous chapters. The importance of different areas of life changes from one phase to the other. The depressive people are those who have extreme problems in wrestling with changing life issues: first professional life, and then private life. But what about the depressives at the so called mid-life point, around the age of 40? People aged 39 to 45 we analysed as a separate group.

The depression here encloses the total person and all aspects of his life. It is not specifically attributed to either professional life or private life; it is attributed to a general feeling that life is not enjoyable or satisfying. Professional life lacks enjoyment, private life lacks enjoyment, but in a more muted way than in the previous two phases. It is above all life itself that lacks enjoyment – now the *single most important* correlate with depression.

Gradually over these 15 years of adulthood, the significance of enjoying life grows, to reach a peak in these years. It is the test of the life structure that has been constructed.

After the age of 45, the depressives appear as lonely and disengaged people. They are not particularly sensitive to any aspect of their lives – career, wife or children (though other results show that the children become the area which engages them the most). They see life as lacking in enjoyment and satisfaction, but it is as if they accept this more than they did before. The most significant correlation is now, curiously enough, with doing what they want to do in the case of a disagreement with their wives. They presumably do what they want without really wanting to do it, thus creating tension in the relationship without compensatory satisfaction. They see life as passive rather than active. They are preoccupied with the mundane task of keeping the wheels of life turning – working at something they don't enjoy to provide for a family in which they are not vitally engaged. The relationship between professional life and private life has become blandly instrumental.

In stressing enjoyment as the criterion for evaluating professional and private life, in saying that the trend in adulthood is towards evaluating personal success not in outward terms but in inner terms of enjoyment, we are not proposing some hedonistic alternative to the

Protestant Work Ethic. The enjoyment principle is described by many labels these days. Behavioural scientists call it 'intrinsic motivation'; but they measure this intrinsic motivation by finding out how long people will carry out tasks where there is no carrot and stick (Deci, 1975). Humanistic psychologists refer to it with the mystic term 'self-actualization', which essentially means doing what you want to do because you want to do it rather than because you have to, and above all finding out what you want to do.

As Hans Selye, the authority on stress, puts it:

> I think we have to begin by clearly realizing that work is a biological necessity. Just as our muscles become flabby and degenerate if not used, so our brain slips into chaos and confusion unless we constantly use it for some work that seems worthwhile to us. The average person thinks he works for economic security or social status, but when, at the end of a most successful business career, he has finally achieved this, there remains nothing to fight for – no hope for progress, only the boredom of assured monotony. ... The question is not whether we should or should not work, but what kind of work suits us best.

He goes on to point out that fishing, gardening, painting, organizing, managing, discussing, building, writing, play-acting, travelling, purchasing, selling – practically any human activity that you can think of – is an enjoyable leisure pursuit for some, work for others. The people who have invested the first part of their lives well never work, either in professional life or private life.

Commenting on how frustration and distress wear out the tissue of body, harden the arteries, clog the veins with chemical waste, Selye goes on to add that

> successful activity, no matter how intense, leaves you with comparatively few such scars; it causes stress but little, if any, distress. On the contrary, it provides you with the exhilarating feeling of youthful strength, even at a very advanced age. Work wears you out mainly through the frustration of failure. Many of the most eminent among the hard workers in almost any field lived a long life. They overcame their inevitable frustrations by the great preponderance of success. Think of Pablo Casals, Winston Churchill, Albert Schweitzer, G. B. Shaw, Henry Ford, Charles de Gaulle, Bertrand Russell, Queen Victoria, Titian, Voltaire ... etc., etc. ... All these people continued to be successful – and, what is more important, on the whole happy, well into their seventies, eighties, or even late nineties. Of course,

none of them ever 'worked' at all, in the sense of work as something one has to do to earn a living but does not enjoy. Despite their many years of intense activity, they lived a life of constant leisure by always doing what they liked to do. (Selye, 1975, pp. 96–7.)

Freud said in 1916:

The difference between nervous health and nervous illness (neurosis) is narrowed down ... to a practical distinction, and is determined by the practical result – how far the person concerned remains capable of a sufficient degree of capacity for enjoyment and active achievement in life. (Quoted by Vaillant, 1977.)

Lieben und arbeiten

Freud saw life in terms of two themes – '*Lieben und Arbeiten*', love and work. This view still seems valid today. What is fundamental is that these two aspects of life come to mutually reinforce each other. This will happen if enjoyment is found in both of them. Enjoyment is the common test.

Our research has shown us that failure in one aspect of life often has a negative effect on the other. Moreover, failure in either work or love cannot be compensated by success in the other. The person who reaches this state inevitably feels that his lifestyle is flawed. The lifestyle of the generative person passes the enjoyment test. And so his life path in the future is full. It has been well launched. The lifestyle of the maintainer fails this test, and so this is a low point in his life. Either he breaks out of this lifestyle, or he comes to accept what he has. Between these two extreme types of people are many others, possibly a majority, for whom mid-life is a period of questioning. Part of their lifestyle is enjoyable, another part is not. They live in what we call 'flawed lifestyles'. For them, the years ahead are often a time of creative adjustment, of search to fill what is missing. The way in which they adjust is the theme of our next chapter.

Chapter 14

How many orchards are you tending?

George Vaillant asked the 50-year-old men, whose lives he had followed for more than 30 years since university, which period in their lives they saw as most happy. Some answered that it was the years since their late-thirties until now. They looked back upon their lives before this point as superficial, one-sided and shallow. It was now that they felt themselves to be whole men. Whatever stress and pain they experienced from time to time, they were enjoying life to the hilt. Others replied that it was the years up until the late thirties. These had been years of adventure and enjoyment, the years when they were going places. Now they did not feel that they were going anywhere. They felt stress and pain, but no enjoyment. Needless to say, at the age of 50 it was the former group of men who were found to have adapted best to life. For the latter, life had taken a turn downhill (Vaillant, 1977).

The former probably have generative lifestyles. They live life to the full. The latter probably have maintenance lifestyles. They may come to accept this with fatalistic resignation. The former have positive self-images, the latter have negative self-images.

These are two extremes. Many people have mixed or ambivalent self-images. Their path for the time being is neither that of generativity nor that of maintenance. The making of life investments is a task that may not be over. They have flawed lifestyles.

Flawed lifestyles

A lifestyle based on enjoyable work but lacking in vital relationships with other people is flawed. Such a person lives with a feeling of loneliness that mars the satisfaction obtained from work. Vaillant finds that lonely people, those who have been unable to achieve a stable marriage and lasting friendships with others, show dramatically more signs of mental ill-health than friendly men. They are more often physically ill and labelled as psychiatrically ill; they miss their vacations more frequently and they make more use of tranquillizers, drugs and alcohol.

A lifestyle based on vital relationships with other people but lacking in any enjoyment in work pursuits is also flawed. It is difficult to maintain the vitality of any relationship, be it with a wife, children or friends, unless one feels competent beyond those relationships. The relationship becomes one of dependence rather than of interdependence.

Both lifestyles are flawed because in each case, the person is only tending one orchard. Life is quite enjoyable but something is felt to be missing. Everyone knows how fulfilment in one activity creates energy to invest in others, whereas frustration or boredom drains energy, leaving one apathetic and lifeless. This is another way of describing the emotional spill-over effect. Furthermore, these lifestyles are built on precarious foundations. If something goes wrong with the career of the lonely prisoner of success, his whole lifestyle is threatened. He has no source of interpersonal support to buffer the shock and help him to reestablish himself. If the spouse of the instrumentally-oriented family man were to die or the children were to leave him, his life's meaning would be threatened.

One of the observable patterns in the years after mid-life, after the phase of life investment, is that of *adjustment*. Sometimes, following a period of self-questioning, depression or crisis, this adjustment takes a dramatic form. Levinson calls it 'breaking out'. (Levinson *et al.*, 1978).

The misfit-become-struggler one day quits his job in business. He leaves with his family for the other side of the country and buys a small store or a farm. He breaks out and launches into a new career, which may or may not work out for the better. The executive with a devitalized marriage leaves his wife and children to marry a much younger girl. As he takes her to discothèques or romantic restaurants or takes extended vacations for the first time in his life, he seems to be trying to catch up on the private life of youth that he missed.

As Levinson points out, radical change is difficult to make at this mid-life point, and while it happens with increasing frequency it still remains a rare and risky phenomenon. It is most likely to occur when a person is particularly fulfilled in one aspect of life, while despairing in the other. The person who makes a radical career change is likely to have a very close family; the support and understanding of the family is vital to pluck up the courage to take a plunge into the semi-unknown, and that support will be a critical asset in the difficult years ahead. Similarly, in the cliché at least, it is the successful top executive who quits his wife for the other woman, not the disgruntled middle manager. Indeed, the less secure and fulfilled he is in his work, the less energy and sensitivity he will have available for the difficult task of shaping a new marriage.

Most forms of adjustment in and after mid-life appear to take a less dramatic, compensatory form. Managers become more sensitive to the importance of relationships outside the family – with friends and work colleagues. People put more effort into developing pursuits and hobbies that they enjoy. Enjoyment and meaning are rediscovered in compensatory ways. Showing how this happens is the theme of this chapter. Life begins to broaden out. The neat distinction between professional and private life fades away.

Let's look at how people adjust to these flawed lifestyles, making them more generative. The first case is the frustrated plateaued manager, a misfit who loves his family but not his work. The second case is the older prisoner of success, who loves his work but not his family.

Finding enjoyable work in leisure

Plateauing, in itself a neutral term though it has negative connotations for the linear person, implies reaching the height of one's career, so that work will not change radically in the future. Paul Evans found in a study of 150 product managers that the majority of the men above the age of 45 saw themselves as having plateaued: they saw the probability of any significant job change in the next five years as very small. However, many of them, described as 'position expanders', saw their jobs as continuing to evolve with market or technological expansion (Evans, 1974).*

The important distinction is between the frustrated plateaued manager and the fulfilled plateaued manager. The fulfilled man finds his work to be interesting and enjoyable. The work fits with his personality, and his lifestyle is not flawed by the absence of enjoyment in work. He only becomes frustrated if this job is not expanding and starts to become

* Plateauing as a career phenomenon has attracted little research attention until recently. It is hardly mentioned except in passing in the first book to review what is known about *Careers in Organizations* (Hall, 1976). To some extent, this reflects the lack of interest in the themes of adjusting to stability or coping with failure, in comparison with the topic of how to be successful. It also reflects the expansive economic environment of the fifties to early seventies. Organizations were growing so rapidly that positions were in constant expansion. The market for managers was open, and new opportunities were constantly being created. All this has changed, irrevocably it seems. We are in an era of stop/go growth. What was unthinkable before, namely the lay-off of managerial personnel, now happens often. Positions are not expanding; openings are not available; the job market is tight. At the same time, the bulge generation – the large number of people born after the war – is entering the mid-thirties, soon the early forties. The combination of limited growth and the bulge generation reaching middle age leads many corporate officers to worry about the reactions of people to widespread plateauing. A fringe concern is likely to become a major social issue.

routine. The frustrated man finds little of his work enjoyable. He is the misfit, now beyond mid-life. He has given up trying to find a professional identity. Or perhaps as the pessimistic Peter Principle would have it, he has risen one or two levels above his level of competence.

One person fits with his job whereas the other does not. This difference is revealed from an organizational point of view by one of the few studies of plateauing, where Stoner *et al.* (1974) contrasted effective with ineffective problem cases. They found six characteristics that distinguished the effective men. These men were:

1. Managers who felt their work was important to the success of their company
2. People who valued particular aspects of their job very highly
3. Individuals who had jobs which closely matched their interests and in which they had an unusually high degree of intrinsic job satisfaction
4. Managers who had positions enabling them to pursue an activity in sufficient depth to develop considerable expertise and recognition as a 'professionals'
5. Managers who tended to have supervisors who consciously provided challenging and interesting work assignments
6. Individuals who derived satisfaction from community and other non-work activities, which were facilitated by their organizational roles

Add up the first five in this list of effective men (ignoring the sixth for the time being), and you have the profile of someone who enjoys his work – who fits with the job that he does.

Even when he does not enjoy his work and is not particularly proud of it, the lifestyle of the frustrated plateaued manager is not a bad lot as long as two conditions are fulfilled. The first is that he is reasonably competent in what he does and thus feels secure in his job; this is likely to be the case where the lack of enjoyment stems from a job that partially fits but simply has become routine. The second condition is that he has a satisfying family life. If these conditions are fulfilled, his work serves the instrumental purpose of maintaining his private life. His lifestyle is satisfactory though flawed. He experiences a low degree of stress, though also a lower degree of satisfaction than the generative individual.

These two conditions are interrelated. If he is a competence misfit in his job and not simply an emotional misfit, then his private life will suffer from spillover. The task of staying on top of his job, maintaining outward appearances, not being labelled as 'deadwood to be cut away', drains emotional energy. Here in contrast we have a maintainer. The relationship between professional life and private life has become instrumental, but there is little energy left to invest in private life. His only dream is retirement, because this means the end of the bitter struggle. One of the two significant relationships that we found in our statistics for older managers probably reflects this struggle: the people who are clearly dissatisfied with their lifestyles are those who are very 'active' in their careers (see Chapter 4).

The case of Noel

Noel is one manager we interview who had a flawed lifestyle. He was a competent but frustrated plateaued manager who described the relationship between his professional and private life as instrumental. He saw himself as bored by his work; his wife believed that this is because he was a misfit who had never discovered his professional identity.

Noel began his career in sales after taking degrees in business and economics. In his early thirties, he left big business to set up his own commercial enterprise. It floundered for several years, years which he now looks back on as both happy and stressful. His firm went bankrupt when he was 35. The strains of professional life led to a divorce a few years later. He rejoined big business, and remarried eight years later. Now he is director of marketing, a senior position, at the age of 56.

Noel describes his work as interesting. But above all he feels that it is easy; it presents no challenge, but nor does he search for that challenge. He feels that he could spend most of the year away from the office without it making one iota of difference; his only point of resentment is that the company will not accept that he stays at home instead of twiddling his fingers at the office. He feels isolated and alone at work.

> Until 15 years ago [when he was 40], I allowed myself to become absorbed by work. I wasn't aware of much else in life. Now, no way! I've learnt to resign myself. Ambitions – well, that would be unrealistic in any case. You have to change your psychology. You have to adapt. The family has become more important to me, but I suppose that's because I'm no longer interested in work.

Much of his private life centres on reading, watching television, and doing household chores; his only other activities are occasional golf and bridge. His wife works full-time as a pharmaceutical researcher. There are no children in the second marriage – those of the first marriage are grown-up and married. His wife talked of his work when asked whether his job suits him:

I prefer my own job. There, there is much more feeling of creating something, of being useful. [pause] You know, that is a fundamental issue. I put a question mark by the whole way he has led his career. I think that it suits him in terms of his studies, his knowledge, his experience. In terms of everything he has actually done. But I'm absolutely convinced that I have a husband who is much more a scientist by interest than – how can I put it – than what he does. Marketing – that's not him.

This means that his work is built on false foundations. It puts a question by everything. It questions what he does now. It questions where we have chosen our home. But I'm convinced that if he were doing what I'm doing now, he would be much more satisfied ...

He isn't content. *I* notice it. Others don't. I think he suffers from working for a large company and not more independently. Being stuck in the middle of a hierarchy, he suffers deeply from that.

One way or the other, Noel has reached an equilibrium in life, a plateau, without ever discovering a strong sense of professional identity. There are no powerful stresses in his existence.

I've no real major worries about work. Or about anything else. Apart from the occasional quarrel with my wife, which upsets me more than her – I guess I'm more sensitive to that than she is – I'm just waiting out until retirement. I had the opportunity for a new job, but that entailed moving. So why bother. After we retire, maybe we'll build a house together. Maybe we'll open a shop. Who knows?

Compensatory adjustment

Unless family life is particularly active, this flawed lifestyle gradually drifts in the direction of maintenance. And that is quite likely because the wife may not necessarily be interested in doing everything with her husband; like Noel's wife; she may be realizing her own career. The children are growing up and lead their independent lives. There may not be a great deal to talk about with friends. There is time to pass but nothing actively to invest it in. But some people re-orient this flawed lifestyle in a generative direction. These men compensate for what is lacking in professional life (usually activities of which they can be proud) by launching new careers – leisure careers.

There was only one manager in our survey who had reinvested himself in this way. But since becoming aware of this form of life adjustment, we have met many people (usually in their forties and fifties) who have developed these leisure careers. What they have in common is frustration with their work careers.

One had taken up his old pastime of riding, building a stable on his land. The point when his pastime had become meaningful was the first weekend he gave riding lessons; first it was on a friendly basis, later for payment. He was finding himself, during the weekends at least, doing what he enjoyed doing and being remunerated for it. He spoke enthusiastically about the dream that was crystallizing in his mind – continuing as a manager in business for a few years with objective of raising enough capital to set up a full-time riding school. His managerial career had provided him with the knowledge and skill to realize this project.

For another man, the revitalized hobby – only now actively invested in – was playing the violin. With some friends in similar positions he had set up a small chamber group which gave paid concerts. The significance of the payment was not that the money was needed but that it accredited the professionalism of the musicians – it made them feel proud. Another man had run out of home-rebuilding projects that he enjoyed. He had creatively broadened out his interest. The first step was buying and remodelling a run-down cottage, originally intended as a second home. The finished project had won a local award, and instead of moving in, the manager had sold it for a handsome profit. This he had used to invest in two other house purchases; finding the work to be a strain on his time, he had hired contractors to do the heavy work – keeping his own role to that of design, interior decorating, and other aspects that he particularly enjoyed.

Most of these people have no intention of giving up their 'professional' jobs in industry, though some do dream of it. They feel more content in their work through having other interests. Work has become instrumental in a positive way. Their work also benefits in the sense that they appear more willing to speak their own minds, more willing to take risks. They worry less about unemployment, knowing that their other pursuits could conceivably provide them with a livelihood. One of the characteristics of effective plateaued managers is indeed that they derive satisfaction from non-work activities.

We could cite many more examples of this generative reorientation – of a passionate reader who founded a national bookclub, of a sculptor who set up an antique shop with his wife to sell his sculptures, of a research manager who founded an international scientific association in his field. We have found these people particularly among French managers, who often see their careers as constrained by the structured and authoritarian nature of their companies (See Appendix 3, Note 3). Indeed, some French managers criticized our questionnaire for focusing too much on work and family life. As they put it, the questionnaire did not adequately emphasize a third arena of life that they called 'para-professional life' – professional life outside work.*

Obstacles to adjustment

Why is it that sociologists find that more people disengage and maintain life rather than reinvest themselves (Cumming, Dean, Newell and McCaffey, 1960)? Why is it that the plateaued managers, in our survey at least, appear more often to choose to maintain life rather that to reinvest in new directions?

One of the reasons is that people do not explore and develop in their earlier adult years what they enjoy doing. Adolescents and young adults tend to have multiple hobbies, interests, pastimes and pursuits. Painting, music, acting, managing a club, amateur electronics, fishing, writing poetry, do-it-yourself work, inventing machines, writing short stories, botany ... the list can be endless. This 'serious play' is an important part of exploration: out of such pursuits may come an awareness of what sort of career one wishes to venture into. But from this time on, most people focus on this single all-or-nothing career; they tend only one orchard.

In the early career years of launching, there is little active leisure time. It is eaten up by spillover. What is left is taken up by the demands of raising a family. In the thirties, non-work energy may be focused on the family or relaxation. Those early active leisure pursuits, each of which might have been developed into a career, are abandoned. If they are not abandoned, they take a passive rather than active form. Instead of playing a musical instrument, one listens to music. Acting becomes an interest in going to the theatre. Amateur electronics expresses itself in a passion for the most sophisticated hi-fi sets on the market. Writing poetry becomes reading poetry. Many passive adult interests have their origins in active childhood pursuits. The active part of oneself becomes progressively invested in *the* career. For the ambitious person, whether he is a prisoner

* There is a close similarity to the way in which some unemployed people break out of their gloom. In a similar way to the frustrated maintainer, unemployed people who have no interests outside their families begin to lose their sense of identity. They become moody, withdrawn. They begin to feel negative about themselves; their standards begin to slip (they demand less of themselves and less of others); they have problems in eating and sleeping, and yet spend much of their time in a passive, somnambulent state. Marsden and Duff (1975), in their British study of the *Workless*, found that the people who adapted reasonably well to lengthy unemployment were those who found an alternative to work in 'fiddling': illegally undertaking odd jobs for people in their houses or gardens. Fiddling was important not only to subsidize unemployment benefits, but more particularly to fill time with some meaningful activity. The people who were found to adapt best to unemployment, to thrive on it, were the active compensators: those who took the opportunity to develop some hobby such as electronics into a very significant interest, setting up an illegal radio repair shop that one day might become an enterprise.

or a misfit, even these passive interests decline in importance until they become distant recollections of childhood pastimes. All the eggs have been placed in one single basket.

The development path of an active leisure interest in fact parallels the launching of the work career. The dynamics of exploration, assessment, and development are the same – only the perilous aspects of launching are absent: risk, moving out, and the dilemma of choosing (these become critical for the person whose hobby becomes his career and livelihood). Where leisure pursuits are abandoned (and one can sympathize with the reasons for abandonment), the man of 40 or 45 finds himself worse off than in childhood – he has little that really interests him. Or there are things that he *enjoys* doing, but he feels he does them badly and that they give him no sense of pride. The investment necessary to learn how to do these things well seems so great that he is discouraged.

Another reason why people succumb to the disengagement impasse is the emotional spillover of unenjoyable work. The stress of struggling to launch a career is replaced by the stress of maintaining a livelihood – maintaining an enthusiastic façade when one does not feel enthusiastic; maintaining an impression of being involved and constructive when one does not feel involved or constructive; worrying about job security, younger competitors for one's position, and the consequences of reorganizations that may destroy one's niche. The task of maintenance requires all the person's active energy. In this stage, the individual who is most likely to compensate by active investment in leisure is the one who has maintained vital leisure interests since adolescence. These 'subsidiary careers' now become valued personal resources. Yet among managers at least, the number of subsidiary leisure interests that have been maintained appear to be few. Maintenance creeps in. If there is any dream, it is that of retirement, a prospect that is appealing to all the instrumentally oriented managers above the age of 45 we have met.

For the person who has an active leisure career, retirement is a positive prospect, the freedom to invest himself in his leisure activities. For the maintainer, retirement is looked forward to but not as something positive. It represents the prospect of freedom from the *struggle* to maintain life. From the moment of retirement, life will be maintained without endless strain. The maintainer's lifestyle will embody what some sociologists believe is the characteristic path of later life, namely disengagement.

Finding vital relationships at work – the older prisoner

The lifestyle of the prisoner of success, the person who finds so much excitement in his work that his private life has always been excluded, is the second flawed lifestyle. We are talking of the person who is divorced and who lives a very lonely private life, or the man whose marriage has no vestige of vitality.

In one sense it is easier to break out of this lifestyle and relaunch a new private life career than it is to launch a new work career, especially at a time in life when the children no longer hold an empty marriage together. But this is a naïve view. The successful executive may find it easy to attract another woman into marriage. He may recapture the vitality of a new relationship for a brief span. But building a vital relationship is a difficult task. He goes through a succession of painful divorces and new marriages in search of that elusive quality. Think of Citizen Kane in the film by Orson Welles.

We have less direct data on this lifestyle after the mid-life years. None of the managers whom we interviewed were in this situation. Some approximated the lonely prisoner, but in a far from extreme way. Their work was fulfilling, and their lives centred on their work. Their marriages were not vital, but they accepted this and viewed them as both happy and important. Their investment in family life took a passive form, and their wives had adjusted to this.

It is an open question whether the post-mid-life prisoner, successful and thriving in his work but lonely in his private life, even exists in an extreme form, other than as a rare exception. Young and Wilmott (1973) described the leisure and family lives of 184 British managing directors. Most of them were prisoners in the sense of enjoying their jobs immensely, and getting most of their satisfaction from their work. But they apparently saw their marriages as stable and happy; such a marriage typically had taken its shape, and this was one where the wife, as many of these managing directors put it, 'accepted her lot'. George Vaillant argues on the basis of his *Adaptation to Life* study that it is difficult to be successful in one's work if one has not achieved a stable marriage and the capacity to build lasting friendships by the age of 50. But Vaillant's criterion was the stability of relationships, not their vitality. The people who had adapted best to life, who had not paid a price for their success, had developed enduring and lasting relationships, but not neccessarily vital and intimate relationships. Cuber and Harroff (1966), who studied the marital lives of 'significant Americans', found that a majority of these successful people had utilitarian marriages – devitalized or passive-congenial in nature. But by and large, they were resigned to this.

Compensatory adjustment

The lifestyle of the older prisoner with a stable but devitalized marriage is flawed by a feeling of having missed out on something, but it is nevertheless a more generative lifestyle than that of the frustrated plateaued man. The latter has difficulty in compensating in leisure life, but the prisoner has greater ease in establishing friendships and relationships outside the marriage, though he may never feel intimate with anyone.

One relationship that becomes a potential source of fulfilment is that with his own children. One of the few clear statistical patterns that we observe in our survey after the age of 42 is the importance attributed to a satisfying relationship with one's own children. In Chapter 4, we saw how the younger manager was most sensitive to the *problems* that his children were having; it is only in the early to late forties that the man who is satisfied with his lifestyle tends to be the one who finds positive satisfaction in the children. These men, like others of their age, begin to regret that they did not share the lives of their children when they were young, and wish to catch up on that sharing now if the children are not already leaving the family nest. The youngest daughter becomes the centre of the father's attention; a friendly relationship develops with the teenage son. The opportunity still presents itself to build a vital relationship within the close family, though outside the marriage.*

Deep and lasting relationships can be developed with children at this stage, as well as with friends. The organizational life of the successful prisoner also brings certain relationships which may superficially satisfy a desire for vital contact with others. These informal friendships may be more meaningful than the contact at home, even when one suspects that other people's friendliness is partly based on the usefulness of that relationship to themselves. One former chief executive officer, now retired, talked candidly of this:

> What do you do if plans go awry, or if things aren't working out and frustration is pushing you? If you're the chief executive officer,

---

* The relationship of parents with their adolescent children are stereotypically stormy. The father wishes to force his values on the son, or at least prevent him from doing stupid things and making choices he will regret. There is talk of a 'generation gap'. We might stress that the father often does not realize that the actions of the adolescent are part of the necessary process of exploration, and do not imply choice.

Vaillant (1977) has some interesting observations here. He found that it is impossible to predict the course of life events from adolescence; an emotional stormy adolescence often precedes a fulfilling life after 30 (as we would also argue, for the exploration process is often stormy).

Vaillant also found that vigorous parental condemnation of things like marijuana and long hair did not create a generation gap; nor did approval of such behaviour bring fathers close to their children. 'The critical factor in creating a generation gap turned out to be not parental conservatism but parental dishonesty' (p. 225). These fathers did the opposite of what they really wanted to do. Themselves wanting to get out of the rut of marriage and play around, they would blow up at the promiscuity of their sons. They were emotionally dishonest and conflicted – inconsistent in their messages and behaviour. Other fathers where the generation gap was particularly apparent were paradoxically those with excellent marriages, but the sort of marriages that excluded the children.

you can always call a meeting and get something off your chest. If you're really in need of stroking, you can have a supervisor's meeting, which brings in hundreds of people from miles around, and when you've finished all of them clap. (Evans, 1977)

Dalton, Thompson and Price (1977) show that among technically oriented people, career progression has an increasingly interpersonal element to it after the age of 40. Pure technical contribution is no longer ranked as high performance. The people who are most valued by their companies are those who have assumed some interpersonal responsibility for other people – as mentors or as sponsors of the work of others.

We describe these types of behaviour as compensatory adjustments because they can rarely substitute for the vital marriage, though they certainly add to it. The friendships are either less intimate or more transitory. Little can substitute for the expressive relationship that has grown out of half a life together. Nevertheless, with this form of adjustment, the prisoner lifestyle comes near to the generative life path – the better the quality of the marital relationship the more this will be true.

Yet the prisoner lifestyle, particularly that revolving around a very instrumental marriage, has its Achilles' heel. All of the person's eggs are in one basket – admittedly, a good basket. But what happens if that basket breaks? That could be due to a performance error, a reorganization, or the like – leading to firing, forced retirement, or reassignment to a less favourable position. The breaking of the basket may result from a growing sense of routine. What was fascinating at age 35, absorbing at 40, interesting at 45, now becomes stale at age 55. At the end, the breaking of the career basket comes irrevocably with mandatory retirement.

In retirement the prisoner faces a serious problem. The enjoyment that he derives from life, the relationships that give life meaning, are all wrapped up with his professional life. Leisure interests? He plays tennis well, though with less vigour than before, enjoys hunting, and likes a light novel after watching television – all a leisure of relaxation and recovery. What he needs is not relaxation, but stimulation; contact with people, of which he is deprived. Active leisure interests are now dim recollections of childhood. His source of life is cut out from under him.

The maintainer welcomes retirement; the prisoner fears retirement. This polarization of attitudes, evident in surveys on mandatory retirement, reflects these two different life-paths. Some prisoners adapt, with pain. In the autobiographical article on the adjustment of a top executive to retirement, the process is described as changing from a 'what' to a 'who' (Evans, 1977). This man's retirement lasted for one year. At the end of that year, he went to the local mayor to say that he felt estranged from the community and wanted to be put to work. He was given a 'can of worms' – heading a community development task force, and took up a job as treasurer and lecturer at a business college.

The successful retirement of the prisoner depends on the availability of meaningful substitute activities (Chown, 1977). Whereas blue-collar retirees who adapt well have hobbies, managerial retirees plunge into political or community activities, where their professional skills and ease of social contact are valued assets (Maas and Kuypers, 1974). Eminent politicians, business leaders and actors write their memoirs. But for those prisoners who have no outside activities, what happens?

Research in the coming years will probably show what happens. They shrivel up and die.

Absurd, you say? We only have the statistics at second hand, from a fellow researcher and a few personnel managers. The statistics that we have are dramatic. In one major high technology organization in the United States, the average time for which the company pays a pension to its managers and professional people after retirement is ... *three months*. In one of Britain's large business concerns, the average is apparently somewhat longer – eight months. Among the senior civil servants in the ministries of one European government, the average life expectancy of the men who have retired is, following the death of their wives, six months. But there is a footnote to this last statistic. If the husband dies after he has retired, the wives apparently live on for an average of seven years ... Perhaps women tend more orchards than men?

The patterns progress into older age

The way in which a lifestyle emerges out of the life investment years and is then adjusted begins to become apparent. Life is settling into a pattern which flows on into older age, after retirement. A basic life philosophy has been moulded, and the projection of the generative path and the maintenance path can be seen in the later years of old age.

Sociologists and psychologists have argued for some time about the best way of describing the ageing process. There are some who view ageing as a process of necessary disengagement (Cumming and Henry, 1961; Cumming, Dean, Newell and McCaffey, 1960). They observe that older people often seem to be less involved with others than younger people. The elderly seem to accept and even welcome comparative isolation. Disengagement is viewed as a process where older people voluntarily withdraw into themselves at the same time as the younger generation reduces contact with them.

Others have put forward an activity theory of ageing (Havighurst and Albrecht, 1953; Havighurst, 1968). Granted, older people do appear to disengage from investment in activities and social contact. But this is because they have little choice – in old age activity remains the ideal lifestyle, but disengagment is forced upon them. These researchers argue that morale and psychological adjustment are significantly higher among elderly people who remain active in social contact and work pursuits.*

The evidence supports both views. Some elderly people are disengaged, some are active well into their eighties and nineties. Some of the disengaged people seem well adjusted to life, while others are less well adjusted. The same is true for the active people, though generally they are better adjusted. Adjustment turns out to depend mostly on acceptance, choice and resignation – whatever their lifestyles, the people who adjust well are those who accept those lifestyles.

By way of illustration, Havighurst (1968) outlines a study undertaken by other researchers of 87 elderly men in the San Francisco area, roughly half retired and half not retired. The men who were found to be adjusted were of three different personality types, to which the following names were given:

Mature people
Rocking chair people
Armoured people

The mature people took a constructive approach to life. They had many activities and social interests, led a balanced life, and looked young for their age. The rocking chair people took life easy, did little with their time, and tended to depend on others. They simply passed time in a pleasant if vacuous way. The armoured men were active individualists, who avoided being dependent or idle, and kept themselves busy. Even the oldest of these people, an 83-year old man, still worked a half-day every day.

The parallel between these three patterns of ageing, all showing high adjustment, and our own patterns emerging after mid-life is striking, though not suprising. A basic philosophy of life is forming in these mid-life years. The generative philosophy continues into old age in the mature

---

* One might expect that the physical capacity to be active declines with old age. But on the basis of thousands of studies on the ageing process it is not clear to what extent this is so, under what conditions, and when this occurs.

With the recent interest in the field of ageing, Birren and Schaie (1977) prepared a first handbook on the process of ageing, where 42 authors reviewed about 4000 studies. These reviews show that there are few clear ageing trends in terms of memory, learning, motor performance, sensual capacity, problem-solving ability, and perceptual ability. Research results are very contradictory. We would expect all trends to be mediated by lifestyle differences, as implied above; almost all gerontological studies have hitherto looked for simple age-related trends.

lifestyle. The maintenance philosophy continues in the rocking chair lifestyle. The prisoner philosophy becomes the armoured lifestyle.

Those elderly people who were less adjusted to ageing were of two different types:

Angry people
Self-hating people

The angry people blamed the rest of the world for everthing that went wrong. They were poorly adjusted to work, and several had been unsuccessful in life. They resented their wives and feared death. The self-hating group also felt angry that things had gone wrong with their lives, either earlier or now in old age, but that anger was directed to themselves. They blamed themselves, and had a very low sense of self-esteem. They were depressed and longed for death as a release from an intolerable existence.

These are less adjusted people, who do not have a life philosophy. They are frustrated, but incapable either of doing anything about it or of resigning themselves. They are the frustrated maintainers who have neither given up nor resolved their dilemmas. They are people who have lost their grip on life.

Later research studies have supported and amplified this assessment of the life patterns that emerge out of the middle adulthood into older age (Havighurst, 1968; Lowenthal et al., 1975; Maas and Kuypers, 1974; Chown, 1977). Older people have a preference to be active, preferably in the multifaceted, generative way. But when life investments have been made in a shallow way, when these investments have been unproductive, when compensatory adaptation has proved impossible, adaptation to older age takes the shape of resigning oneself to the stress free but satisfaction-less life of disengagement.

Part Five

Conclusions

Contrary to the cliché of the price of success and its underlying assumption that professional and private life are in conflict, our research leads us to conclude that under certain conditions these two dimensions of life can come to reinforce each other. However, these conditions are not easy to achieve, even assuming that one wishes to achieve them. Until now, we have described what the individual can do. Before finishing, let us turn to the organizational perspective.

What organizations can do

In this book, we have insisted that the main responsibility for managing professional life as well as the relationship between professional and private life rests with the individual executive. However, organizations bear responsibility for practices and policies that may make this unnecessarily difficult. In fact there are several things that organizations can do to help rather than hinder this process.

Broadening organizational values

Our first recommendation to organizations is likely to be the most heretical. Managers can help their people by encouraging them not to be devoted solely to career success. Many executives attach too high a value to effort, dedication, dynamism, and energy. Managers often take long hours at work and apparent single-minded dedication to professional success as indicators of the value of a subordinate. Attachment to private life and efforts to protect it by working 'only' 45 hours a week are interpreted as signs of weakness in today's middle aged; in younger managers, this pattern signifies an erosion of the work ethic, a symptom of what is wrong with the younger generation.

We find little evidence, however, of an erosion of the work ethic among younger managers. Their professional commitment is strong, but it represents a commitment to what interests them rather than a blind commitment to their companies. They resist simply doing what has to be done and conforming to organizational practices, even if they are compensated by incentives. They are aware that a lot of office time is wasted by engaging in ritualistic, nonproductive 'work' and that few people make a real success of activities that fail to excite and interest them. Above all, they appreciate that the quality of an individual's work life has an enormous impact, positive or negative, on his private life.

What organizations ideally need are a few ambitious high achievers who fit with their jobs, and a majority of balanced, less ambitious but conscientious people more interested in doing a good job that they enjoy and are adequately rewarded for than in climbing the organizational pyramid. Organizational practices that overvalue effort and climbing, while undervaluing pride in one's job and good performance, are counterproductive. Economic recessions in years to come will make this even more apparent. As the growth rates of organizations stabilize, the possibilities for advancement and promotion will diminish. People will be productive only if they enjoy the intrinsic value of what they are doing and if they draw their satisfaction simultaneously from two sources – work and private life – instead of one.

Creating multiple reward and career ladders

Since external rewards often pressure people into accepting jobs that do not fit them, our next recommendation concerns the reward policies and ladders of organizations. The reward ladder of most organizations is a very simple, one-dimensional hierarchy; the higher, the more 'managerial' one is, the more one is rewarded. People come to equate being successful with climbing the managerial ladder. That would be appropriate if skilled managerial people were the only skilled people we needed. But this is far from being the case. Most organizations have relatively few general managerial positions and, while these are important posts, the life blood of the company is the people who fit with their jobs in other ways. To encourage these people, reward ladders need to be far more differentiated than they are at present.

The obvious implication is that organizations must create multiple career and reward ladders to develop the different types of people required for their operations. Some high technology companies that rely heavily on technical innovation have indeed experimented with offering both managerial and technical reward ladders. In the future, we will probably see the development of reward ladders that reinforce creativity and entrepreneurship as well.

The problem with the simple structures of many organizations is that they channel ambition and talent in only one direction, creating unnecessary conflict for the many individuals who are ambitous or talented but do not walk the single prescribed path. We can warn individuals against being blinded by ambition to the emotional aspects of fit; yet we must also warn organizations, not against fostering ambition, but against chanelling it into a single career path.

Facilitating job mobility

Since the key to launching a career successfully is exploration, organizations need to help executives, particularly those in their twenties and early thirties, to explore by providing opportunities for job mobility. This implies readiness to offer opportunities not only to people who are doing well in their jobs, but also to those who are struggling. These in particular may be eager for new opportunities. Only if the organization takes this attitude will individuals be prepared to take risks rather than narrow their career exploration.

By job mobility, we do not mean systems of quick job rotation to familiarize a person with the organization. Brief assignments in different departments may provide the individual with some knowledge about different activities; but they neither give him the opportunity to test and assess himself nor the opportunity to develop skills. Real exploration requires real challenges – having at least a year in a job to meet those challenges. Nor are we talking of planned moves, where the man's career is mapped out long into the future. The organization can never know for sure what will be in a person's best interests in the future – each job should increase his self-awareness and clarify his ideas for his own future steps.

Opportunities for mobility are typically created either by expansion or by one person's move, or departure, which creates a vacancy for another, and so on in a chain reaction. Since business expansion has slowed in many sectors, the management of the fewer opportunities that now exist requires greater skill. Posting openings on the notice-board is no longer sufficient. Periodic and genuine discussion to find out what sort of opportunities a manager might envisage has become essential. The mentor's role has become very valuable to an organization. All this requires that bosses should interpret the desire to move as a healthy desire to explore, not as adverse criticism of their departments, or disloyalty, or an indication of a flighty nature.

Improving performance appraisal and self-assessment

Our fourth recommendation is that managers help individuals in their own self-assessment, thus reducing the chances that they will either move into positions that do not fit them or be promoted to beyond their level of competence. To do this, managers need to pay greater attention to their subordinates' performances and be honest in discussions of their strengths and weaknesses. Managers should also encourage self-assessment. Contrary to standard assessment practices that only emphasize skills and competence, assessment should focus as well on the extent to which an individual enjoys his job both as a whole and in its component parts. Many researchers have called for accurate and realistic feedback in performance appraisal (for instance Levinson, 1964). We also ask that managers be as concerned and realistic about enjoyment and values as about competence.

Of all managerial omissions, lack of candour about a subordinate's chances for promotion can be most destructive. At one time or another, to one degree or another, most managers have agonized over their insincerity in trying to motivate an individual with the lure of promotion while knowing that he does not have much of a chance. Candor may result in employees short-term unhappiness and even in their leaving the company, but we suggest that the long-run effects of dissembling are far worse. Eventually truth will out, and the negative effects of disappointment are likely to harm not only the individual's performance at work but also, through the spillover effect, his private life – at a time when perhaps it is too late for him to change jobs.

Recognizing that executives are human beings

Probably the most important thing than an organization can do to facilitate the professional development of its members without jeopardizing their private lives is to recognize that the issues described in this book are real and legitimate issues for the organization to care about. In attributing responsibility for these issues separately to the individual and the organization, we make an artificial distinction. An organization is a group of managers and employees, all of whom struggle with personal dilemmas in professional and private life at one time or another. These same people then put on an organizational hat as hierarchical superiors, dealing with subordinates sometimes in ways in which they would not like to be dealt with themselves. In effect, some executives have a Janus face: they adopt a personal perspective when reacting to the organization above them, and they become 'the organization' when influencing the lives of their subordinates.

Perhaps optimistically, we believe that if the executive becomes sensitive to these issues in his own life and better able to balance the demands of professional and private life, he is likely to become more sensitive and skilful when dealing with them in the lives of his subordinates. When enough managers feel and act this way, the 'organization' starts to change.

Top executives may worry that this may lead people to work less, or be less interested in professional success. We do not believe that this will happen. The manager who becomes sensitive to these issues will be better able to design policies and establish practices which do not bring individual and organizational interests into conflict, but which measure up to the challenge of matching individual and organizational needs – rightly seen by Schein (1978) as the central problem in managing the human resource system in an organization.

But the organization is often not to blame

Failure in private life is often attributed to either organizational demands or to excessive work involvement. Certainly, organizational practices sometimes make private life more difficult. And it is so difficult for most people to launch their work careers that few can attend to this and at the same time attend well to their private lives. But this is sometimes too easy an alibi. Recently, the film *Kramer versus Kramer* portrayed the cliché of the price of success and was a box office winner. People leaving the cinema commented on how accurate the film was; they readily bought the thesis that Mr Kramer destroyed his private life because he was too involved with his work. This may well have been the case for Mr Kramer and may be true for many young men who divorce. But it would be a mistake to assume that it describes the case of all ambitious executives.

We do not deny that work involvement often does have a negative effect on private life. But there may be other reasons for a poorly functioning marriage. Do people always have the attitudes, skills and even knowledge they need to manage a marriage successfully? It is only when one knows that a person does have these that one can accept the explanation that his failure must have been caused by excessive involvement in work.

People must recognize what they intuitively know, that it is as difficult to succeed in private life as it is to succeed in the professional world. Marriage is also a career, as is one's relationship to one's children. Just as people learn to assess their professional skills, so they must assess their strengths and weaknesses in private life. Not understanding a son should be as much a concern as not understanding a balance sheet or computer printout. In private life, one may throw up one's arms and conclude that it is impossible to understand a child, a woman, or one's own problems in a way that one never would if confronted with a professional problem.

Most managers will agree that where there is a problem, there is a solution; where there is a will there is a way. This applies to private as well as professional life. Executives know that the success of their subordinates on professional projects depends on how these assignments are planned: the assignment should lead to specific results and should be feasible. 'Increase market share on product X,' is an assignment that has a poor chance of success; 'Increase market share by 2 per cent within six months by intensive publicity of product X in the Southerby area,' is a project that has a much better chance of success. The same applies to private life. The general target of 'improving my relationship with my wife' or 'relating better to my children', however deeply felt, is unlikely to succeed. But the opportunities we have had to follow up on the work executives did on these issues in the aftermath of some of our seminars have shown us that people have a high chance of succeeding on specific projects: 'Making sure that I spend at least three hours a week *alone* with my wife doing something we both enjoy,' or 'spending time this month with Mary telling her how she was when she was little.' The concreteness of these projects has the important consequences of knowing if one has succeeded and of feeling rewarded by success. A private life success spiral is created; skills in handling private life begin to develop.

Must success cost so much?

We have seen how some people become so successful in one area of life that it becomes more satisfying to invest in that area than in others that need investment. We have seen how others pay a price, not for success, but for their mistakes in trying to achieve it, leading to eventual failure. We have seen individuals who launch their careers while skilfully maintaining their private lives, and others who neglect their private lives, sometimes turning painfully towards them in their late thirties and early forties, sometimes never turning. We have seen people who entered late adulthood with a feeling of despair and resignation, having paid a price in most life ventures; we have seen others who experienced their lives as full and generative, having paid no unreasonable price in any life venture. In summary, we have encountered no simple stereotype, no easy cliché among these managers, but a variety of life patterns and implicit choices.

What is encouraging is to find some people in the business world, no more privileged than others at the beginning of adulthood, who have been able to manage the relationship between their professional and private lives well, ultimately achieving a synergistic relationship between the two. Their lives have not been free of stress, conflict, or pain – quite the contrary. These are people who appear to have a high degree of sensitivity to the emotional aspects of work. Rather than settling early for a particular path to success, their career exploration has been wider and richer. Their capacity for self-assessment is deeper. They have an ability to keep their marital relationship vital through reciprocal expressiveness. Success in one area of life has been a cue to invest in other areas. They have developed relationships which allow them to cope with the stress of responsibility. They have investments in so many areas of life that inevitable blows in one aspect of life can be adjusted to, with the support of others. If a few people achieve this state of life today, what about the future?

New frontiers

Our findings reflect the social values and conditions in western society at the time the survey was undertaken.* These values and conditions are certainly undergoing change, and some of those changes may facilitate the process of launching three careers and attaining success in all three life ventures. Yet there are other undeniable trends that may make it more difficult.

One such trend is towards the dual-career family. The couple where both husband and wife pursue a full-time career and have children, both launching their careers as young adults, is rare in our survey. Indeed, we have argued that it is the most stressful situation for both husband and wife in the first of our three life phases. Yet it is not an impossible situation, as studies of dual-career couples show. It is possible where both husband and wife skilfully succeed in launching their separate careers as well as in managing their family relationships. Knowing how to do this becomes very important, and the ways in which organizations aggravate the problems become more serious.

Also making the task more difficult is the trend towards greater environmental uncertainty. The economic, political and social scene in our societies is becoming more unstable, less predictable, and less favourable to leading a balanced life. In times of recession there are fewer jobs available and greater competition for those openings; managers take

* It was surprising to find few differences in our findings between one country and another. Where there were major differences, we have mentioned them. See also Appendix 3, Note 3.

fewer risks with their careers, settling for what they have rather than for what they might have. The organization persuades a person to accept a job abroad knowing well that the job will not suit him and that his wife is reluctant, but also knowing that there is no better opportunity available. Organizations are more frequently restructured; changing political and market conditions lead to redundancies and company shut-downs. The social mores about what a woman should do with her life change. Children become independent at an earlier age, aggravating the worries of their parents. Again, none of these trends make the management of professional life and private life impossible. They mean that people have to show more skill in how they do this.

This leads us to a fundamental observation. Skills develop through experience, and there are limits to the complexity of experience that a person can handle at one time. The evidence suggests that no-one is able to achieve success in all dimensions of life and develop a stable life structure by the early thirties. Levinson found this among the men he studied (Levinson *et al.*, 1978), and our survey confirms it. And if one cannot expect a person to successfully launch three careers – professional, marital and parental – at the same time, it is even less reasonable to expect a couple to launch six careers simultaneously.

The logical prescription would seem to be sequential development. Life investments should be sequenced, as they are, unconsciously and imperfectly, in the lives of our survey managers. In the case of a couple, the developmental sequences of the two parties would have to be coordinated. This would mean attempting to develop solid foundations and skills in one or two areas before launching into a new venture. It may imply avoiding permanent commitments in private life, such as marriage or having children, until such time as professional life is reasonably well established. At the level of society, this might involve allowing people the option to develop private life before launching their careers, rather than labelling such people as having no personal ambition.

'Staging' life in this way is untraditional, unlikely to appeal to most people who wish to be successful in different careers. However, some, particularly dual-career couples and young adults who deliberately decide to marry late, are exploring these new formulas. It is possible that these men and women, the exceptions of today, are establishing the patterns for tomorrow.

For the time being, however, the majority of people launch five careers simultaneously, three for the man and two for the woman – and there is a trend towards the six career family. This involves managing an immensely complex life. The ideas and findings in this book are, we hope, of interest and assistance to these men and women who courageously search for true personal success without paying too high a price.

Appendix 1

The questionnaire (abbreviated)

A STUDY OF THE PROFESSIONAL AND PRIVATE LIVES OF MANAGERS

You have been asked to help us in this study by answering this questionnaire on your professional life (your career and work) and your private life (your family and leisure). So let us tell you a little about the purpose of the project.

Our interest is in the life styles of managers, and in particular how they satisfy the demands of their professional and private lives. There are many myths and clichés about managers as people. We would like, with your help, to obtain some facts. Our final objective is to provide some information and ideas that may be useful in managing one's life.

Our interest in the topic goes some way back. Fernando Bartolomé carried out a study of the private lives of managers leading to a *Harvard Business Review* article, 'Executives of human beings', since reprinted in several books. Paul Evans undertook a study of managerial careers at MIT, analysing how managers resolve various career conflicts such as the one of concern here.

We might emphasize that this questionnaire is anonymous. Our interest is in the aggregate results. We hope to obtain the assistance of several hundred people in completing it, primarily from various European countries. In addition, we will be undertaking a programme of interviews with managers.

Many thanks for your help,
Fernando Bartolomé and Paul Evans
Department of Organizational Behaviour
INSEAD

1. How you spend your time

(a) During an *average weekday* in the last three months, how much time did you spend at your place of work or away on business? *Excluding commuting time*, please indicate the length of a typical working day in hours.

.... hours

(b) During the last three months, how much time did you spend on the following activities on average?
   (i) Sleeping

.... hours per day

   (ii) Business travel – the number of *nights per month* away from home

   None

   1–2 nights

   3–4 nights

   5–6 nights

   7–10 nights

   More than 10

(c) The next two questions concern the relationship between your professional life and your personal life.

   (i) Which of the following statements most closely reflects your *beliefs* about the relationship between professional and private life? (tick one box)

   Professional life and private life should never be mixed.

   One should *try* to separate professional and private life; it is annoying if one has to think of professional matters at home.

   While one should at least try to separate professional and private life, it is natural that one sometimes has to attend to business matters at home.

   The distinction between professional and private life is very unclear.

There is no reason for any clear distinction between professional and private life. ☐

(ii) Tick the box by the statement which most closely describes your usual *behaviour* when you come home from work:

After I leave work I never give a thought to professional matters. ☐

After I leave work, I don't think about professional matters except on the few occasions when I have to. ☐

After leaving work, I gradually unwind from my work. ☐

A considerable amount of my spare time during the week is spent on professional matters. ☐

Most of my spare time during the week is spent on thinking about or attending to professional matters. ☐

(d) When do you consider that your *'weekend'* normally begins and ends – the time free of professional commitments and concerns?

It normally begins on .... at about ....
                 (day)   (time)
and ends on .... at about ....
                (day)   (time)

(ii) Of the weekend time that you have indicated above, how many hours if any would you say that you usually spend thinking about or attending to professional matters?

.... hours

(e) During a typical working week, do you feel that you get:

Less sleep than you would like ☐

As much sleep as you would like ☐

More sleep than you would like ☐

No feelings one way or the other ☐

(f) The following is a list of different *types of activities* in which one may engage during one's private life or free time. Please indicate how you spend your free time during a seven-day period by ticking one place on the scale opposite each activity (there are of course overlaps between the different types of activities listed).

	more than 30 hours	21–30 hours	11–20 hours	6–10 hours	3–5 hours	1–2 hours	rarely or never
Simple relaxation (e.g., light reading, TV, a siesta, a relaxing hobby)							
Being a companion to your wife (i.e., talking or doing things with her)							
Playing with the children							
Bringing up or educating the children (e.g., help with their work, discipline)							
Household chores (e.g., shopping, repairing, cleaning)							
Going out with wife and family (e.g., excursions, cinema, sport events)							
Active hobbies or pastimes, playing sport for fun							
Keeping fit (i.e., running, playing sport to keep healthy)							
Self-development (e.g., reading, studying or activities to develop yourself)							
Entertaining or visiting relatives							
Entertaining or visiting friends							
Entertaining business clients or acquaintances							
Participation in community, civic or political activities							

(g) Most people must share their limited waking hours and energy between their work/career and their family/leisure life. We would like to measure how people rate the proportions of time and energy they invest in work and career, relative to their family and leisure. Firstly, consider the question of *time*. During a typical *seven-day period* over the last three months, what proportion of your time did you invest in your work and career, relative to your family and leisure?

Percentage of time spent on work/career	0	10	20	30	40	50	60	70	80	90	100
Percentage of time spent on family/leisure	100	90	80	70	60	50	40	30	20	10	0
Tick the appropriate box:											

Using the above scale, what would you say was the *time* ratio, *two years ago?*

Please indicate this by writing the percentages in the spaces below:

Percentage of time spent on work and career ....

Percentage of time spent on family and leisure ....

————
100
————

What about the future? What do you *exepct* the *time* ratio to be in *three years from now?*

Percentage of time spent on work and career ....

Percentage of time spent on family and leisure ....

————
100
————

(h) Now, please consider the question of *energy*. During a typical *seven-day period* over the last three months, what proportion of your energy did you invest in your work and career, relative to your family and leisure?

Percentage of energy spent on work/career	0	10	20	30	40	50	60	70	80	90	100
Percentage of energy spent on family/leisure	100	90	80	70	60	50	40	30	20	10	0
Tick the appropriate box:											

Using the above scale, what would you say was the energy ratio two years ago?

Please indicate this by writing the percentages in the spaces below:

Percentage of energy spent on work and career ....

Percentage of energy spent on family and leisure ....

$$\overline{100}$$

What about the future? What do you *expect* the *energy* ratio to be in *three years from now?*

Percentage of energy spent on work and career ....

Percentage of energy spent on family and leisure ....

$$\overline{100}$$

(i) In the previous question, you summarized how you spend your time and energy. We would also like to know *how you feel* about this distribution of your *time* and *energy* between work and family.

Please indicate how you feel about your distribution of time and energy:

Very satisfied with my present distribution of
time and energy

Satisfied

I have no feelings one way or the other

Unsatisfied

Very unsatisfied with my present distribution of
time and energy

If you feel 'unsatisfied' or 'very unsatisfied' about the way you are currently using your *time*, please indicate how you would like to modify the present situation. Tick *one* of the three boxes below:

I would like to devote more time to my work:

| 5–10 per cent more | 10–20 per cent more | 20–30 per cent more | beyond 30 per cent |

I would like to devote more time to my family/leisure:

| 5–10 per cent more | 10–20 per cent more | 20–30 per cent more | beyond 30 per cent |

I don't think that it is a question of time but a question of how well you use your time at work and at home.

(j) How does your wife feel about the distribution of the time and energy you devote to your private life today?

She is very satisfied with my present distribution of time and energy.

She is satisfied.

She has no feelings one way or the other.

She is unsatisfied.

She is very unsatisfied with my present distribution of time and energy.

2. Your wife

(a) Is your wife currently working? (Tick one box)

No

Working full or part-time

Very active in community affairs (voluntary organizations, etc.)

How many hours per week?

40 or more

30–40 hours

20–30 hours

10–20 hours

Less than 10

(b) *If* she is working or very active in community affairs now, or has been so during the last three years, what is her *main* reason? (Tick one box only)

Financial (to have her own income, supplement family income, etc.)

To build a career

To occupy herself, keep herself busy

To develop her interests

For contact with other people

Other (please specify):

....

....

(c) If your wife is *currently* working full or part-time:

   (i) Please indicate the type of job she has

....

   (ii) To what extent do you see her as *emotionally involved* in her job or professional activity?

Extremely involved

Very involved

quite involved

Not very involved

Not at all involved

(d) For how many years in total *since you were married* has your wife had a *full-time job* – working more than 30 hours a week?

.... years

(e) If your wife has worked in the past or is working now, to what extent do you think that her working had or has an influence on the quality of your marital and family life? (Please circle the appropriate number on the scale below.)

1	2	3	4	5	6	7

A clearly negative influence   A balance of positive and negative, or no influence   A clearly positive influence

(f) Are you in favour of married women engaged in a *career* – i.e. where there is a long-term occupational commitment? (Please tick one box.)

In favour

Mixed or neutral feelings

Against

3. Your marriage

(a) Taking things together, how do you feel about your marriage? (Tick one box)

Very happy

Pretty happy

Sometimes happy, sometimes unhappy

Not very happy

Unhappy

(b) (i) When you come home in the evening, if your wife starts talking about herself or about what she has done, the children or problems with the household, do you ever find that you are only half listening – that your mind is on other things or that you feel impatient?

Most of the time

Often

Sometimes

Rarely

Never

(ii) Some people look forward to the weekend as a time to pursue their own interests; for others, the weekend is a time to relax and build up energy for the next week. How do you view your weekend?

Primarily as a time to relax from work

Slightly more as a time to relax rather than as a time to pursue my own interests

Partly as a time to relax, partly as a time to pursue my own interests

Slightly more as a time to pursue my own interests than as a time to relax

Primarily as a time to pursue my own interests

(iii) Would you say that you devoted more time and energy, less, or about the same as your immediate work colleagues, to actively taking care of your family?

Much less time and energy than other colleagues

A little less than others

About the same as others

A bit more than others

Much more than others

(c) In your relationship to your wife, how do you see yourself? Please tick one place on the following scale opposite each statement.

1 = essentially so
2 = very much so
3 = to a large extent
4 = to a certain extent
5 = not really

	Scale				
	1	2	3	4	5
As a provider of financial security for her					
Someone to actively help her take care of the household and children					
Someone who shares times of mutual relaxation with her					
As a provider of social status for her					
As a provider of an interesting leisure or social life for her					
As an active support in her self-development, assisting her to develop her capacities in the work or interests she herself chooses					
As a provider of affection for her					
As someone with whom she can talk about herself, her interests and problems					

(d) With respect to each one of the roles that you see yourself as performing in your family, *how* well do you think you *perform* each one of them?

1 = very well
2 = well
3 = it varies
4 = not too well
5 = poorly

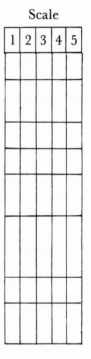

Scale

	1	2	3	4	5
Providing financial security for my family					
Helping my wife take care of the household and children					
Sharing mutual relaxation with my wife					
Providing my wife with social status					
Providing an interesting leisure or social life for my wife					
Being an active support in my wife's self-development, assisting her to develop her capacities in the work or interests she herself chooses					
Providing my wife with affection					
Being someone with whom my wife can talk about herself, her interests and her problems					

(e) How do you see your *wife's role*? (Please tick one alternative on the following scale opposite each statement)

1 = essentially so
2 = very much so
3 = to a large extent
4 = to a certain extent
5 = not really

Scale

	1	2	3	4	5
As another wage earner in the family					
As someone to look after the household					
As someone to look after the children					
As someone who shares times of mutual relaxation with me					
As a social asset to me					
As a provider of an interesting leisure or social life for me					
As an active support in my self-development assisting me to develop my full potential					
As someone responsible for her own self-development					
As a provider of affection for me					
As someone with whom I can talk about myself, my interests and problems					

(f) How well do you think your *wife performs* each one of the roles described below?

1 = very well
2 = well
3 = it varies
4 = not too well
5 = poorly

Scale

	1	2	3	4	5
Contributing financially to the family					
Looking after the household					
Looking after the children					
Sharing times of mutual relaxation with me					
Being a credit to me in social situations					
Enlivening our leisure and social life					
Supporting me					
Taking care of her own self-development					
Providing me with affection					
Listening to me when I want to talk about myself, my interests and my problems					

(g) The following are a few characteristics of the relationship between a husband and wife.

Using the scale below, please indicate the extent to which they are to be found in your marriage at the present time.

1	2	3	4	5	6	7	8	9	10

Very little
indeed

Very much
indeed

Place the appropriate number from this scale in the box by each category of behaviour:

Communicating openly how you feel towards each other

Listening and understanding how the other person is feeling

Being able to ask for help from the other person

Feeling mutual attraction

Being able to bring out and openly explore the conflicts which may exist between you

Having as much concern for satisfying the needs of your spouse as your own

Being able to satisfy each others' needs

Explicitly expressing to your wife your love for her

Adapting to the changing needs and expectations of your wife

Playing, joking, teasing each other in a friendly way

Allowing each other the freedom each one desires

To what extent do you and your wife experience conflict in the following areas?

Please tick one place on the following scale opposite each statement.

1 = very often
2 = often
3 = sometimes
4 = rarely
5 = never

Scale

	1	2	3	4	5
What to do during the weekend					
Coming home late from work					
Not doing things that you have promised to do					
Sexual behaviour					
The short amount of time you spend with the children					
Not doing things as she would like them done					
Her not doing things that you want done					
The handling of family finances					
Friends (i.e. disliking one's spouse's friends)					
Relationships with in-laws					
Proper behaviour in social situations					

When the two of you disagree about what to do, you end by doing what *you* want to do . . .

In most cases	
Often	
About half the time	
Sometimes	
Rarely	

On the occasions, few or many, when you and your wife get involved in heated arguments or disputes, does one of you ever feel resentful or hurt at the end?

On most occasions

Often

Sometimes

Rarely

Never

4. Your feelings about your life

(a) (i) Which of the following gives you the *most* satisfaction in life?

(ii) Which gives you the *second most* satisfaction?

(iii) Which gives you the *next* greatest satisfaction?

Place a 1 by the activity which gives you the most satisfaction; place a 2 by the activity which gives you the second most satisfaction; and a 3 by the one which gives you the next most satisfaction:

Your career and its achievements

The work you do

Family relationships

Leisure time recreational activities

Social relationships with other people

Religious beliefs or activities

Participation as a citizen in civic affairs

Running a home

Other (please specify):

....

....

(b) Do you ever experience any of the following? (Please tick one place on the scale opposite each statement.)

1 = often
2 = now and then
3 = very rarely
4 = never

Scale

	1	2	3	4
Moodiness				
A sense of fatigue				
A need to be left alone				
Depression				
Boredom				
Not being able to sleep at night				
Worry about a nervous breakdown				
Irritability (small things annoy you)				
Worry about your health				
Restlessness and agitation				
Difficulty in concentrating				

Other questions asked

Other questions, not included in the abbreviated questionnaire above, were asked of the 532 survey respondents. These covered the following issues:

(a) *Personal background:* nationality, age, education, marital history, number of children in the family and their ages.

(b) *Work experience:* current job, type of company and its size, salary, level in the managerial hierarchy, age when the person first assumed supervisory responsibility, number of times the person had moved home to a place more than 60 miles away since marriage.

(c) *Career:* where the person situated himself on a career ladder relative to the beginning of his career and the position he expected to attain at its height; the type of position he expected to reach at the height of his career; his expected salary at this point; whether he saw himself as working harder than colleagues in his company; how successful he saw his career relative to colleagues.

(d) *Type-A behaviour:* 20 questions about behaviour, frequently associated with executives, that has been found to bear some correlation to coronary heart disease. These are known as Type-A behaviours (Friedman and Rosenman, 1974). The questions asked for a 'Yes-No' answer. Examples are as follows:

Do you find that you take on too many commitments and demands?

Do you enjoy competition and try hard to win?

Do you often wish that you had more free time?

(e) *Feelings about different aspects of life:* This lengthy question was introduced as follows:

'The next five questions ask you to describe your feelings about various aspects of your life at present. The five aspects of your life are:

Your career

Your work

Your relationship with your wife

Your relationship with your children

Your life in general

Describe your feelings about each of these, ticking the appropriate point on the scale between each pair of words. For example, if you feel that your career is '*fairly rewarding*', you should tick as follows:

	1	2	3	4	5	6	7	
Rewarding	—	✓	—	—	—	—	—	Disappointing

If you feel that your career has been '*very disappointing*', then you would tick:

	1	2	3	4	5	6	7	
Rewarding	—	—	—	—	—	—	✓	Disappointing'

Respondents were asked to indicate their feelings by marking the appropriate point on a seven point scale between the following word pairs:

rewarding – disappointing
satisfied – unsatisfied
interesting – boring
enjoyable – unenjoyable
enthusiastic – unenthusiastic
successful – unsuccessful

easy – hard
relaxed – tense
free – tied down
active – passive
changing – constant

The additional word pairs were included in the lists concerning feelings about one's wife and children, namely: warm – cold, and close – distant.

Appendix 2

The survey methodology

The results of any survey are only as good as its methodology. For example, our interpretation of some results would obviously be biased if only half of the managers who were asked to complete our questionnaire did so, and these men, unknown to us, were those most happy with their marriages. In the design, administration, and analysis of the survey, we went to great lengths to deal with methodological issues such as this. Some readers may be interested in knowing how we went about this and arrived at the conclusions in this book.

Past research experience has taught us that the risk of methodological problems can be minimized by careful design, but never eliminated. One becomes aware of inevitable problems in one's design only when one is half-way through the analysis. To arrive at meaningful results we decided to put several irons in the fire, employing an approach we think of as 'triangulation'. One point of data is a questionnaire; this can be administered to a large number of people, giving quantitative data that can be objectively analysed. Another point of data is an interview; this provides an in-depth feeling for the questions one is researching, but one's hypotheses, based on the lives of a few interviewees, have to be tested out on the questionnaire data. This leads us to certain tentative conclusions – the third point is then the discussion of these conclusions with the type of people one is researching: in this case managers attending seminars. The discussions at hundreds of seminars often led us back to the questionnaire or interview data. The findings in this book are those which satisfied these three tests: they were supported by the questionnaire results, they were reflected in the lives of the people interviewed, and they seemed to be meaningful to managers with whom we discussed them.

The questionnaire

Since a literature search revealed few standard and validated questions relating to our research, we designed most of the questions ourselves. The single most helpful source of ideas was a survey undertaken by Pahl and Pahl (1971). A first questionnaire was administered between August and October 1977, and at that time we were particularly interested in discussing with the 90 respondents any problems they had in filling it out. Two months were then spent on a full analysis of the data. This led us to eliminate many questions which did not seem important, to revise the wording of a few others, and to add some new ones (for example, on Type-A behaviour (see Appendix 1)). This became the final questionnaire.

The respondents

The questionnaire was administered to executives attending programmes of at least two weeks duration at INSEAD in Fontainebleau, France. English was the language of these programmes (except for those held in French, where we gathered most of the French responses to a questionnaire translated into that language). They were typically general management seminars, and one or the other of us was an instructor on most of them. The purpose of the research was explained to these managers, and they were asked to help us by spending more than an hour of their time in the next week by filling out the questionnaire.

One cannot legitimately expect this degree of serious cooperation unless one provides some feedback. So in all cases, we promised and provided this, usually spending four hours as part of the course we were teaching. We presented their own results on various key questions, as well as discussing our emerging findings. Although we never kept any formal tally of response rates, we would estimate that the response rate to our questionnaire was in excess of 90 per cent. Thus, we are reasonably sure that our survey results do not suffer from response bias, though they do reflect the type of people we studied.

As mentioned in the Prologue, these people are probably more successful in the eyes of their companies than a representative group of managers, as well as being married and male. Another characteristic is that there is probably a higher proportion of internationally-mobile managers than on a similar programme in Britain or the United States. However, although INSEAD is an international management school, a minority of the managers on seminars there are pursuing a career as international executives. The fact that they come from different national backgrounds is commented on in Appendix 3.

The interviews

The interviews with the 22 British couples (one turned out to be American) were conducted in London in April 1977 by Olivia Grayson, an American woman who is an economist by education but who had become interested in our study. Similar interviews were carried out in Paris with the 22 French couples by Catherine Leblanc, a French psychologist. Let us outline how we went about the British interviews; the French procedure was similar.

We wished to undertake interviews with at least 20 couples, and we constructed a list of alumni from certain programmes in the recent past, all of whom lived in the London area. We randomly picked 25 names and adjusted this list so as to have a fair distribution of people in terms of age. These 25 people were contracted by phone and the project was explained to them. At that time, we requested their cooperation, but no immediate response. A letter followed this up, as well as various telephone calls after the man had discussed our request with his wife. Some indicated that their wives were reluctant but willing. Only one person said no in the end (we do not know his reasons). In fact, 22 and not 24 interviews were carried out, owing to scheduling constraints. The men and women were interviewed separately, half the men at their offices and half at home, while the women were all interviewed at home.

Each interview lasted for one and a half to three hours, and was recorded on tape. The interviews followed a semi-structured format: the interviewer had a list of questions to ask, some to code on her printed schedule, but she was also asked to encourage the men and women to elaborate at length. Examples of the more open questions that were asked of the men are as follows (expressed here in summary form):

> What sort of things happen at work or because of your work which have an effect on your family life?
>
> Do you feel that you have given anything up for the sake of your career?
>
> How have your wife and family influenced your career?
>
> Could you describe yourself as a person, as a husband, as a father? And your wife as a person, as a wife, as a mother?
>
> How do you spend your free time?
>
> Has your family life increased or decreased in importance to you during the last three years? And what about in the next three years?
>
> Could you describe the things that have happened to you during the

last year which have been a particular source of satisfaction to you? And those that have dissatisfied you?

What are the things, general or specific, that have been sources of worry or concern to you during the last few years?

The interview schedule for each wife was longer, in that questions were asked not only about herself but also about how she viewed her husband and his behaviour; furthermore, the wives were asked to complete a questionnaire that paralleled the main survey questionnaire. Examples of specific questions asked in the interview were:

What proportion of your husband's time and energy does he invest in his professional life? And how do you feel about that? How does he feel about it?

Could you describe his job, and how he feels about it?

In an ideal world, what would you like to change about his work or his work-related behaviour?

How do you invest your own time, and how do you feel about each of these roles?

What do you feel about your own work (if she has a professional job), and what influence does it have on your private life? Do you think of going back to work (if she is not working now)?

What is the most pleasurable aspect of being married to a business executive? And the most difficult aspect?

Data analysis

The quantitative questionnaire data was analysed using standard statistical procedures, first for exploratory analysis and later, after the interviews had been transcribed and analysed, for hypothesis testing – principally using tabulations and cross-tabulations, correlations, factor analysis, and methods for analysis of variance. Tentative conclusions were drawn after analysis of 370 responses. These conclusions were later retested for their reliability after analysing the final 532 responses.

In terms of statistical significance, the findings reported in this book are significant at the level of $p < 0.01$ (and in most cases at $p < 0.001$). Where the level of statistical significance is less than this, we have qualified ourselves by saying something on the lines of, 'There is a certain indication that ...', or 'There appears to be some association between ...'.

However, as we noted above, statistical significance is only one indication of the importance of findings, for statistical relationships or differences sometimes turn out to be confirmations of commonsense, or occasionally of spurious associations. Consequently, the final test of our conclusions was the later reactions, comments and supplementary data gathered at seminars with nearly 4,000 other managers and 600 wives, conducted before writing this book.

Appendix 3

Methodological notes

NOTE 1: On subjective versus objective measurement
(see Chapter 1, page 10)

We chose to measure time investment in a subjective way for a number of reasons. The 'objective' measurement of time budgets requires expensive and painstakingly detailed research; the methodological problems are enormous (Robinson and Converse, 1972). But more important, objective measures of time spent on different activities do not allow us to draw conclusions about the psychological significance of that time investment. To give an extreme example, time spent at church is supposedly invested in a religious activity; but one study concluded that for a small number of people, church activities represented sexual entertainment or protection from hunger and cold (quoted from Robinson and Converse, 1972).

People often asked us whether they should consider commuting time as professional or private time. Our answer was to say that it depends; only the person himself can answer that. Some people do crossword puzzles while commuting, and consider that to be leisure time. Others run through work problems of the day in their minds, and thus consider it as professional time.

All things taken into account, we considered that the person's own judgment would be the best indicator of investment behaviour, though we recognize the subjectivity of this measure. This is still more true of energy investment. Energy investment turns out to be even more significant than time investment, and yet there is no objective way of evaluating energy invested in different activities. People nevertheless have little problem in evaluating their energy investment.

Indeed, most of our questionnaire items measure the various aspects of professional and private life in a subjective way, as does any questionnaire. But this survey concerns itself with the *experience* of life rather than with objective truths. For example, from an 'objective' point of view, no-one can deny that every individual pays a price for his success in any particular venture of life. This is the price of having chosen to invest one's limited time in one particular activity rather than in another. But few people experience themselves as paying a price when they act in this way.

NOTE 2: On marital role concepts (see Chapter 11, page 146)

How the husband saw himself in his relationship to his wife (his marital role concept) was analysed by factor analysis. The eight questions are reported in the questionnaire (Appendix 1, question 3-c). Three factors or general role concepts explained two-thirds of the variation in replies to these questions – in other words, there appear to be three separate dimensions to the way in which husbands view themselves in their relationships with their wives. These three dimensions are separate and independent.

We called the first and statistically most important dimension *expressiveness*, as outlined in Chapter 11. The expressive husband sees it as important to provide affection to his wife, and to be available to talk with her about herself, her interests and her problems. Forty-five per cent of the 532 men saw expressiveness as a very important aspect of the relationship, checking '1' or '2' on both items. Twenty per cent saw it as fairly important (averaging 2 to 3 on the two items). The remaining 35 per cent saw expressiveness as a less important element in the relationship. The only other role concept that is a significant part of this dimension is seeing oneself as someone who shares times of mutual relaxation with her.

The second dimension consisted of three items: providing an interesting leisure and social life; providing support in her self-development, and providing social status. We called this role concept being the *active provider*. The husband sees himself as actively bringing something into the marriage.

The third dimension consisted of two related items, providing financial security and providing social status. This was called the *passive provider* role concept. Without any active investment in the family, he provides for its maintenance through his work.

NOTE 3: On cultural differences (see Part Five, page 209)

Since the managers in our survey come from different cultural backgrounds, we had expected to find big cultural differences in our survey. In its early stages, we expected that these cultural differences would allow us to assess how social conditions in some countries ease the difficulties of balancing professional and private life, while aggravating them in others.

There are indeed significant differences between cultures in terms of what people believe and how they behave (Hofstede, in press), but not in terms of the issues we investigated. The fact of being a manager in a large business organization and having a wife and children appears to override these differences. Statistically controlling for culture, as we did with the four large groups in our survey (the British, French, Scandinavians, and Germans) made, in general, little difference to the results. Let us summarize here the differences we found.

If one compares managers of various nationalities, there is little difference in the rhythm of preoccupations at the three life phases. The French are slightly more sensitive to career tensions at all phases, possibly a reflection of working as middle managers in relatively structured and authoritarian organizations. Young British managers are particularly insensitive to their marriages, though this changes strongly in the mid-thirties, while the Scandinavians are more preoccupied than other nationalities with their wives during their twenties and early thirties.

While French managers believe more in a rigid separation of professional and private life – work should not in principle be allowed to interfere with family and leisure – the British executive perceives a much less clear boundary between the two domains. Yet, in terms of *actual* investment behaviour, there is no difference – both invest on average the same proportion of time and energy in work, travel about the same amount, and their wives react to overinvestment in similar ways.

Their time in private life is spent differently. The British are more passive and companionable, spending time relaxing, doing chores, and simply being together. The French are more active – playing sports, spending time with children, friends, or the extended family. In their marital lives, the British allow their wives more freedom within their marriages. Furthermore, while there is no difference in the percentage of wives who are working from one country to another, the French are most likely to see this as having a negative effect on the marriage. One of the most significant cultural differences is reported in Chapter 11 – the British attached the most importance to expressiveness in the marriage, while the Scandinavians attached the least. Nevertheless, this seems to reflect different norms regarding the appropriate degree of expressiveness in a relationship; in all cultures, the more expressive the marriage relative to these norms, the more likely it was to be seen as happy.

Perhaps the most striking difference is in feelings towards life, and the career in particular. On average, the French saw their careers as more bland – work was less tense and stressful, more constant, but less satisfying. In contrast, one might stereotype the British as more volatile – high on tension and stress, perceiving their careers as changing rather than constant, but higher on satisfaction. (These differences do not, however, apply to the private life domain.) Above all, the French feel most 'tied down' in their careers, whereas the British and particularly the Scandinavians feel 'free'. All of these differences are paralleled by slightly less significant differences in feelings about life in general. There appears to be a carry-over of career feelings to overall life feelings. This observation, based on the questionnaire, was independently supported by the impressions of those who interviewed our 22 British and 22 French couples. In some way, counter to the stereotype, the British managers who were interviewed often led stormy but interesting lives, while the French managers often appeared to lead lives of quiet but controlled unhappiness. In our view, this reflects the relatively rigid, structured, and authoritarian career environment of many French companies in comparison to the more open structure of opportunities in the British organization. The career strategy of the Frenchman is necessarily more defensive and risk-avoiding, while that of his British counterpart is more aggressive and risk-taking.

References

Andrews, F. M. and Withey, S. B. (1976) *Social Indicators of Well-Being: Americans' Perceptions of Life Quality*. New York: Plenum.

Ansoff, H. I. (1978) The next twenty years in management education. *The Library Quarterly*, **43,** October, 293–326.

Argyris, C. (1962) *Interpersonal Competence and Organizational Effectiveness*. Illinois: Dorsey Press.

Argyris, C. (1971) *Management and Organizational Development*. New York: McGraw-Hill.

Bailyn, L. (1970) Career and family orientations of husbands and wives in relation to marital happiness. *Human Relations*, **23,** 97–113.

Bailyn, L. (1978) Accommodation of work to family. In Rapoport, R. and Rapoport R. N. (eds) *Working Couples*. New York: Harper Colophon; London: Routledge & Kegan Paul.

Bailyn, L. (1978) The 'slow burn' way to the top: implications of changes in the relations between work and family for models of organizational careers. Working paper: Alfred P. Sloan School of Management, MIT.

Bailyn, L. and Schein, E. H. (1976) Life/career considerations as indicators of quality of employment. In Biderman A. D. and Drury T. F. (eds) *Measuring work Quality for Social Reporting*. New York: Halstead Press.

Baltes, P. B. and Schaie, K. W. (1973) (eds) *Life-Span Developmental Psychology*. New York: Academic Press.

Banner, D. K. (1974) The nature of the work-leisure relationship. *Omega, 2:2*.

Bartolomé, F. (1972) Executives as human beings. *Harvard Business Review*, November-December, 62–9.

Bartolomé, F. and Evans, P. L. (1980) Must success cost so much? *Harvard Business Review*. March–April, 137–48.

Bernard, J. (1973) *The Future of Marriage*. London: Penguin.

Birren, J. E. and Schaie, K. W. (1977) (eds) *Handbook of the Psychology of Aging*. New York: Van Nostrand Reinhold.

Bradburn, N. M. (1969) *The Structure of Psychological Well-being*. Chicago: Aldine.

Bray, D. W., Campbell, R. J. and Grant, D. L. (1974) *Formative Years in Business: A Long-Term AT & T Study of Managerial Lives*. New York: Wiley-Interscience.

Brim. O G. (1976) Theories of the male mid-life crisis, *Counselling Psychologist*, **6,** 2–9.

Bronfenbrenner, U. (1970) *Two Worlds of Childhood: U.S. and U.S.S.R.* New York: Touchstone 1972; London: Penguin.

Bruner, J. (1966) *Toward a Theory of Instruction*. New York: Norton.

Campbell, D. P. (1977) *Manual for SVIB-SCII*. Stanford, Cal.: Stanford University Press.

Chaikin, A. L., Derlega, V. J., Bayma, B., Shaw, J. (1976) Neuroticism and disclosure reciprocity. *Journal of Consulting and Clinical Psychology.*

Chown, S. M. (1977) Morale, careers and personal potentials. In Birren, J. E. and Schaie, K. W. (eds) *Handbook of the Psychology of Aging.* New York: Van Nostrand Reinhold.

Collin, A. (1977) Mid-life crisis: working paper no. 14. Department of Management studies, University of Technology, Loughborough.

Cuber, J. and Harroff, P. (1966) *Sex and the Significant Americans.* Baltimore, Maryland: Penguin.

Cumming, E., Dean, L. R., Newell, D. S. and McCaffey, I. (1960) Disengagement: a tentative theory of aging. *Sociometry,* **23,** 23–5.

Cumming, E. and Henry, W. E. (1961) *Growing Old: The Process of Disengagement.* New York: Basic Books.

Dalton, G. W., Thompson, P. H., Price, R. V. (1977) The four stages of professionals. *Organizational Dynamics,* Summer, 19–42.

Deci, E. L. (1975) *Intrinsic Motivation.* London: Plenum Press.

Driver, M. (1980), Career concepts – a new approach to career research. In Paap, J. (ed) *New Dimensions in Human Resource Management.* Englewood Cliffs, N.J.: Prentice-Hall.

Erikson, E. (1968) *Identity: Youth and Crisis.* New York: Norton.

Evans, D. F. (1977) Changing from a 'What' to a 'Who'. *Business Horizons,* November, 14–17.

Evans, P. L. (1974) The price of success: accommodation to conflicting needs in managerial careers. Unpublished doctoral disseration, Alfred P. Sloan School of Management, MIT.

Evans, P. L (1975) Orientational conflict in work and the process of managerial career development. INSEAD Research Paper No. 166, Fontainebleau.

Evans, P. L. and Bartolomé, F. (1979) Professional lives versus private lives – shifting patterns of managerial commitment, *Organizational Dynamics,* Spring, 2–29.

Evans, P. L. and Bartolomé, F. (1980), The relationship between professional and private life. In Derr, C. B. (ed) *Work, Career and Family.* New York: Praeger.

Faunce, W. A. and Dubin, R. (1975) Individual investment in work and living. In Davis, L. E. and Cherns A. (eds) *The Quality of Working Life,* Volume I. London: Collier Macmillan; New York: Free Press.

French, M. (1978) *The Women's Room.* London: Deutsch; New York: Summit.

Friedman, M. and Rosenman, R. H. (1974) *Type-A Behaviour and Your Heart.* London: Wildwood House.

Furstenberg, F. F. (1974) Work experience and family life. In O'Toole, J. (ed) *Work and the Quality of Life: Resource Papers for 'Work in America'.* Cambridge: MIT Press.

Gavron, H. (1966) *The Captive Wife.* London: Penguin edition 1978.

Glueck, W. (1974) Managers, mobility, and morale. *Business Horizons,* December 1974.

Goldthorpe, J. H., Lockwood, D., Beechhofer, F. and Platt, J. (1969) *The Affluent Worker in the Class Structure.* Cambridge: Cambridge University Press.

Gould, R. L. (1978) *Transformations: Growth and Change in Adult Life.* New York: Touchstone edition 1979.

Gowler, D. and Legge, K. (1975) Stress and external relationships: the 'hidden contract'. In Gowler, D. and Legge, K. (eds) *Managerial Stress.* Epping, Essex: Gower Press.

Gurin, G., Veroff, J. and Feld, S. (1960) *Americans View Their Mental Health*. New York: Basic Books.

Hall, D. T. (1971) A theoretical model of career subidentity development in organizational settings. *Organizational Behaviour and Human Performance*, **6**, 50–76.

Hall, D. T. (1976) *Careers in Organizations*. Pacific Palisades, Cal.: Goodyear.

Hall, D. T. and Gordon, F. E. (1973) Career choices of married women: effects of conflict, role behaviour, and satisfaction. *Journal of Applied Psychology*, **58**, 42–8.

Hall F. S. and Hall, D. T. (1978) Dual careers – how do couples and companies cope with the problems? *Organizational Dynamics*, Spring, 57–77.

Handy, C. (1978) Going against the grain: working couples and greedy occupations. In Rapoport, R. and Rapoport, R. N. (eds), *Working Couples*. New York: Harper & Row; London: Routledge & Kegan Paul.

Havighurst, R. J. (1968) Personality and patterns of aging. *Gerontologist*, **8**, 20–23.

Havighurst, R. J. and Albrecht, R. (1953) *Older People*. London: Longman.

Henning. M. and Jardim, A. (1976) *The Managerial Woman*. New York: Pocket Books edition 1978.

Hicks, M. W. and Platt, M. (1970) Marital happiness and stability: a review of research in the sixties. *Journal of Marriage and the Family*, November, 553–74.

Holahan, C. K. and Gilbert, L. A. (1979) Inter-role conflict for working women: careers versus jobs. *Journal of Applied Psychology*, **64**, 86–90.

Holmes, T. H. and Rahe, R. H. (1967) The social readjustment rating scale. *Journal of Psychosomatic Research*, **11**, 213–18.

Hofstede, G. (1976) Occupational determinants of stress and satisfaction. Working Paper 76–39, European Institute for Advanced Studies in Management, Brussels.

Hofstede, G. (in press) *Cultures Consequences*. New York: Sage.

Jacques, E. (1965) Death and the mid-life crisis. *International Journal of Psycho-Analysis*, **41**: 4.

Jones, M. C. (1969) A report on three growth studies at the University of California, *Gerontologist*, **7**, 49–54.

Jourard, S. M. (1971) *The Transparent Self*. New York: Van Nostrand.

Jung, C. G. (1934) The stages in life. In Campbell J. (ed.) *The Portable Jung*. New York: Viking, 1971.

Kahn, R., Wolfe, D. M., Quinn, R. P., Snoek, J. D. and Rosenthal, R. A. (1964) *Organizational Stress*. New York: Wiley.

Kando, T. M. and Summers, W. C. (1971) The impact of work and leisure: toward a paradigm and research strategy. *Pacific Sociological Review*, **14**: 3.

Katz, R. (1977) Job enrichment: some career considerations. In van Maanen J. (ed.) *Organizational Careers: Some New Prospectives*. Chichester: Wiley.

Katz, R. and van Maanen, J. (1976) The loci of work satisfaction. In Warr P. (ed.) *Personal Goals and Work Design*. New York: Wiley.

Keene, P. G. W. (1977) Cognitive style and career satisfaction. In van Maanen, V. J. (ed.) *Organizational Careers: Some New Perspectives*. Chichester: Wiley.

Kets de Vries, M. F. R. (1977) The mid-career conundrum. McGill University Working Paper No. 77–4.

Klinger, E (1977) *Meaning and Void: Inner Experience and the Incentives in Peoples' Lives*. Minneapolis: University of Minnesota Press.

Kohn, M. L. and Schooler, C. (1973) Occupational experience and psychological functioning: an assessment of reciprocal effects. *American Sociological Review*, **38**, 97–118

Kolb, D. A. (1971) Individual learning styles and the learning process. Sloan School of Management Working Paper 535–71, MIT.

Kolb, D. A. and Plovnick, M. S. (1977) The experiential learning theory of career development. In van Maanen J. (ed.) *Organizational Careers: Some New Perspectives*. Chichester: Wiley.

Kornhauser, A. (1965) *Mental Health of the Industrial Worker*. New York: Wiley.

Kotter, J. P., Faux, V. A., McArthur, C. C. (1978) *Self-Assessment and Career Development*. Englewood Cliffs, N. J.: Prentice Hall.

Langner, T. S. and Michael, S. T. (1963) *Life Stress and Mental Health*. New York: Free Press.

Leslie, G. R. (1976) *The Family in Social Context*, (Third Edition). New York: Oxford University Press.

Levinson, D. J. Darrow, C. N., Klein, E. B., Levinson, M. H., McKee, B. (1978) *The Seasons of a Man's Life*. New York: Knopf.

Levinson, H. (1964) *Emotional Health in the World of Work*. New York: Harper and Row.

Lidz, T. (1976) *The Person: His and Her Development Throughout the Life Cycle*. New York: Basic Books.

Lowenthal, M. F., Thurner, M. and Chiriboga, D. (1975) *Four Stages of Life*. San Francisco: Jossey Bass.

Maas, H. S. and Kuypers, J. A. (1974) *From Thirty to Seventy*. San Francisco: Jossey Bass.

Maccoby, M. (1976) *The Gamesman*. New York: Simon & Schuster; London: Secker & Warburg.

Marsden, D. and Duff, E. (1975) *Workless*. London: Penguin.

Maslow, A. H. (1971) *The Farther Reaches of Human Nature*. New York: Viking.

McClelland, D. C. *et al.* (1972) *The Drinking Man*. New York: Free Press.

McGill, M. E. (1977) Facing the mid-life crisis. *Business Horizons*, November, 5–13.

Mussen, P. H., Conger, J. J., Kagen, J. (1969) *Child Development and Personality* (Third Edition). New York and London: Harper and Row.

Neugarten, B. L. (1968) (ed.) *Middle Age and Aging*. Chicago: University of Chicago Press.

Neugarten, B. L. (1977) Personality and aging. In Birren, J. E. and Schaie, K. W. (eds) *Handbook of the Psychology and Aging*. New York: Van Nostrand Reinhold.

O'Toole, J. (1974), (ed.), *Work and the Quality of Life: Resource Papers for 'Work in America'*. Cambridge: MIT Press.

Orthner, D. K. (1975) Leisure activity patterns and marital satisfaction over the marital career. *Journal of Marriage and the family*, February, 15–28.

Pahl, J. M. and Pahl, R. E. (1971) *Managers and their Wives*. London: Penguin.

Parker, S. (1972) *The Future of Work and Leisure*. London: Paladin.

Payton-Miyazaki, M. and Bradfield, A. H. (1976) The good job and the good life: the relation of characteristics of employment to general well-being. In Biderman, A. D. and Drury, T. F. (eds) *Measuring Work Quality for Social Reporting*. New York: Halstead.

Peter, L. J. and Hull, R. (1969) *The Peter Principle*. New York: William Morrow; London, Pan (1971).

Peters, R. K. and Benson, H. (1978) Time out from tension. *Harvard Business Review*, January–February 1978.

Rapoport, R. and Rapoport, R. N. (1971) *Dual-Career Families*. London: Penguin.

Rapoport, R. and Rapoport, R. N. (1975) *Leisure and the Family Life Cycle*. London: Routledge & Kegan Paul.

Rapoport, R. and Rapoport, R. N. (1978) (eds), *Working Couples*. New York: Harper Colophon; London: Routledge & Kegan Paul.

Robinson, J. P. and Converse, P. E. (1972) Social change reflected in the use of time. In Campbell, A. and Converse, P. E. (eds) *The Human Meaning of Social Change*. New York: Sage.

Rogers, C. R. (1961) *On Becoming a Person*. Boston: Houghton Mifflin.

Rose, J. B. (1974) The shorter work week and leisure time, *Omega*, **2**: 2.

Rosenblatt, P. C. (1974), Behaviour in public places: a comparison of couples accompanied and unaccompanied by children. *Journal of Marriage and the Family*, November.

Ryder, R. G. (1973), Longitudinal data relating marriage satisfaction and having a child. *Journal of Marriage and the Family*, November, 604–6.

Schneider, B. and Hall, D. T. (1972) Toward specifying the concept of work climate: a study of roman catholic diocesan priests. *Journal of Applied Psychology*, **56**, 447–55.

Schein, E. H. (1978) *Career Dynamics*. Reading, Mass.: Addison-Wesley.

Selye, H. (1956) *The Stress of Life*. New York: McGraw-Hill; London: Longman (1957).

Selye, H. (1975) *Stress Without Distress*. New York: Signet; London: Hodder & Stoughton.

Sheehy, G. (1974) *Passages*. New York: Dutton; London: Corgi (1977).

Sommers, D. and Eck, A. (1977) Occupational mobility in the american labour force, *Monthly Labor Review*, January, 3–18.

Stoner, J. A. F., Ference, T. P., Warren, E. K. and Christensen, H. K. (1974) Patterns and plateaus in managerial careers. Working Paper No. 66, Graduate School of Business, Columbia University.

Tausky, H. and Dubin, R. (1965) Career anchorage: managerial mobility motivation, *American Sociological Review*, **7**: 4.

Toffler, A. (1970) *Future Shock*. New York: Random House; London, Bodley Head.

Vaillant, G. E. (1977) *Adaptation to Life*. Boston: Little, Brown.

White, R. W. (1959) Motivation reconsidered: the concept of competence, *Psychological Review*, **66**, 297–333.

Whyte, W. F. (1956) *The Organization Man*. New York: Simon & Schuster.

Wilensky, H. (1960) Work, careers and social integration, *International Social Science Journal*, **7**: 4.

Winterbottom, M. R. (1958) The relation of need for achievement to learning experience in independence and mastery. In Atkinson, J. W. (ed.) *Motives in Fantasy, Action and Society*. Princetown, N.J.: Van Nostrand.

Work in America (1973) Report of a Special Task Force to the Secretary of Health, Education, and Welfare. Cambridge, Mass.: MIT Press.

Young, M. and Wilmott, P. (1973) *The Symmetrical Family*. London: Penguin.

Index

adjustment *see under* lifestyle
age: and relation between private and
    professional life, 41, 42–58; and ambition,
    44; and sense of guilt, 100; *see also* life,
    phases of
ageing, 199–201
alcohol, 24, 74, 188
ambition, 77–8, 84–5, 95, 124, 205
anchors *see* career anchors
Andrews, F. M. and Withey, S. B., cited, 22,
    45n
Ansoff, H. I., cited, 70n
anxiety *see* distress
Argyris, C., cited, 144n
assertiveness, 144 & n
assessment (self), 86, 87–8, 206
attitudinal and behavioural spillover, 16
autonomy *see* independence

Bailyn, L., cited, 57, 103–4, 137
Bailyn, L. and Schein, E. H., cited, 10
Baltes, P. B. and Schaie, K. W., cited, 43n
Banner, D. K., cited, 29
Bartolomé, F., cited 16, 144, 145, 153
Bernard, J., 118, 132, 137, 140, 159–60
'Bill', 78–81, 87, 99
Birren, J. E. and Schaie, K. W., cited, 200
Bradburn, N. M., cited, 22, 45n
Bray, D. W., Campbell, R. J. and Grant, D.
    L., cited, 47
breakdown, 36, 40, 155, 179, 183
breaking-out, 188–9
Brim, O. G., cited, 180n, 182
Bronfenbrenner, U., cited, 114
Bruner, J., cited, 83

Campbell, D. P., cited, 87n
career: importance of, 9–10; time and energy
    spent in, 10; failure and anxieties over, 17,
    23–6; compensation for failure in, 34–5;
    effect of private life on decisions in, 40–1;
    life-phases and fulfilment in, 42–3, 59–60;
    launching, 45, 46–9, 60, 65, 71, 76, 82,

124, 166–7; and mid-life managers, 49–52;
    and older managers, 52–3; effect on
    personality, 60–1; fits and misfits in, 62–7,
    71, 76; exploration in, 82–4, 86–91, 166–7;
    Driver's four forms of, 84–6; mistakes in
    starting, 94–6; women in, 102, 105, 164,
    166–9, 209; as constraint on wives' choice,
    108, accommodating to family, 120;
    women's part-time, 170, and enjoyment,
    183, 185; value of technical contribution
    to, 198, 204–5; promotion ladders, 204;
    and job mobility, 205
career anchors, 67–70
catharsis, 153–4
Chaikin, A. L. *et al*, cited, 143
'Charles', 100
children: and paternal absence, 4, 18,
    111–13; anxiety over, 23, 113; and
    parental life-phases, 42; and younger
    manager, 49, 112–13; importance in
    midlife, 50, 113; and older managers,
    52–3, and misfits, 75; guilt towards, 100;
    as constraint on wives, 109; effect on
    marital happiness, 110n; effect on career
    decisions, 112–13; postponement of
    attention to, 113; and broken homes, 113,
    144; and paternal consistency, 113–14;
    effect of spillover on, 114; and achieving,
    114; effect of marriage conflict on, 138;
    expressiveness towards, 145; wives'
    attitude to bringing up, 160–1; and
    depressive parents, 184; as source of
    fulfilment, 197; *see also* family
choice: in career exploration, 86–7, 92–3, 96,
    107; wives' freedom of, 106–7, 161–2, 164,
    168–72; in leisure activities, 131
Chown, S. M., cited, 199, 201
civic participation, 9
compensation, 27–9, 34–5, 37–8; defined, 28
competence, 62–4, 67–9, 94
confidence, 63
confirmation, 118
conflict, 27–9, 31–2, 36–7, 89